OCR

D1558801

R. D. LAING

A Biography

R. D. LAING

A Biography

ADRIAN CHARLES LAING

THUNDER'S
MOUTH
PRESS

Published by
Thunder's Mouth Press
632 Broadway, Seventh Floor
New York, NY 10012

First published in Great Britain 1994
© A. C. Laing 1994, 1996

First Thunder's Mouth Press Edition

ISBN 1-56025-105-0

Library of Congress Catalog Card Number: 96-61499

Distributed by
Publishers Group West
4065 Hollis St.
Emeryville, CA 94608

Contents

R. D. LAING

A Biography

Acknowledgements

My warmest thanks to all those individuals who let me interview them for hours (sometimes days) on end, and those who spent precious time dealing with my unsolicited correspondence. I would also like to thank the organizations that provided me with research material, library access and goodwill. In particular, I wish to express my gratitude to Ethel Laing, Sid Briskin, Dr Joe Berke, Dr Charles Rycroft, Dr Jock Sutherland, Penry Jones, the Philadelphia Association, Arbours Association, the Society of Existential Analysis, the Tavistock Centre, Dr Thomas Szasz, Professor Anthony Clare, Dr Leon Redler, Chris Oakley, Haya Oakley, Dr Morton Schatzman, James Greene, Dr John Heaton, Dr Loren Mosher, Francis Huxley, Calvin Hernton, Captain Brian Hogan of the National Institute of Mental Health, Bethesda, Dr Ross Speck, Joan Speck, Dr Herbert Phillipson, Rollo May, Arthur Rosenthal, Anne Laing, Fiona Laing, Karen Laing, Paul Laing, Jutta Laing, Marcelle Vincent, Sally Vincent, the Reverend Baird, Dr James Templeton, Kay Carmichael, Johnny Duffy, Dr Lenny Davidson, Dr James Hood, Dr Mike Scott, Dr Norman Todd, Walter Fife, Dr Jock Wilson, Dr Marion Milner, Peter Morrish, Bernie Simons of Simons Muirhead and Burton, David Goldblatt, Theo Itten, Bernard Spalding, Robert Dando, Dr Steve Ticktin, Dr Aaron Esterson, Mary Garvey, Professor Jennings, Mary Barnes, Ian Spurling and Jeff Nuttall. I wish to thank my editor, Jill Foulston, for innumerable improvements to the text.

My long-suffering wife, Deborah Fosbrook, deserves special gratitude. Not only did she put up with R.D. Laing when he was alive, but also with her husband's obsession with 'Ronnie' for over four years thereafter. To Deborah I am eternally grateful.

9

for Susie

INTRODUCTION

In Search of the Old King

During the course of writing this book I was often confronted by psychoanalysts and psychiatrists who felt compelled to ask me: 'Has writing this book made you feel closer to your father?', to which I could only answer: 'My relationship with Ronnie has greatly improved since his death'.

I have interviewed more than two hundred people over a period of nearly four years; I have corresponded with and spoken to countless others about R.D. Laing. I travelled from Iona to Mount Joy in search of the old king, often having to remind myself that my 'subject' was, in addition to being R.D. Laing, my father. I rarely felt close to that person others talk about – 'Ronnie', and never personally referred to him as such. He was 'Dad' or 'the old man'. In rare moments of filial respect I might have talked about 'my father'. In writing this book I have battled against prejudice, both for and against my father; the fundamental approach I adopted was to accept that my father was correct about fifty per cent of the time. But which fifty per cent?

When I visited the United States, for example, I learned that much of what I thought Ronnie had originated concerning families and madness had its roots in theoretical and clinical practice on the West and East coasts of America, going back to the 1930s: Nathan Ackerman in New York, the Gregory Bateson group in Palo Alto, Ross Speck in Philadelphia, Murray Bowen, Lyman Wynne, Jay Haley, Albert Scheflen and Raymond Birdwhistell in Bethesda, Maryland, among many others. I also learned that these people were not merely representatives of academic schools of thought, but dedicated practising professionals, most of whom Ronnie met during the period 1962 to 1967. Whatever disillusionments I experienced, I none the less became aware that Ronnie possessed a widely recognized energy and charisma, an outstanding intellect, an almost masochistic dedication to his work, and an extremely rare ability to communicate with others, particularly those individuals whose behaviour had led them to be clinically diagnosed as schizophrenic.

Books will continue to be written about R.D. Laing, the psychiatric profession, psychoanalysis and lay psychotherapy for many years to come. I therefore decided not to attempt an analysis of the professional legacy of R.D. Laing. Besides, I am a lawyer, not a therapist. The material legacy which R.D. Laing left to the world is embodied in his fifteen books (particularly *The Divided Self*), his other writings both published and unpublished, and his nine surviving children.

More importantly, the legacy of R.D. Laing in the sense of his influence on others is best encapsulated by the therapeutic houses currently operational: the Philadelphia Association and the Arbours Association in London; Burch House and Crossing Place in the United States. These four voluntary and charitable organizations are principally run by individuals who received their training at Kingsley Hall in the 1960s, and at the subsequent households which were run under the auspices of the Philadelphia Association during the 1970s and 1980s: Haya Oakley, Dr Joe Berke, David Goldblatt and Dr Loren Mosher, respectively. To their credit, they have learned many lessons from the experiment called Kingsley Hall, and although they now have their own special *modus operandi*, their collective ethos is firmly rooted in the intensity and courage of those extraordinary days during the sixties under the charismatic leadership of R.D. Laing. All of these households have the same aim: to provide a caring and humanitarian alternative to mental health institutions.

Finally, there are the innumerable books, chapters of books and articles written about the works of R.D. Laing to which I have referred extensively, though not exhaustively. An analysis of the works of R.D. Laing, embracing an analysis of all previous references to R.D. Laing, would not only be an entirely different project to the one I embarked upon but would require at least twice the space. If there is one lasting legacy that Ronnie Laing left to the world it was the unquantifiable degree of humanity that his life infused into his profession.

It was only in the immediate aftermath of Ronnie's death on the afternoon of 23 August 1989 that I began to appreciate the number of people from all over the world who had been influenced by the works of R.D. Laing. By the end of that day I, together with other members of Ronnie's immediate families, had received condolences from people living in nearly every European country. Calls were received from friends living across the length and breadth of the United States, and I even had one phone call from a friend of Ronnie's living in South America, who had heard of Ronnie's death from a satellite news channel uplinked from China. Obituaries appeared in most of the major newspapers around the world and memorial services in honour of R.D. Laing were held from New York to Los Angeles, London to Austria. During the course of researching Ronnie's life, many tributes were made on a more private and intimate level. Rollo May, the renowned American existential analyst, described Ronnie in correspondence to me as 'a kind of angel set loose in a world he never made'. I was also strangely heartened by a reply I received from the Buddhist Publication Society based in Kandy, Sri Lanka, which informed me that R.D. Laing had been 'a very devoted Buddhist and read all our books published on Theravada Buddhism. He must have collected much merit and should be happy throughout his journey in Samsara'. Charles Rycroft, Ronnie's own analyst, described him as a 'special case'. Of that I now have no doubt, for the name R.D. Laing, I have come to accept, provokes not only joy and love but deep anger, resentment and bitterness.

There will be some, I have no doubt, who will feel this book is a betrayal of my father. I do not share that view. One cannot, with a man such as R.D. Laing, ignore the 'down' side of his life. He was obsessed with experience, with phenomenology, with existentialism, with life itself. Those personal experiences – his two divorces, the death of his daughter Susie, the breakdown of his daughter Fiona, his financial worries and his excessive drinking and drug-taking cannot be conveniently swept under the proverbial carpet. He had bad times as well as good. I have tried to balance one against the other and to give to specific events in his life the prominence they seemed to merit – no more and no less. Whether I have succeeded is not a matter for me to judge.

CHAPTER ONE

Ancestral Voices

'Have a Caesar, and Keep Your Passage Honeymoon Fresh', was emblazoned across a large billboard advertising Caesarean births. Many people, arriving in Los Angeles in 1972, would have thought no more about it; they might not have even realized what was being advertised. For R.D. Laing, in the midst of a gruelling lecture tour, it was a perfect example of the crazy world we live in. It was worse than the five-star hotel with plastic grass, in a different league from the plastic Buddha converted into a lampshade, more horrible than de-homogenized milk, more threatening than an armed policeman.

Such matters affected Ronnie to the core. He cried over less. He was painfully sensitive, and had an empathy with the bewildered and downtrodden, an intellectual awareness that set him apart from others. But Ronnie's distinguishing feature was his heartfelt desire to do something about what he perceived to be the injustices of the world. Despite his many faults, Ronnie maintained his defiant personality until his last breath. But what made him the man he was?

The forebears of R.D. Laing were deeply Scottish lower-middle-class lowland Presbyterians; a quiet lot consisting of weavers, teachers, engineers, architects, craftsmen and the like. The family tree going back to the early eighteenth century reveals no major events, traumas or achievements, with the notable exception of a 'Great Uncle Tom', who obtained a Master of Arts from Aberdeen University in his seventy-third year in the 1920s.

Ronnie's father's side of the family is firmly rooted in the small, quiet communities around the north-east of Scotland. In the mid-nineteenth century a John of Bogbain married and moved to Strichen, a tiny Scottish village a few miles south-east of Fraserburgh, a fishing port on the Moray Firth. The eldest child of John married a local lady by the name of Isabella Barclay. Eventually this family moved south to the larger town of Aberdeen in search of work, and it was in Aberdeen that their six children were born, the first being another John, in 1867, who married Ann McNair. John and Ann had four Laings: David Park McNair (Ronnie's father), Isabella Barclay, John and Ethel. This family moved to Glasgow, where they made their home at 21 Westmoreland Street in Govanhill, on the south side of the city.

Glasgow, which has evolved around the estuary of the River Clyde on the west coast of Scotland, is a Scottish city with a rich history. During the Roman period, the Antonine Wall was built just north of Glasgow to keep out the fierce Pictish tribes, and it is next to the remainder of this wall that R.D. Laing lies buried today. Glasgow Cathedral was consecrated in 1136 in the presence of King David I, and during the mid-fifteenth century Glasgow University was founded. By the time of a nationwide survey, the 'Report on the Sanitary Condition of the Labouring Population of Great Britain' by Edwin Chadwick in 1842, the Industrial Revolution had rendered Glasgow 'possibly the filthiest and unhealthiest of all the British towns of this period'. During a period of 'squalor and delinquency' in 1891, the Glasgow city boundaries were extended to Govanhill, Ronnie's home district for the first twenty-two years of his life, to ease the problem of over-crowding caused by the rapid growth of its cosmopolitan population. Due to its heavy reliance on ship-building and engineering, Glasgow suffered badly during the depression of the early 1930s, the time of Ronnie's childhood.

Ronnie's mother, Amelia Glen Kirkwood, was the second youngest of six children, having two elder brothers (William and Archie), two elder sisters (Netty and Sarah), and a younger sister, Mysie. Amelia's mother, Elizabeth Glen, was born in Australia, where her parents had a sheep farm. Amelia's father, John, originally from Scotland, met Elizabeth in Australia and wanted to make a visit back to the 'auld country'; he brought Elizabeth with him sometime in the early 1880s. It apparently broke Elizabeth's heart that he would not take her back to Australia. John and Elizabeth settled in Rankinston in Ayrshire, where John became the cashier at the local colliery, and there they started their family. Later, the family moved north from Rankinston to Uddingston, a suburb of Glasgow, and later still, to Garturk Street, close to Westmoreland Street where the Laings were resident.

Located in Govanhill, Westmoreland Street and Garturk Street were then, as now, a good walk away from a very different part of Glasgow known as the Gorbals, much of which disappeared during the 1930s. For many years, the image of the Gorbals, circa 1930, was portrayed in books like *No Mean City* by McArthur and Long – 'the best-selling novel of the Glasgow slums' – as desperately poor, horribly violent, and as deprived a place as any on this earth.* Govanhill, however, was 'respectable', lower-middle-class in character, and separated by two miles or so from the Gorbals. Although near to the Gorbals, the area of Govanhill was a different world.

No one seems to know how David and Amelia first met. It was certainly an event to which Ronnie was never made privy. As the two lived close to each other it seems likely that proximity was the reason for their first contact. The fact is that in 1917, David Park McNair Laing, a handsome twenty-four-year-old, second lieutenant in the Royal Air Corps, married the equally handsome Amelia Glen Kirkwood, then aged twenty-six, in Burlington House in Glasgow. After they were married, David and Amelia moved to 21 Ardbeg Street, almost equidistant between 39 Garturk Street and 21 Westmoreland Street, and they ended up living there for most of their married lives. Ten years later Ronald David Laing, their only child, was born.

David, the eldest of four and having a slightly wayward father, turned out to be a responsible member of the community, 'a solid and respectable chap'. As an adult David Park McNair Laing was a tall, handsome man whose upright demeanour and strong Scottish voice at once indicated the righteous and hard-working character typical of the respectable lower-middle classes. In Glasgow in those days, a clean suit, crisp shirt, sober tie, polished shoes, hat, overcoat, scarf and gloves were an essential part of the apparel of such God-fearing, though not church-going, folk. Cleanliness was next to godliness, and a slovenly appearance was indisputable evidence of a weak spirit. David

---

* Ralph Glasser's *Growing Up in the Gorbals* provides a historical insight into the Gorbals between the wars and the difficulties that faced the Jewish communities in Glasgow. More recently, Jeff Torrington has written a widely acclaimed and prize-winning book about the Gorbals in the 1960s, entitled *Swing Hammer Swing!* (London, 1992).

was clean-shaven and short-haired all his life, and was never known to take anything to excess. Leaving Bottlefield school in 1907, aged fourteen, David worked as an apprentice in the Mavers and Coulston shipyard on the River Clyde. In 1910, he joined the Royal Tank Corps and eventually served in the Royal Air Corps during the First World War. Although David was never engaged in battle, he informed his teenage son of an occasion during the Great War when he was in an aeroplane that cut out over the Dead Sea – the most frightening moment of his life. The only other combat story David told his son concerned a soldier he had witnessed being decapitated by an aeroplane propeller. It is quite likely that David saw a fair amount of live action as a lieutenant stationed in Egypt during the Great War, but these two stories epitomized the war experience as related by father to son.

In 1927, the neat row of sandstone tenement houses in Ardbeg Street were as clean and tidy as their inhabitants. Coming out of the communal entrance referred to as the 'close' of 21 Ardbeg Street and turning left, one comes into Calder Street. Crossing Calder Street to the right, two streets on the left is Westmoreland Street where David's parents, John and Ann, with David's younger brother, Jack, then aged 30, and his younger sister Ethel, aged fifteen, lived at number 21. David's other sister, Isabella, then thirty-two, had gone to London to seek her fortune as a singer.

One might have presumed that with three generations living so closely together there existed a close family network. This was not the case. The Laings and the Kirkwoods did not get on; not in any sense of positive animosity, but there was an absence of any overt friendliness. David's parents thought that he had married beneath himself, that he was too good for Amelia. The Kirkwoods felt much the same about the Laings. Ronnie's closest relative outside his immediate family was his Aunt Ethel, David's younger sister. The fifteen-year age difference between Ethel and Ronnie was the same as between Ethel and her elder brother, Jack (confusingly referred to as John, the name of Amelia's father, which did not amuse Amelia). Although Ronnie had no brothers or sisters, his Aunt Ethel was as close to him as an elder sister.

When Ronald Laing came into the world, Amelia's two elder brothers, William and Archie, had long since left the nest to find their fortunes in America and Australia, respectively. Amelia's elder sister, Sarah, was married and living in Manchester. Her younger sister, Mysie, then aged thirty, was still living at home in Garturk Street, but yearning to return to Australia where the family had originally come from many years previously. The other elder sister of Amelia's, Netty, had died (probably of scarlet fever) in 1901, when she was seventeen and Amelia was nine years old. Netty's existence was a non-subject, not to be talked about under any circumstances. Throughout the whole of his life, Ronnie was unaware that he had had an Aunt Netty.

In 1927 David was working at the West of Scotland Electricity Board as an electrical engineer employed by the Glasgow Corporation. His wages were sufficient to pay the five-shillings-a-week rent and have enough left over for him and Amelia to live comfortably above the bread line. Home, for them, was the three-roomed, second-floor flat owned by David's employer, the Glasgow Corporation. At the beginning of October 1927, Amelia was nine months pregnant. It was a particularly depressing and anxious time for Amelia's family, since her father was dying. Sarah, Amelia's elder sister, was seven months pregnant. Sarah was living in Manchester but anxious that her baby should be born in Scotland. As difficult as it is to believe now, the fact is that no one at 39 Garturk Street or 21 Westmoreland Street had been remotely aware that Amelia was pregnant. Had the baby not survived the birth, no one in the family would ever have known of its existence other than David and Amelia. As an accomplished feat of social deception this should not be underestimated. Amelia was not particularly stout and lived in a real community, where pregnancy and births were at the very heart of local gossip. Her only means of physical disguise was a favourite old coat, which hid the terrible truth that she had been penetrated by a man.

Into 21 Ardbeg Street at 5.15 p.m. on Friday the 7th of October 1927 came a wee boy. Amelia decided to call him Ronald after the dashing matinée idol, Ronald Colman. David was to be his second name, after his father. Several days later Amelia realized that she had to come clean. Avoiding the fact of her pregnancy was no matter; to continue the charade now was impossible. The news was greeted by the family with a stunned silence; the implications arising from the lies and deceit required for such a *fait accompli* were immediately buried, and all concerned quietly adopted their new identities as grandma, grandpa, aunt and uncle. Wee Ronald was, after all, the only baby around at that time, and would be the centre of attention, no matter what.

Ronnie's upbringing, in relative terms, was materially privileged. The flat in Ardbeg Street was humbly furnished but there was always warmth, a piano and sufficient food and clothing for the Laings to consider themselves one up from the working classes who lived their lives toiling at the nearby tramworks or down at the shipyards.

Ronnie's nauseating desire to rationalize external events began at a very early age. Whatever the material privileges he experienced, his emotional world was one of bewilderment and confusion. He felt emotionally deprived, a fact that he freely confessed throughout his life. Although Amelia no doubt loved her son a great deal, she was not particularly adept at expressing her feelings towards Ronald, the name she always called him. As an adult Ronnie was always ready to portray Amelia as the classic nutty mother. The sad fact was that they never had a close relationship and by the time Ronald reached his teens Amelia was quite sure he had taken 'a bad turn'. Even when Ronnie was in his fifties, a visit to his mother was an excruciatingly painful experience. He retained a childish habit of stashing any food provided by Amelia into his pocket, discreetly wrapped in his handkerchief. Any liquid provided (usually over-milky, sickly-sweet tea) would be poured into some pot-plant or other vessel during a well chosen moment. Ronnie and Amelia certainly had a communication problem; not because of the absence of love but because of the absence of a genuine friendship.

Two months after Ronnie was born, Amelia's father died. Christmas of 1927 should have been a celebration of Sarah's child (now the Reverend William Baird, who still lives in Inverkeithing on the Firth of Forth, north of Edinburgh). Instead, the family retreated into deep mourning. Apart from his position as the cashier at the local colliery in Rankinston, Ayrshire, little else is known of Amelia's father. Amelia's relationship with him, as indeed with her whole family, was not a subject for open discussion, and Amelia was very thorough in eliminating any clues. It is clear, however, that once Amelia's father died, his past died with him. The following year, 1928, David's mother Ann McNair died and, as was the custom, Ronald was taken to the funerals. To wee Ronald, 'Grandpa' would always mean his father's father, and 'Grandma', his mother's mother.

Grandpa, a naval architect by trade and irreverently known to Ronald as 'Old Pa', was a character, overfond of the bottle and none too keen on working His drunken outbursts were a constant source of fear and embarrassment to the whole family, especially Amelia. Physical encounters between David and John, although rare, were memorable.

David felt that his father had systematically destroyed his mother over the years. This was a real old-fashioned, perpetual clash between a father and son with the consequential dispute as to what actually happened, Glasgow early-thirties style. 'Old Pa' harboured high hopes of not having to work past the age of forty, but he is remembered for suffering sobriety on Sundays. Ethel Laing (Ronnie's aunt on his father's side) describes him as others would later describe Ronnie – 'a very charismatic character – good appearance, speaking voice and great charmer *when sober*'. Unfortunately for Old Pa, economic and familial pressure ensured a continued working life into his sixties, as a lowly clerk. In contrast, Ronnie's maternal grandmother is remembered as the kindliest of ladies, who was consulted by the local community about all and sundry – a type of communal agony aunt for whom no one had a bad word.

As a mother, Amelia was devoted to the point of being over-protective, always fussing about 'wee Ronald' and making absolutely sure that he was not 'contaminated' by the 'riff-raff' down the road. Although she was a fair-looking lady in her day, as evidenced by photographs taken before her marriage, it is probably true, as Ronnie came to believe, that the only time his parents ever had sex was at the time of his conception. The relationship between David and Amelia was totally without outward affection; even David's side of the family thought he had made a great mistake in marrying a person so unsuited to his own character. Amelia's real problem was her inability to express affection to any other human being, including her only child. Perhaps because her father had favoured her two sisters, she developed a coldness, which was the one aspect of her personality remembered above others. She was quick to dismiss others as 'bothersome' and made few friends in life.

Ronnie's father David was a likeable and popular chap. He had a good singing voice, which compensated for his shyness, and overall nobody speaks a harsh word against him. As a father he was strict but fair during Ronnie's early days, and a generous, warm friend to Ronnie as time moved on. Amelia was by far the emotionally stronger of the two and it is in this opposition that one sees the basis for the emotional confusion that troubled Ronnie throughout his life.

David's passion was his music; he was an accomplished baritone who had studied music with Frederick Lemont, a well known and respected music teacher of the time. David's social status was derived more from being the principal baritone at the Glasgow University Chapel choir than being second in command at the West of Scotland Electricity Board. Amelia, by all accounts, had no musical inclinations at all, and was clearly resentful of David's talent. He often expressed himself musically to her open derision.

The relationship between David and Amelia was never a happy one, as far as any one knows; they shared the same flat, ate the same food, were parents to the same child and, on occasions, shared the same bed. Beyond that they shared an emotional void. Sex, even within the sanctioned ground of the matrimonial bed, was an activity which obviously repelled and revolted Amelia to the core. Even after Ronnie's birth, she denied having had sex with David. Were it not for the birthmark on Ronnie's right knee, which was in the same place as David's, Amelia's case for an immaculate conception might have gained further ground. As it was, her denial of carnal knowledge was treated with the humour it deserved.

The relationship between David and Amelia was strained partly due to the constant friction between their respective families. Ethel, for example, could walk down to the local shops and pass one of Amelia's sisters without so much as a 'good-day'. In the emotional bleakness in which Ronnie grew up, the one saving grace was his father's interest in music. It was not uncommon for musical evenings to take place at Ardbeg Street with David singing and Isabella, during her visits to Glasgow, at the piano. Amelia would, if she felt so inclined, turn her back on the lot of them.

The extent to which those evenings filtered through to the well-fed, well-scrubbed and well-tucked-up baby boy during these very early years is difficult to say, although anyone who knew Ronnie and heard him sing 'Roses of Picardy', an old family favourite, would be hard pushed not to see a direct connection between his father and himself. Not just a musical influence but an overlapping of personalities. There exists a recorded duet between Ronnie and his father, which probably dates around 1942. Listening to David sing a few of his old favourites (including 'Roses of Picardy' and 'I Will Not Chide'), accompanied by his teenage son on the piano, one cannot help but feel that there was an extremely close relationship between Ronnie and his dad. Ronnie certainly never enjoyed such an intense musical relationship with any of his own children.

Early photographs show Ronnie to be a bright and bonny wee boy: alert, enthusiastic, mischievous and quick to learn. He was, compared with others in the neighbourhood, well looked after and, undoubtedly, spoiled rotten. The toys which came his way were exceptional treats: one was a wooden horse, which Amelia removed and destroyed when she felt Ronald had become 'too attached' to it. For the remainder of his days, Ronnie was openly embittered about this wooden horse. To him, the destruction of his wooden horse, to which he really had grown very attached, was an act of unmitigated emotional brutality, by his mother. Another favourite plaything of young Ronnie's was a grand toy car. When this toy was broken, Amelia decided to give it away in its dilapidated condition to a 'less fortunate lady' down the road for her boy to play with. As an adult that boy made it clear that Amelia, acting as she did in an aloof and pompously charitable fashion, slighted and insulted the whole street and was never to be forgiven. Amelia, for her part, no doubt thought the lot of them an ungrateful shower.

For most children then and now there are two annual events which lighten up one's life: birthday and Christmas Day. Christmas 1932, shortly after Ronald's fifth birthday, was the an event that might be called his first existential crisis. Ronnie's world was shattered when his parents informed him that Santa Claus was none other than themselves. Could he ever believe them again? Ronnie's written version of this Santa Claus episode exists in manuscript form in about a dozen guises. Always the same story, always told with the same immediacy and passion. Ronnie felt that the shattering of his illusion was an unforgivable conspiracy by his parents. What else were they lying about?

David set high standards for his son. On the occasions when David was performing he was dressed impeccably: starched wing-collar, best tie, dinner suit, waistcoat, cuff-links, spit-and-polish shoes. The highlight of David's musical career was probably during Ronald's fourth year. On 21 February 1932, at a regular, well-attended social event called 'pleasant Sunday evenings' held at the venue, St Andrew's Hall, a couple of serious speeches by Rosslyn Mitchell (a well-known Glasgow lawyer) and Dr T.J. Honeyman (a curator of the Kelvingrove Art Gallery, responsible for purchasing Salvador Dali's 'Christ of St John of the Cross') interlaced the musical entertainment. Top-billing was given to the internationally renowned soprano Maria Marova. In between a piano recital by the pianist Joan Singleton and the violinist David McCallum (father of the well-known actor of the same name) was David Laing, baritone. Despite third billing it was David who started the vocal part of the evening with 'Invictus', later followed by his rendition of 'The Auld Plaid Shawl'. To young Ronald, his father must have seemed a very important figure indeed.

What violence there was at Ardbeg Street rarely centred on Ronnie, and it is difficult to believe that he felt too hard done by despite certain passages in his autobiographical work, *Wisdom, Madness and Folly*, written many years later. In all likelihood, Ronnie received one, maybe two, thrashings throughout the entirety of his childhood and these were precipitated, as far as one can ascertain, by an act which gave David a reluctant excuse for ritualistically chastising Ronald. (Compared to his own father David must have thought of himself as quite liberal.) Ronald's main crime, in his early days, was to disobey his mother's instructions about eating sweets. There was no hiding such transgressions, as Ronnie's body would flare up in an acute form of eczema requiring the expense of ointments and bandages.

At the age of four, Ronnie went to school. Ronnie's education was one subject which united David and Amelia. The young boy would get, like it or not, the education they never had. The local primary school might seem an inauspicious beginning to such a task but the Sir John Neilson Cuthbertson Public School was only a few, safe, minutes' walk from Ardbeg Street, and was highly regarded. So anxious were Amelia and David to have Ronnie enrolled that the records show he had to be turned away due to his premature age on their first attempt. They succeeded, however, in having the name Ronald D. Laing entered into the register on 2 May 1932, when Ronald was still four years old. Three weeks after he started school in mid-August 1932, Ronnie was being lectured on the life and work of Sir Walter Scott.

'Cubby's' was a good choice. Despite the size of the school (there were over 800 pupils), Mr James Reid, the headmaster, was reported to know each pupil. The teachers were not overbearing crypto-sadists, but decent folk who had mastered the art of teaching young children how to read, how to write, how to count, how to say their prayers, how to exercise, how to recite and how to obey. In other words, a solid Presbyterian education with particular emphasis on singing, recitation, verse speaking and drill. The school was also proud of its gramophone, wireless set, cinema and epidiascope. The Inspector's report of Cuthbertson's Primary School of the year 1934–5, when Ronnie, aged seven, was in his third year, proclaimed: 'the children's performance both in the basic subjects and in the lighter side of the curriculum, bespoke most conscientious and efficient teaching.'

By this stage, another important component of Ronnie's education had been set in motion – piano tuition. David knew of a music school for young children called the 'Misses Ommer School of Music'. Julia Ommer, the proprietor, was a well-regarded teacher of music to young children. Ronnie was to share a close relationship with her for many years to come.

The motivation behind the musical regime into which Ronnie was placed was, undoubtedly, David and Amelia's desire to ensure that he received the best they could afford. A secondary consequence was that David had a trained accompanist in the years to come. Indeed, so keen was David to keep tabs on Ronnie's progress that Julia Ommer was forced to reprimand David for teaching Ronnie his own technique instead of hers. This battle was short-lived. Ronnie soon sunk himself into his finger exercises with a self-discipline expected of a would-be concert pianist.

During the mid-1930s Ardbeg Street boasted three budding musicians: Ronnie playing the piano, a girl who practised singing her scales, and another boy who played the violin. So popular were these individual practice sessions that it was not uncommon, as a school friend of Ronnie recollects, for a group of workmen coming home from the tramworks in Crown Street to pause at the corner of Calder Street and Ardbeg Street and listen to the strangely reassuring combination of such musical talent, like three professionals warming up for a concert. Ronnie was a serious, devoted musical scholar who was recognized at an early age as having real potential as a professional musician.

When Ronnie left primary school on 26 June 1936, aged eight, it was, no doubt, with the same exhilarating feeling shared by most boys and girls of that age and of that time. He knew when he left that he was going not to Queen's Park, a good but by no means an outstanding school, nor, indeed, Strathmungo, an educational establishment that concentrated on woodwork for the boys and secretarial skills for the girls. Instead, he had got into Hutchesons' Boys' Grammar School, commonly referred to as 'Hutchie'. Attending Hutchesons' was Ronnie's first step up the school ladder, and David and Amelia were as proud and happy as any parents would be. Young Ronald even had a 'reputation' as the best wee boy at Sunday School: punctual, well behaved and hard-working.

Ronald David Laing was on the path to becoming what his parents had always dreamt of – a musician, a scholar and, above all, 'a perfect gentleman'.

CHAPTER TWO

Hutchesons' Grammar School

Ronnie's days at secondary school (1936–45) coincided with the Second World War and although Glasgow was geographically remote from the front lines, none the less school children were required, occasionally, to carry gas masks, and were drilled in the emergency procedure of donning the masks in the event of an aerial attack by the Germans. By early 1941, this threat of annihilation, although relatively distant, was extremely real to those concerned; once, when aiming for Glasgow's shipbuilding industry, the German bombers went off target and destroyed a Greek church near Queen's Park, not far from Ardbeg Street. In Ronnie's case this ever-present fear lasted from age twelve to seventeen – a fact reflected in his school essays, many of which survive to this day. This dark cloud dominated the lives of children then growing up. Perhaps for this reason, life seemed extremely precarious. Death was a real and constant reality.

In pre-Second World War Glasgow there were five schools recognized as being in a substantially higher academic league than all the others: Glasgow Academy, Hillhead High, Kelvinside Academy, Allen Glens and Hutchesons' Grammar School. As with these other schools, entry into Hutchesons' was either by competitive examination or through the payment of fees. Ronnie sat the exams. There was no doubt in David and Amelia's minds that Ronnie would get in, as he did. The irony was that Hutchesons' was situated in Crown Street, the very heart of the Gorbals. Ronnie walked to school together with a friend called Walter Fife who lived two doors down at number 17 Ardbeg Street. Coming back from school, they might stand at the bottom of

Ronald's close, talking until Amelia's gloved hand would pull back the curtains and tap on the window. This was the signal that the 'bleathering' (idle chatter) was to stop – immediately – and for Ronald to get on with his homework and his piano lessons. Ronnie, for the most part, had a quiet life while he lived at home. In *Wisdom, Madness and Folly* he described the routine of a typical school day:

I would be back at four-thirty unless it was an afternoon at the playing field, when it would be later. Then out for a music lesson or out to play. Back by six for tea when my father would have come home, practice before it was too late for the neighbours, maybe a bit of radio, 'The Brains Trust' (C.E.M. Joad, Julian Huxley, the anonymous Scottish doctor whom I later discovered to to have been Edward Glover, the psychoanalyst), 'Henry Hall's Guest Night', Charlie Krunz [*sic*] and Chopin; and then homework, and then bath, bed, prayers and sleep, negotiated through a reverse process from the morning of undressing, bathing, peeing, doing No. 1, washing my hands and then to bed, lights out, no reading no talking.

For most of the time . . . provided I looked all right, smelt all right and sounded all right, as long as my thoughts were good and my heart was pure, I was as free as a bird.

Hutchesons' Grammar School was to be the foundation of Ronnie's education; there he learned Greek and Latin and, in the process, read the cornerstones of Western intellectual thought in the original languages. The curriculum included the pre-Socratic philosophers, Homer, Sophocles, Euripides, Aeschylus, Ovid, St Augustine, St Francis of Assisi, Plato, Aristotle, the lives of the Roman emperors, the Cynics and Sceptics, Plotinus and the fathers of Catholic and Protestant thought. As a schoolboy Ronnie came across *Oedipus Rex* in Greek prior to reading Freud in English or German many years later. The ground was also laid for Ronnie's public debating life. By all accounts he was a well-respected member of the Hutchesons' debating society, which pupils were encouraged to join in their third year. The debating society was of an unusually high standard; open enquiry was encouraged. Ronald was in his element.

The level of intellectual and cultural education on the inside of

Hutchesons' School was in stark contrast to the immediate world outside. The Gorbals had two main 'teams' – Glasgow street gangs – the Cumbie and the Crosbies. To some of the pupils at Hutchesons', these gangs were nothing more than a remote threat, further removed from everyday concerns than the war. To others they were a source of constant fear, especially on the way home from school. Their violent reputations were awesome; their favoured 'tools' (weapons) were bicycle chains and knives. It requires a special mentality to enjoy fighting with open blades; it was a world which Ronald studiously avoided.

Ronnie was not particularly athletic at school. Sports was something in which he could participate without disgrace or distinction. However, what he lacked in talent he compensated for with enthusiasm, and, considering his lack of physical prowess, it was an achievement to reach the relative heights of the second fifteen rugby team. There was even a short period during which his father insisted that he took boxing lessons, but the threat which this contact sport posed to his potential musical career meant that the boxing lessons were short-lived.

During the course of Ronnie's rugby career he once broke his left wrist and on a separate occasion, his collar-bone. These episodes were heart-stopping blows to his musical technique. Luckily, these setbacks were not sufficiently serious to prevent Ronnie being elected a Licentiate of the Royal Academy of Music on 30 March 1944, aged sixteen – an event which prompted the headmaster to announce the fact to the whole school at morning assembly.

Ronnie was a reluctant Glaswegian. For the majority of young boys in Glasgow then and now, the most important part of life apart from the family is football – an activity which generates an almost iconoclastic passion. The main football team around Govanhill at that time was Queen's Park, based at Hampden. In addition, there was another local football team called Third Lanark. For most Glaswegians based in Govanhill, Saturday afternoon during the football season meant attending one or the other of the football matches. Whether Ronnie had no time for football due to his other interests, or whether Amelia would not have permitted such an 'idle pastime' is difficult to say. During the term time there was only one hour or so for unsupervised play after school and before his tea at six o'clock. During this time, when most other kids were out playing, Ronnie was expected to be practising the piano or doing his homework. He was simply not permitted to join in 'kicking the can' and the like. As far as David and Amelia were concerned, Ronnie was destined for better things.

The school and the Church were powerful forces over young boys in those days, and even more so when acting in league with each other. Male puberty was a time when evil thoughts were likely to take over impressionable and innocent young minds and the Scripture Union or 'The Covenanters' were there to save as many wayward souls as they could. The leading Christian light at Hutchesons' was a man called Michel John – the 'Boss' – who ran a centre for teenagers, a large house off Byres Road in the West End of Glasgow. There the boys could play table tennis and plan their camping trips to Perthshire or the banks of Loch Tay; a weekend with the Covenanters in the summer of 1939 provided Ronnie with his first holiday away from home. Ronnie and a school friend, James Templeton (now one of the few practising psychoanalysts in Glasgow), both joined the Covenanters at about ten or eleven years of age, while they were at the Junior School. They had met in the 'A' group studying Latin and Greek. Also in the same class was Tom Burnett ('the Boss's right-hand boy'). Ronnie's involvement with the Covenanters was, however, brief, and by the time he was fourteen he made a break from the 'Boss' and 'all that stuff' about the word of God, Jesus dying on the cross, the Resurrection, sinfulness, the evils of cinema-going and – the most evil sin of all – physical contact with girls. Even ballroom dancing was claimed to be the work of the devil by virtue of the possible physical contact between the male and female genitals (albeit with the superficial protection of the clothing). The Church recruited boys at an impressionable age and it was not unusual for widespread desertion around the age of fourteen or so, when boys had to make a decision between the Covenanters and girls. Ronnie's departure was a sad loss; his organ playing was greatly missed.

Ronnie was generally in the top four of the 'A' class but never first; the top boy in Ronnie's year was Gordon Smiley who, along with Tom Beg, Tod Ritchie and James Templeton, constantly kept Ronnie away from being top dog. James Templeton, who left Hutchesons' in the fifth form to go straight into the Army while Ronnie stayed on for the sixth form, has very clear memories of those days: music and reading were Ronnie's great passions while at secondary school.

Ronnie's life at Hutchesons' Grammar School consisted mainly of school-work, music and reading. These concerns left little else for Ronnie's attention and there is no evidence that while at Hutchesons' he ever had a girl-friend ('serious' or otherwise). Like many young boys of that age his emotional life was dominated almost entirely by his mother. It was not until Ronnie was fifteen that he was allowed to have a bath on his own without his mother scrubbing his back, as he confessed in *Wisdom, Madness and Folly*. At about the same time his relationship with his father was reaching the stage when theological debate between them was becoming commonplace and their musical relationship was, by any standards, extremely sophisticated. Indeed, family discussions on religious issues were commonplace, as Ronnie's Aunt Ethel clearly remembers.

From the window in his room in Ardbeg Street, Ronnie could see the local library, on top of which sat a stone-carved angel, similar to the statue of Eros in London's Piccadilly Circus. Throughout Ronnie's early days, this angel had an almost hypnotic effect on him, representing magic, wisdom, truth, innocence, and – above all – the possibility of freedom through learning. Govanhill Library was where Ronnie spent more time than anywhere else during the long school holidays; he realized from an early age that his best bet of getting out of his immediate environment was through the cultivation of his mind. For others it would be football, boxing, singing, dancing, acting, sex – anything to get out and get away.

Ronnie went through a rebellious stage at school between the ages of twelve and thirteen, although James Templeton does not recall Ronnie holding the record throughout this period for being strapped more frequently than anyone else by the headmaster, as Ronnie suggested in *Wisdom, Madness and Folly*. Physical punishment (a leather strap or 'tawse' being swiped against the bottom or on up-turned hands in front of one's peers) was commonplace until a few years ago, when the European Court of Human Rights intervened. But by all accounts Ronnie was fairly lucky to be able to record as he did in *Wisdom, Madness and Folly* that 'none of the masters were *serious* sadists'.

Ronnie studied seven subjects at school: mathematics, Greek, Latin, geography, history, drawing and gymnastics. From his final examination results, disclosed by the Scottish Records Office, it is clear that his strong subjects were Greek, Latin, English and history. He was clearly put off both geography and mathematics because of his dislike of the teachers – a feeling that was probably mutual. But as far as mathematics was concerned it was a subject which he simply found too difficult. As was clear from his attitude to mathematics later in his life, and his friendship with the mathematician and author David George Spenser-Brown, he enjoyed the intellectual stimulus from philosophical questions such as 'what is a number?'; 'is the difference between 0 and 1 the same as 1 and 2?'; and 'can one determine the square root of a negative number?'. But differential and integral calculus had Ronnie beaten.

Ronnie left Hutchesons' Grammar School in 1945, aged seventeen, shortly before Armistice was declared. One of his teachers told him that his level of classical knowledge was that of a post-graduate student. He was a gifted and fearless debater. His musical accomplishment then was probably at its highest point in his life. In addition to being elected a Licentiate of the Royal Academy of Music in 1944 he was made an Associate of the Royal College of Music the following year, in April 1945. There was even a family debate as to whether he should pursue a musical career. However, it was David and Amelia's view that although Ronnie was a competent and classically trained musician, he was none the less not good enough to risk everything on such a perilous course. A severe lesson had already been learnt from Isabella, David's sister, who had tried unsuccessfully to make it in London as a singer. On the purely academic side Ronnie had come away from Hutchesons' with two prizes – *Gray's Anatomy* and two volumes of the *Shorter Oxford English Dictionary*. There is no doubt that he was a star pupil with a brilliant career ahead of him.

When Ronnie left school his immediate ambition was to qualify as a doctor, on the grounds that

> it was one of the things approved by my parents, and to me it offered entry into the secret rituals of birth and death, and would give me access to sexual knowledge. Besides there seemed no point in studying anything that was really important, like philosophy or psychology in a University curriculum. These things were matters of personal apprenticeship and I did not know of any master philosopher or psychologist teaching at a University in Britain, and my personal horizons had not stretched beyond the shores of the British Isles. . . . I had not even seen

much of Glasgow. I couldn't imagine Dostoevsky studying literature at a University, or any great writer. But I could imagine such a person studying medicine.*

When he left school, Ronnie was not considering psychiatry. He saw the empirical world through the eyes of a dedicated, albeit confused philosopher. Philosophy was, he thought, in opposition to medicine. However, it was time to put his head down and get through the exams; Glasgow University beckoned.

---

* From an unpublished work, 'Elements for an Autobiography', written while on holiday on Patmos during July 1968.

CHAPTER THREE

Glasgow University

Ronnie spent nearly six years at Glasgow University, from October 1945, less than a week before his eighteenth birthday, until graduation in February 1951, at the precocious age of twenty-three. His contemporary world throughout University consisted of fellow medical students Douglas Hutchinson, Mike Scott, James Hood, Norman Todd and Lenny Davidson. Walter Fife, Ronnie's classmate from Hutchesons' who was studying philosophy, and George Paul, a classics student were, in addition to Johnny Duffy from the Merchant Navy, among the wide range of close friends Ronnie mixed with during those years. George MacLeod, a senior figure in Glasgow at the time who had rejuvenated the Iona Community, and Joe Schorstein, a surgeon at the West of Scotland Neurosurgical Unit in nearby Killearn, were among the elder generation who took a shine to the budding doctor. Last, but by no means least, was his first love, whom he met during the second year through George Paul – a beautiful French student called Marcelle Vincent with whom he talked of Camus, Sartre and Marx.

During his undergraduate years Ronnie played the piano a great deal both for recreation and financial reward. He enjoyed reading, debating, croquet, tennis, climbing, camping, swimming, hitch-hiking, walking, and competitive cross-country running, although his running career came to an abrupt halt during the course of a race with Dublin University in the first year as the result of an asthma attack. At Glasgow University Ronnie was a popular guy with an ever-growing reputation for the extreme. Mike Scott, for example, recalled an epic tennis match between two equally obstinate spirits, which lasted all day. Too tired to keep the score, Ronnie and a fellow student played from sunrise to sunset, just to see who could keep going the longest.

The days at Glasgow University were among the most influential in Ronnie's life. He, like other students, grew up, and grew up fast. It was only later in life that Ronnie talked of University in 'anti-psychiatry' tones. It would appear that Ronnie had as full and rewarding a time as any undergraduate could wish for.

Relative to Ardbeg Street, the main campus of Glasgow University is merely a couple of miles further up the road from Hutchesons' Grammar School. One peculiarity at the university is the large proportion of undergraduates who remain at home throughout their studies – quite consistently around eighty per cent. Until the age of twenty-three, Ronnie lived at home except for a few months during 1950 when he was a houseman at Stobhill Hospital. There is no doubt in the minds of those who knew Ronnie in those days that this prolonged, day-to-day contact with his parents was a major factor in the breakdown of his relationship with them, particularly with his mother, Amelia.

In the year Ronnie enrolled there were about two hundred medical students. Once in the large lecture rooms, the students tended to group themselves by reference to which school they had just left. From Paisley Grammar School there was Mike Scott, Norman Todd and Douglas Hutchinson, all of whom, at Ronnie's suggestion, later went into psychiatry. The 'Hutchie' group included Tom Beg, who had the reputation as the scholar and the 'Dux' (the best academic student) of Hutchesons'. In addition, there was the usual crop from Allen Glens, Kelvinside, Hillhead High and Glasgow Academy. There was also the distinction between those who had been in the Army and those who had not. Naturally there was rivalry and one-upmanship between these factions. The ex-servicemen were goaded by the schoolboys and vice versa, although some thought schoolboy humour had gone too far when the younger students started a fad by making imitation whistling-bomb noises during the lectures to freak out the ex-servicemen. Those were the days. . . .

The formidable five-year medical course is a well-trodden path for the fresh-faced, bright and eager teenager, with the basics of biology, physics and chemistry in the first year and those of anatomy, physiology, and embryology in the second. These initial two pre-clinical years are followed by three clinical years studying pathology, obstetrics and gynaecology, and, finally, anaesthetics. The tactics used to get the students through are many and have evolved over several generations. An important component, brought into play in the first clinical year, is the 'pairing-up' between students. Ronnie was paired up with Douglas Hutchinson, perhaps the closest friend Ronnie ever had in his life next to Johnny Duffy or Lenny Davidson.

The clinical training for obstetrics and deliveries was in Dublin, which was where Ronnie and 'the boys' went. Students were expected to make a total of twenty deliveries over a period of several weeks, sometimes in the middle of the night, assisted only by a midwife. They learned how to deliver babies having had little sleep for days on end, how to deliver babies when hung-over from the night before, how to deal with the emotional aftermath of the delivery of a still-born or deformed child. This was an extremely intense period, during which the schoolboy became initiated into the real, hard world of everyday life. Hard drinking was the necessary complement to a hard day.

One of the marks that Ronnie left on Glasgow University was the creation of the 'Socratic Club', formed for the purpose of non-dogmatic discussion on matters relating principally to theology and philosophy. Although there seems no doubt that Ronnie was the moving spirit behind the creation of the Socratic Club, its successful functioning was equally attributable to many other fellow students, including Robert Gouldie, Allen Garrett, John McQueen, Allen Heath, Jimmy Willcox, Robert Colville, Douglas Hutchinson, Mike Scott, Norman Todd and a lady called Helen. The debates at the Socratic Club are remembered as 'impressive', and Ronnie quickly established a reputation for himself as an excellent debater with a razor-sharp mind. Mike Scott remembers one occasion when Ronnie was chairing a debate between the Catholics and the Communists. As the end of a prolonged and acrimonious discussion, Ronnie dismissed their respective positions with the words, 'a plague on both your houses'.

It was also through the Socratic Club that Ronnie came across his first real mentor – Joe Schorstein – who was a respected practising surgeon at the West of Scotland Neurological Unit based in Killearn, outside Glasgow. Ronnie describes Schorstein in *Wisdom, Madness and Folly* as a substitute father figure, as well as an intellectual companion. Joe was against 'the mechanisation of medicine' and a strong advocate against the growing use of leucotomies and electric shock therapy. He also passionately felt medicine had 'taken the wrong path'. The writings of Karl Jaspers, Nietzsche, Kierkegaard and Kant were common ground to Joe and Ronnie.

Walter Fife believes that Ronnie missed out by not formally studying philosophy and/or theology. It was as if Ronnie, one of the founder members of the Socratic Club, was filling an intellectual lacuna created by studying medicine, and sorely missed the heady, far-off days at Hutchie studying Latin and Greek. The function of the Socratic Club, from Ronnie's point of view, was threefold: firstly, Ronnie could bring together people from all walks of life and persuasions to discuss issues that troubled him intellectually; secondly a means of making contact with people of influence was established; and, thirdly, Ronnie could be part of a scene over which he could exercise authority in a manner which was disproportionate to his actual status. According to Glasgow University, the Socratic Club survived well into the 1970s and then petered out, quietly and without ceremony.

Douglas Hutchinson was Ronnie's closest friend and contemporary throughout university. In the second year, Ronnie became involved in the Glasgow University Mountaineering Club (referred to as G.U.M.). Its secretary was Stan Stewart (later a lawyer) and, at the time, Angela Hood, sister of Ronnie's friend James, was the toast of the club. This interest in mountaineering was inspired as much by the onset of Ronnie's asthma in the preceding year as by his tenuous interest in putting his life at risk climbing over the treacherous Scottish countryside. The asthma attack during the race against Dublin University had rocked Ronnie. At a stroke, all sports requiring intense physical activity such as running and rugby were considered 'too risky'. Mountaineering, of the less energetic type, provided the solution to a tricky problem. Ronnie enjoyed hanging out with the lads but had to be careful of the activities which preceded the 'jollies' (heavy drinking sessions). Those who later became psychiatrists as a result of Ronnie's influence, Mike Scott, James Hood and Norman Todd, were all met through G.U.M. These friendships were sustained throughout the long summer holidays. During the summer of 1947, Mike Scott worked with Ronnie in hotels in Torquay and youth hostels around the country. It was also through Mike Scott that Ronnie met one of his most enduring and long-suffering friends – Johnny Duffy.

In 1947 Johnny was sponsored by the Merchant Navy to study at the Royal College of Science and Technology. Although not at the university, Johnny would join G.U.M. for a weekend and occasionally attend the Socratic Club. Johnny was an important part of Ronnie's life, one of the very few people with whom Ronnie kept in contact throughout his turbulent career. More importantly, Johnny was one of a very small group of people who could tell Ronnie, when necessary, to 'cut the crap'. Johnny still remembers vividly the occasion when they first met, at lunchtime in Waterloo Station on a beautiful sunny Saturday morning. The two immediately clicked together.

Another G.U.M. connection was Norman Todd, who knew Ronnie from 1945 through to 1951, although Norman was never really close to Ronnie – he found him 'too intense'. Norman went into psychiatry in 1957 and worked as a psychiatrist for nearly thirty years at Leverndale Hospital, where Ronnie's father lived out the remainder of his days in the psychogeriatric ward.

Ronnie was not committed to the G.U.M to the same extent as Norman Todd, Douglas Hutchinson and James Hood, all of whom were serious and accomplished mountaineers. Ronnie mucked in, joining G.U.M. for the not-too-serious expeditions, although he would go on relatively adventurous walks, including climbing over Scotland's highest mountain, Ben Nevis, during the winter, and conquering the mountainous regions of Inverness. G.U.M. was an open club, and a weekend would be arranged with short notice; whoever turned up would be welcomed on board. Setting off, normally by bus on a Saturday morning, rucksacks packed to bursting point, the group would venture into the Scottish hillside and spend the evenings talking about whatever cropped up. Norman Todd still recollects Ronnie's obsession with issues such as the relationship between madness and genius. Mike Scott was left with the memory of Ronnie's sense of humour, which he described as consistent throughout Ronnie's university days: 'daring and anti-conventional'. G.U.M. provided Ronnie with a great team of mates, and the G.U.M. annual dinner was one event in the year when everyone was expected to get completely wrecked on a lethal combination of whisky and bottled Guinness. Ronnie was no exception.

Complex relationships were a perpetual feature of Ronnie's life. Hidden as a club within a club was a group that called itself 'The Trinity', whose members were Ronnie, Bill Donaldson and Johnny Duffy. Ronnie, Bill and Johnny 'cut about' together. Stories of The Trinity are, quite rightly, kept well within the memories of its former members. On the fringes of The Trinity, but never a fully-fledged member, was Aaron Esterson, with whom Ronald would later write *Sanity, Madness and the Family* (vol. I). Aaron became a drinking friend of both Ronnie and Johnny Duffy, but for some reason the camaraderie which existed between Ronnie and Douglas or between Ronnie and Johnny was never established between Aaron and Ronnie. The relationship between Aaron and Ronnie, which evolved over the years and was later to come to a bitter and acrimonious end after the setting up of Kingsley Hall in 1965, is rooted in these early days at Glasgow University.

Ronnie's musical training served him well throughout his university days. As his repertoire ranged from the classical to the bawdy, he was in constant demand, whether around the piano in the students' recreational area or as a paid performer for a formal social event, such as a birthday party or a wedding. These were memorable and hilarious evenings, often preceded by a hair-raising journey to the venue on Johnny Duffy's 500cc motor bike. On one occasion Ronnie was even requested to play at a social function in the house of a retired Admiral.

The pattern of these events became familiar. The formal part (which never lasted too long) was inevitably followed by complete disintegration into drunken bawdiness, signalled by the opening bars of 'Four and Twenty Virgins', which became one of Ronnie and Johnny's popular party pieces. This ever-popular drinking song opened with the words:

> *Four and twenty virgins*
> *Came down from Inverness*
> *And when the Ball was over*
> *There were four and twenty less*

followed by the chorus:

> *Singing balls to your partner*
> *Your ass against the wall*
> *If ye canna get fucked on a Saturday night*
> *Ye canna get fucked at all*

and then by Johnny's verse, which Ronnie remembered throughout his life:

> *Septimus Branigan he was there*
> *He put a jolly good show*
> *He shoved his tagger up his arse*
> *And tied it in a bow*

Then one of Ronnie's favourite verses might be sung:

> *First lady forward*
> *Second lady back*
> *First lady's finger*
> *Up the second lady's crack*

And so, back to the chorus, which was followed by as many verses as the assembled crowd could drag out in their inebriated condition.

The drinking was heavy but not excessive by the high standards expected of medical students and Merchant Navy characters such as Ronnie and Johnny. Indeed, Johnny did not think that Ronnie's drinking was 'over the top' – it was just that others who thought along those lines only said so because they did not have the capacity to keep up.

Ronnie and Johnny did not spend all of their time together becoming inebriated; they often attended concerts and recitals together or went swimming with other university medical students, such as David Gould, in Cuilness, on the banks of Loch Lomond. A lodge was found, where Ronnie, Johnny and David Gould could go for weekends. These swimming ventures lasted from about 1948 to as late as 1955.

Of constant concern to both Ronnie and his friends was the intense asthma which beset Ronnie from his first year. Johnny remembers that it practically went away shortly after he married in 1952, but recalled one incident when they were camping. Ronnie had such a bad asthma attack that Johnny had to persuade him to swap his old Army blanket for Johnny's top-of-the-range quilted sleeping bag. At about the same time in 1947, Julia Ommer, who had been Ronnie's music teacher from the age of seven, became very ill. Ronnie was terribly upset, in tears, when he visited her. He was her star pupil and their relationship, according to Johnny, was like mother and son.

For Ronnie, like many students, university life was a combination of serious socializing and serious study. His early interest in psychiatry is evidenced by his voluntary participation in the Saturday morning sessions at Duke Street, where a Dr Isaac Sclare gave extra-curricular talks on psychiatry. Despite Ronnie's lack of interest in his formal studies he was none the less awarded an informal first prize by Isaac Sclare. Douglas Hutchinson came an honourable second. Ronnie's other involvement with psychiatry was with the Medico-Chirurgical Society which organized an annual visit to Gartnavel Mental Hospital. For many students this was akin to Bedlam-like entertainment, but for Ronnie it provided a first encounter with the type of behaviour that obsessed him throughout his adult life. At the first lecture, two people appeared on the lecture room floor – Professor McNiven and a psychiatric patient from Gartnavel. Ronnie genuinely believed that the professor was the psychiatric patient, a fact that he later put to Professor McNiven, who took it 'with no hard feelings'.

That Ronnie's path lay in the field of philosophy and medicine is indicated by two papers published by *Surgo*, the Glasgow University medical journal. The first, entitled 'Philosophy and Medicine', was published in June of 1949. Ronnie's second paper, his 'Winning Senior Address at the Medico-Chirurgical Society Members' Night', was published in the Candlemas edition of 1950, under the title 'Health and Society'. The combination of the these two papers provides the clearest evidence of a serious scholar and skilled debater. Ronnie was also awarded the Medical Student's Prize of £25 during the year 1948–9, for his essay 'Health and Happiness'.

Ronnie was a well-regarded student of great promise. He was expected to sail through all his exams, perhaps even win a prize or two. Quite unexpectedly, he failed the lot. Failing *all* of the exams was practically unheard of in those days, and brought great shame on his mother. Ronnie blamed his dramatic and unforeseen failure on the combination of the 'Health and Society' speech (during which he talked of the 'syphilisation of society') and a drunken discussion with a professor at the latter end of his studies, during which he unwisely argued that medical exams were merely examinations in the ability to pass exams. But more likely, Ronnie's spectacular fall from grace was due to the absence of any foundation in science and his obsession with extra-curricular interests, which distracted him from his formal studies. Ronnie's failure was a hard blow, which he forever held against 'the establishment'.

However, failing the exams in the early part of 1950 meant that Ronnie could take a job as a houseman in the Psychiatric Unit at

Stobhill Hospital on the outskirts of Glasgow before sitting the exams again in December. Stobhill housed about eighty men and women who had caught what was thought to be a form of influenza, but turned out to be encephalitis lethargica. It was here that Ronnie's aim crystallized: 'I knew what I wanted to go for. Neurology, neuropsychiatry, psychiatry, not forgetting hypnosis.' Ronnie's flirtation with hypnosis is well documented in *Wisdom, Madness and Folly*.

Ronnie re-sat all of his exams and was confirmed to have passed in late December 1950. Ronnie's belated success was much to everyone's relief; Amelia's weight had sunk to a mere five stones with the worry and shame of it all. But he had passed and that was the end of that.

Upon qualification, the medical students were required to make a declaration based on the Hippocratic oath; until 1868, it had to be recited in Latin. One part of this oath stuck with Ronnie: 'I will not knowingly or intentionally do anything or administer anything to them to their hurt or prejudice for any consideration or from any motive whatever.' Throughout his professional life, these words were a constant reminder of what he considered to be his humanitarian duty – not to impose 'treatment' upon those who did not want it.

Ronnie graduated from Glasgow University on 14 February 1951. Unlike most students, he did not participate in the ritual of graduation photographs, and opted instead for a drink with his buddy Johnny Duffy. His undergraduate days were now behind him. The road ahead pointed towards a small community based in Killearn, about five miles north-east of Glasgow. Although only a few miles outside the centre of Glasgow, the small community of Killearn lies deep in the Scottish countryside and is as beautiful a part of the world as one could wish for. As a bonus Ronnie was under the tutelage of his mentor, Joe Schorstein. The year 1951, in Killearn, turned out to be one of Ronnie's most fulfilling.

CHAPTER FOUR

Killearn and National Service

A few miles from the centre of Glasgow, heading north-east towards Stirling, lies the small community of Killearn, where the West of Scotland Neurosurgical Unit was situated. Here, Ronnie spent from February to October 1951 under the wing of Joe Schorstein. These were days when he was stretched – physically and mentally – to the limit. It was also during this relatively short period that two fainting bouts during operations confirmed that Ronnie had not the stomach for surgery.

During 1951 there were three neurosurgical chiefs at the West of Scotland Neurosurgical Unit: Professors Paterson, Robertson and Schorstein. Much of their work was the result of motoring accidents on the treacherous, winding roads that lead further north into the Cairngorms along the west banks of Loch Lomond. This was unpretentious and well-praised work performed by hard-working and dedicated surgeons who had learned their trade during the war.

However, Killearn was also the unit to which psychiatric patients of a particularly disturbed and violent nature were sent for lobotomies. Of the three surgeons *in situ*, Professor Robertson was the only one willing to perform lobotomies, although it would appear that Paterson and Schorstein refused for very different reasons. The primitive method of entering the skull with ice-pick and hammer, followed by the use of an instrument which could easily be confused with an industrial manual drill, resulted in undisputed, irreversible brain damage. This was justified on the basis of the change in the post-operational behaviour of the patient. But even in those days, a surgeon would not be criticized for refusing to perform a lobotomy on the grounds that the medical evidence was insufficiently persuasive to justify the damage caused during the operation itself. This was Paterson's view. Joe Schorstein, on the other hand, was against lobotomies on far wider grounds, believing that there were serious ethical objections to such brutality masquerading as treatment.

The debate, as one might imagine, was a furious one. At Killearn, Ronnie was in the midst of real medical issues, with real consequences for real people. Even Joe Schorstein was unduly conservative in Ronnie's view, since Ronnie believed that a lobotomy was the final act in the destruction of the will of the subversive, as drastic and inhumane as ever conceived by man against man. Ronnie was forever surprised why more people, both inside and outside the medical profession, did not share his unabashed anger. However, the fact of the matter was that he was straight out of 'school'. His opinions carried no weight. What did he know – a twenty-three-year-old who had yet to master the art of maintaining consciousness during a routine brain operation? It would be a long time before his voice would be listened to – and he knew it. There was one consolation. Joe Schorstein was a deeply cultivated and educated character who had great respect for Ronnie's intellect. They became closer to each other than Ronnie was to his own father, David. Although Ronnie's style of expressing his dissent was seen as part of his immaturity, he none the less realized that his feelings were shared, albeit in a diluted form, by others.

Ronnie recalls much of the detail of his few months at Killearn in *Wisdom, Madness and Folly*. He describes his intellectual relationship with Joe Schorstein, and the routine duties at the unit: 'general systemic and neurological examinations, assisting at operations, accompany consultants on ward rounds; above all, to set up "drips" without thrombosing the patient's arms, to do lumbar punctures without turning the lower back into a pincushion, and to get a cannula through a burr-hole (a hole made in the skull by the surgeon) to draw off cerebral spinal fluid from the lateral ventricle without turning the temporal lobe into mush'. Above all, Ronnie learned that surgery would not be his future – he was beginning to focus, for the first time, upon psychiatry.

In the meantime, conscription was looming on the horizon. With others of his generation, he faced two years in the Army, possibly (as with old university friends such as Mike Scott) based in Korea. Ronnie's mind was working overtime on how to 'beat the rap'. As a doctor he was classified as a non-combatant, but this argument only served to prevent medical students from engaging in actual battle, not from National Service itself.

Two prime years of his life in the army! Ronnie always thought that the 'powers that be', as represented by an Army panel in Edinburgh, would be persuaded to let him live a dream life he had constructed for himself, which consisted of living with his university girlfriend Marcelle in Montmartre in Paris, and studying in Basel with Karl Jaspers, with whom he had already made contact. Glasgow University had sanctioned the idea with the promise of some funds and Marcelle was waiting for the return of her university love. However, the Army panel recognized a promising student with great potential in psychiatry, and decided that as Karl Jaspers was merely 'an armchair philosopher', the best road forward for young Dr Ronald Laing would be in the Army, in psychiatric practice. As a consolation prize, the two years would be counted as one of the years required towards his Diploma of Psychiatric Medicine. Ronnie felt that this was heavy-handed interference with his own plans, but realized there was no getting away from this decision. Marcelle was heartbroken as the sad fact dawned on the couple that all their plans were unattainable dreams. Ronnie realized for the first time in his life what it meant to break another's heart. The extent to which Marcelle's love was reciprocated is difficult to determine; Ronnie expressed his love to her on many occasions and at one stage contemplated marriage. But it would seem that once they went their separate ways after university, their love was destined to be unfulfilled.

Marcelle was undoubtedly an important person throughout Ronnie's university life. Ronnie later wrote of his university and Killearn days, while in the Army, and while suffering from a rare pique of nostalgia:

I would like to tell others about MacLeod, about the acting of Duncan MacCrae, and Eillen Worth; about Johnny Duffy, George Paul and Douglas Hutchinson − about times in tents, on the hills; about Marcelle; and also experiences of 'the night side of life', above all about Joe Schorstein. But I shall never do so − lack of sustained interest in recording, lack of ability in written communication.

The Army, for Ronnie, meant being part of the Royal Army Medical Corps from October 1951 until September 1953. Whatever expectations he might have had of Army life, he little expected what horrors awaited him in the deep insulin ward in the Royal Victoria Hospital in Netley, near Southampton, or the detention barracks in Catterick, Yorkshire. Lobotomies at Killearn may have been extreme, but they were quite rare. During his Army days Ronnie was, for the first time in his life, very much part of 'the system'. He administered drugs, he gave electric shocks, he induced comas and epileptic fits through the injection of insulin. Strait-jackets and padded cells were integral to psychiatric practice at the time. Doctors were not expected to speak to psychiatric patients. The early 1950s were dark ages in the history of the treatment of the insane.

Norman Todd, one of Ronnie's former Glasgow University Mountaineering Club friends, was called up in September 1951, as was Ronnie himself. Both were posted to Aldershot, south-west of London, for their initiation into the Army. Norman was a welcome face among the sneering Sassenachs who thought civilization ended at Watford. Coming from Scotland, the two were treated as foreigners by their English counterparts. Some of their peers had never heard of Glasgow University and believed Edinburgh to be the only place where medicine was taught in Scotland. The bullshit was of a particularly memorable nature. New internees were required to state to which religious belief they subscribed. The answer, for some reason, had to be entered into the Army pay book. The entry in Ronnie's book read 'Church of England'. At a later stage this was noticed by Mike Scott, who queried why the entry was not Church of Scotland. Ronnie explained. During enrolment at Aldershot, a steely-eyed Sergeant Major had asked Ronnie his religion. Ronnie said: 'I am an atheist – I haven't got a religion.' The sergeant told him that as a member of the Army he *must* have a religion. Ronnie said Church of England, as 'that was the closest to atheism I could think of. . . .'

Mercifully, Aldershot only lasted two weeks. Anyone who knew Ronnie can only begin to imagine the righteous indignation with which he took to the compulsory 'square-bashing', marching round and round and round the Army grounds. The cockney voice of the drill sergeant was still ringing in his ears thirty years later. 'Left! Right! Left! Right! Get yer knees up lad you bleeding poofter! Yer bleeding granny could do better you bleeding fairy! Left! Right! Left! Right! On the double! MOVE IT!'

Ronnie consoled himself reading Sartre in French during those few moments when he was left alone. Everyone else lay asleep with exhaustion.

Following the two weeks at Aldershot there was two weeks' 'theoretical' training at Millbank in London, at the Royal Medical College, near the Tate Gallery. These were no-holds-barred lessons on germ warfare and nuclear attacks. Norman Todd was, again, Ronnie's sole companion. Norman remembers that the literature they were required to study was widely available and was not 'secretive and classified', as Ronnie made out in *Wisdom, Madness and Folly*. In that book Ronnie tells the story of walking out of a lecture complaining about the fatally high X-ray shots given to human guinea pigs during the war by the Nazis. As a well-deserved break from all this, Norman and Ronnie would go out and about to the London theatre-land. This was Ronnie's first taste of London. Following Millbank, Norman and Ronnie parted ways. Norman was posted to Salisbury, Ronnie to the British Army Psychiatric Unit in Netley, a sweet English town near Southampton. Here he would meet his first wife – Sister Hearne – who was working in the hospital where Ronnie was to be stationed as Lieutenant Doctor Ronald David Laing R.A.M.C.

Although the central British Army Psychiatry Unit of the Royal Victoria Hospital at Netley contained many wards other than those involved in deep-insulin coma treatment, it was the stark horror of this particular form of 'modern treatment' that stayed with Ronnie. As he recalled in *Wisdom, Madness and Folly*:

Insulin was administered at six o'clock in the morning and within four hours the patients began to go into coma. The course of insulin started off with ten units, increased daily by ten units until the patients went into deep comas and sometimes epileptic fits. The policy was to put it in at a level at which epileptic fits were liable to occur, but to avoid them if possible. Backs could break. Light is extremely epileptogenic under a lot of insulin. The ward was entirely blacked out. When people started to go into coma we, the staff, moved around in total darkness, penetrated only by the rays of the torches on hinges we had strapped to our foreheads. It was essential to get each patient out of his or her coma before too long, because if we did not, the coma became 'irreversible'. Around ten o'clock, we poured quantities of 50 per

cent glucose into the patients through stomach tubes. We hoped
we had got the tube into the stomach rather than the lungs.
Difficult to tell sometimes with someone in a coma. We often
had to put up pressurized glucose drips in the darkness for
patients already completely collapsed whose veins had
disappeared. There were those who 'had no veins left' because of
thrombosis everywhere caused by veins bursting under pressure,
and needles would 'miss the vein', glucose solution pouring into
tissues. One might have to take a scalpel to 'cut down' and stick
a needle into something one just hoped was not an artery or a
nerve. We only had our headlights.

It is difficult for a non-medic to get to grips with the rationale
behind such treatment, of which insulin-induced comas, electric shocks,
strait-jackets, tranquillizers and padded cells formed the main components. A Dr Mayer-Gross had produced 'results' in insulin-based courses
in Dumfries. Ugo Cerletti, Professor of Psychiatry at Rome University, produced encouraging statistics on the benefits to diagnosed schizophrenics who were given electric shocks. There was no dispute that
Cerletti had this brainstorm witnessing pigs being given electric shocks
in slaughterhouses: not all the pigs died. Cerletti reasoned that schizophrenics might benefit from electric shocks. As far as Ronnie was
concerned, the practice of electric shock treatment was totally crazy.
'Would you think of doing that to a normal person?' he would say.
'If not, why on earth is it being done to disturbed people?' But there
were *results*. Ronnie did his duty and administered insulin comas, electric
shocks and drugs. He felt, however, that all of this was wrong, unjust
and counterproductive. Why, therefore, was it all the rage? Was he
alone in thinking that this was yet another form of brutality masquerading as treatment? Could there not be a better way than this irra-
tional and inhumane treatment? A single patient was to provide Ronnie
with the confidence to think in 'inter-personal' terms. Ronnie became
a pupil, while at Netley, of 'schizophrenese'.
One night, instead of ordering a ranting and raving patient to be
injected with tranquillizers, Ronnie decided to spend time with him in
the padded cell.

I had the padded cell opened and went in and sat down to listen
a bit more before he would have to be stopped by injection. He

calmed down. I stayed for half an hour or so. He did not need an injection. On the next few nights I stayed for longer until I was almost 'hanging out' during the night with him in his padded cell. I felt strangely at home there, lounging on the floor.

During those nights, Ronnie gradually came to understand the disjuncted utterances of this patient. Ronnie joined in 'John's' fantasies, talked with him, drank whisky in the padded cell with him, but most importantly, *listened* to him. As Ronnie describes in *Wisdom, Madness and Folly*, he was nominated 'Horatio' to John's 'Hamlet'. (A thankful letter was later sent to Ronnie after John had been discharged: 'Dear Horatio', it began.) They had become friends. 'His padded cell had become a refuge for me and his company a solace.'

'Hanging out' with John in the padded cell was not an idle pastime. These sessions went on for some time, encouraging Ronnie's growing belief that mainstream psychiatry had got it all wrong. The textbooks provided no support for his way of thinking and there was no one around with whom he could share his sentiments. Ronnie knew that he was on to something – but what? All he was advocating was, in effect, giving no 'treatment', as understood and accepted at the time. Treatment, in Ronnie's eyes, meant how people treated other people. Listening to people was, therefore, treatment. Seeing patients as people was treatment. While at Netley Ronnie even went so far as to take one of the patients from the insulin ward to stay at home with his mother and father in Glasgow during a week's leave, and he later used 'the case of Peter' as the basis for a chapter in *The Divided Self*. It took Ronnie the next six years of his life to articulate his concerns, and culminated in his first two publications: *The Divided Self* and *Self and Others*.

Ronnie's diaries of that period provide a rare insight into his thoughts and feelings. The pressure of leading what seemed to him a double life, which betrayed his innermost beliefs, was getting him down. He was drinking too much. By February 1952, when still a young man of twenty-four, he wrote: 'The essence of what it is that I seek to achieve by drunkenness is still unrevealed to me.' The cause of his excessive drinking at this stage in his life was probably the torment created through the conflict between his real life as an Army lieutenant and his fantasy life, in which there were no insulin coma wards, no electric shock therapy, no drugs. To Ronnie, the concept of madness was always as much a philosophical problem, if not more so, than a medical one. His diary at the time provides the evidence: ' "Sanity" is determinism and totalitarianism. It is death to the soul and the end of freedom. Against this self-justified tautology, this invincible and inevitable self-rectitude, the romantic revolt takes its origin.'

The 'romantic revolt' would, however, have to wait. The time was not right — yet.

Despite the frustrating reality of having the relatively lowly status of a lieutenant in the Army, Ronnie decided it was time to put pen to paper for the first time in a professional capacity, and 'say something'. The radical stuff would have to wait. Ronnie came across a patient who had all the classic symptoms of 'The Ganser Syndrome', otherwise known as the syndrome of 'approximate answers' or 'talking past the point'. This was an opportunity for the serious young doctor, not yet qualified as a psychiatrist, to make a contribution, to make his voice heard.

In July of 1953 the *Journal of the Royal Army Medical Corps* published 'An Instance of the Ganser Syndrome', by Lieutenant Ronald D. Laing, Royal Army Medical Corps, Psychiatric Division, Royal Victoria Hospital, Netley. The article reads like many others — well researched, well written and very *calm*. Ironically, it might have seemed to Ronnie that the article itself was 'talking past the point'. A young man found himself in serious trouble with the Army through his desertion and was up for court-martial. Ronnie's duty was to recommend whether the chap was 'genuinely crazy' or 'merely malingering'. By all accounts this poor sod was suffering from everything the psychiatric textbooks mentioned, and had also suffered a recent road accident resulting in severe chest injuries and lacerations. His wife had betrayed him and had had a child by another man, resulting in divorce. He went AWOL and then surrendered himself to the authorities. Ronnie concluded in his paper: 'It would seem that this Ganser-like reaction may be understood as a massive, desperate, and temporary defence to a situation fraught with both internal and external danger to the ego. In this case the most intense and immediate danger was intra-psychic.'

This was Ronnie in 1952, aged twenty-four. From the earliest opportunity he declared that madness was behaviour, to be understood within the context of the patient's own world. He was, none the less, holding a great deal back: his real intention was to find a way in which he could articulate his anger against mainstream psychiatric practices, which he always felt to be infinitely more crazy than the utterances and behaviour of the so-called patient.

Ronnie's days at Netley were coming to a rapid end. Ardbeg Street, Cuthbertson's Primary School, Hutchesons' Grammar School, Glasgow University, Stobhill Hospital, Killearn – i.e., Ronnie's Glasgow – were now part of his distant past. Occasionally he was reminded of those far-off days with a letter from one of the 'auld gang' – perhaps from Mike Scott in the China Sea, or from Johnny Duffy remembering the days of The Trinity; from an increasingly distraught Marcelle, or from Joe Schorstein with the latest gossip from the Socratic Club; perhaps a letter from his Aunt Ethel with the latest family comings and goings. His thoughts would drift back to encounters with George MacLeod in Killearn, whose words of wisdom he recalled in his diary entry for 16 January 1952:

> You are an artist Ronnie and also a scientist. . . . You're done for, unless you become a Christian. . . . You will never be a good psychiatrist unless you become a Christian – and if you are a good psychiatrist it doesn't matter anyway. . . . You will never become a Christian, Ronnie, until you are physically sick.

The year at Netley soon passed. As Ronnie had successfully completed the first half of National Service, the authorities had no difficulty in promoting the young Lieutenant to Captain and placing him in charge of Catterick Military Hospital in Yorkshire. Ronnie briefly described the set-up in *Wisdom, Madness and Folly*:

> After a year at Netley, I was transferred to Northern Command at Catterick in Yorkshire. I became a captain and had the job of being, in effect, in clinical and administrative command of the psychiatric ward and detention ward of Catterick Military Hospital, which contained any sort of prisoners in detention in any sort of medical or surgical condition, psychiatric or not. The two wards were separated by steel grilles, the detention ward

being doubly secured behind a double-locked grille and two double-locked doors. These wards were my domain. In addition, my duties included any sort of psychiatric referral. I liaised with the rest of the hospital in terms of neurological, neuropsychiatric problems, had to visit various units in Northern Command, to visit and give a psychiatric report on any soldier on whom it was deemed appropriate who had got into a civilian prison....

Ronnie's principal function was to make a professional judgement as to whether an individual was a genuine 'psychiatric case' or a malingerer. This was no easy task, even putting aside Ronnie's philosophical beliefs, which always centred on the intrinsic ambiguity of 'madness'. Ronnie and a colleague, Murray Brookes, wrote an unpublished paper* on 'the difficult clinical problem' of soldiers whose auditory functions seemed perfectly normal, but who claimed to be unable to hear. Although Murray Brookes and Ronnie became friends for only a few months, Murray recalls an aspect of Ronnie's personality to which many witnesses are keen to testify: his incredible empathy with disturbed patients. Murray went so far as to describe Ronnie as being 'on the side of Angels, gentle to the fallen'.

Despite Ronnie's undoubted generosity of spirit towards 'the fallen' and his extremely rare empathy with the insane, he had little patience with those who thought they could pull the wool over his eyes in order to get out of the Army. As with any Army doctor there were very difficult decisions to be made on a day-to-day basis and during the course of the year at Catterick Ronnie was required to make frequent professional judgements of a highly discerning nature.

While at Catterick, Ronnie's girlfriend from the Royal Victoria Hospital in Netley, Sister Hearne, informed Ronnie out of the blue that she was expecting his child. Ronnie, despite some initial reservation expressed during a period of consultation with Joe Schorstein and Johnny Duffy, decided to take the honourable course. Anne and Ronnie married on 11 October 1952 in Richmond Registry Office and Fiona was born on 7 December of the same year; Douglas Hutchinson was Ronnie's best man. Two days after his marriage Ronnie wrote a farewell love letter to Marcelle Vincent, complaining bitterly of his predicament. The love between Ronnie and Marcelle appeared des-

* Extensive reference to the content of this paper is made in *Wisdom, Madness and Folly*, pp. 105–6.

tined to be unfulfilled although they remained in contact throughout the remainder of Ronnie's life.

Throughout this period – late 1952 and 1953 – Ronnie was still in close contact with his old friends from university, in particular Mike Scott, now in the First Battalion Royal Fusiliers. Ronnie and his mates did not seem to enjoy the Army one bit. There was considerable resentment to military service – quite understandably. The 'class of '51' was now reaching the stage in their lives when the gossip was beginning with routine consistency, to be taken up with marriage, children and promotion. However the taste which military service left in Ronnie's mouth was a bitter one indeed. He recorded some personal thoughts on the matter on 18 May 1953:

> Almost finished national service – 4 months to go. What have
> I achieved? Fuck all. Yet I now have a baby girl, I am married,
> I own a flat, a great deal of piss has been knocked out of me, I
> have retained my friends, I have done perhaps inestimable harm to
> one person, I have become more reconciled with my parents, I have
> been forced to my knees, forced back to the Bible, Plato, Kant.
> I can hardly say that I have furthered my career.

And from notes made while in Catterick 1953, which reflect his attitude to the Army social scene: 'At a cocktail party. Colonel to rather pissed nursing sister: My dear, do you know when you have had enough? Sister: Oh yes, I always fall flat on my fucking face.'

What a relief it must have been to be demobbed! Now the real battle could begin.

CHAPTER FIVE

The Return to Glasgow

Ronnie returned to Glasgow in late 1953 to complete his psychiatric training at Gartnavel Hospital, the clinical base of the Glasgow Royal Mental Hospital. This was a much older Ronnie than the one who had left his ancestral Scottish home on the long journey to Aldershot in October 1951. He had now been through two years in the Army, having gone in as a rookie Lieutenant and come out a seasoned Captain. He was married, a father, and, through the financial assistance of Anne's parents, the owner of a small tenement flat in Nova Drive, in the relatively up-market west end of Glasgow.

His relationship with his parents was becoming increasingly difficult. On returning home to Ardbeg Street to see his folks he discovered that his prized possession, a writing desk with a roll-down front, had disappeared. The story of what happened to it is to this day the subject of family dispute. Ronnie later spread the rumour that Amelia had taken an axe to it, having decided at an earlier stage that he had gone 'evil'. Another version is that the desk was sold since Amelia and David did not use the desk and preferred, understandably, to have the money rather than an unused and cumbersome piece of furniture. Possibly Amelia, now cast in the role of an interfering mother-in-law, was jealous of Anne. Ronnie and his father David still got on well with each other; ironically, their relationship seemed to prosper just when Ronnie's relationship with Amelia deteriorated. Ardbeg Street was too far away from Nova Drive for Amelia and David to make a habit of popping in unexpectedly. All Ronnie had to do was to ensure that the visits were not embarrassingly far apart from each other and keep his head down. With no telephone in their home, Amelia and David were as far away as need be. Ronnie could get on with his career as a psychiatrist and writer.

Ronnie's intellect during the mid-1950s was in overdrive. Since adolescence he had studied carefully the works of the most difficult Germanic philosophical writers: Immanuel Kant, Georg Hegel (acknowledged even by Bertrand Russell as 'the hardest to understand of all the great philosophers'), Arthur Schopenhauer and Friedrich Nietzsche. Throughout university and the early 1950s Ronnie read avidly – Søren Kierkegaard, Edmund Husserl, Martin Heidegger, Sigmund Freud, Carl Jung, Karl Jaspers, Martin Buber, Karl Marx, the French *philosophe* Jean-Paul Sartre – and was particularly interested in the little known works of the French psychiatrist and philosopher Eugene Minkowski.*

Ronnie's reading was not confined to works of philosophy, theology and psychology and his intellectual ambitions lay not solely within mainstream psychoanalysis. He wanted, above all, to be recognized as a world intellect, fully educated in a wide range of fields including poetry, music, fiction and not 'just' philosophy, theology and psychology (embracing psychoanalysis, psychopathology and, to a lesser extent, psychiatry). His interest in the Eastern perspective on the condition of man within Western civilization would shortly be awakened, but he was already aware of the existence of the Upanishads through the works of Schopenhauer before he left school at seventeen.

It was crucial to Ronnie's ambition as a would-be intellectual to maintain the pace of cultivation to which he had become accustomed since early adolescence. Throughout the late 1940s and 1950s Ronnie kept a detailed record of books he was reading. Between October 1951 and July 1954, for example, he records ploughing his way through the works of Kafka, Camus, Sartre, Wittgenstein, Descartes, Bergson, Henry James, Waugh, Simone Weil, Coleridge, J.S. Mill, Bleuler, Rex Warner, Schoenberg, T.S. Eliot, Tolstoy, Freud, Schweitzer, Rousseau, Husserl, Huxley, Tillich and Dylan Thomas, with what would appear to be an insatiable appetite for knowledge, truth and wisdom.

Between February and March of 1957 he further records having read *The Collected Poems of Marianne Moore*, *The Revolution in Philosophy* by Ayer, *The Less Deceived* by Philip Larkin, *The Meaning of*

---

* Eugene Minkowski (1885–1972) was a psychiatrist by training whose main work, *La schizophrénie*, was published in 1953 at his own expense.

Meaning by C.K. Ogden and I.A. Richards, John and Anne Tribble's work on John Clare, and *The Poetry of Ezra Pound* by Hugh Kenner. From an early age he felt destined to write a book which would be an existential-phenomenological analysis of *something* (including at one stage biographies of Gerard Manley Hopkins and William Blake) but throughout the early fifties his mind focused on the application of the philosophical traditions of existentialism and phenomenology to that form of behaviour which, one way or another, is labelled 'crazy'.

Ronnie's professional responsibility centred on the clinical wards of Gartnavel Hospital. He now had sufficient clout to initiate an experiment that would provide some empirical basis for the hard-fought lessons learnt in Netley and Catterick. He persuaded two psychiatric colleagues, Doctors Cameron and McGhie, to participate in an experiment that received virtually no recognition at the time, but was repeated by many others in years to come in different forms.

The experiment took place between 1954 and 1955, in the refractory ward of Gartnavel Hospital. Following his experiences in the Army, Ronnie felt certain that if the hospital staff stayed calm during a patient's outburst, the crisis would pass as surely and unexpectedly as it had arrived. Ronnie's central argument was that there was simply no need to inject patients with drugs of any sort, give them electric shocks, or physically restrain them with a strait-jacket – just ride things out. There was, of course, much resistance to such a perilous course. Would there not be a dramatic increase in suicides? Would the patients benefit in any way? What of all the physical damage and personal injury the patients would inevitably cause? Ronnie must have been at his persuasive best. The turning point in the debate, as he told others later in his life, was his demonstration of the fact that the cost of replacing the broken windows and furniture would be less than that of the drugs to be administered. He was given the go-ahead. The details of what became known as 'The Rumpus Room' were described in the article published in *The Lancet*:*

In the last twelve months many changes occurred in these patients. They were no longer social isolates. Their conduct became more social, and they undertook tasks which were of

* The paper, formally entitled 'Patient and Nurse: Effects of Environmental Changes in the Care of Chronic Schizophrenics', by Dr Cameron, Dr Laing and Dr McGhie, was published 31 December 1955.

more value in their small community. Their appearance and interest in themselves improved as they took a greater interest in those around them. These changes were satisfying to the staff. The patients lost many of the features of chronic psychoses; they were less violent to each other and to the staff, they were less dishevelled, and their language ceased to be obscene. The nurses came to know the patients well, and spoke warmly of them.

We started this work with the idea of giving patients and nurses the opportunity to develop interpersonal relationships of reasonably enduring nature. A physical environment was supplied which was clean and pleasant: and materials for knitting, sewing and drawing, a gramophone, foodstuffs, and facilities for cooking were made available, and the patients and nurses were left to make what use of them they wished. But our observations on the results seem to us to support the view that what matters most in the patient's environment is the people in it. The nurses found it useless merely to try to get the patients to do something; but, once the patients liked the nurses, attempts to help them became the basis for apparently autonomous activity in which the patients used the material in the environment. Disturbance and rupture of the relation, perhaps because of the absence of a particular nurse, or to some failure in her understanding interrupted this activity.

The material used or the nature of the activity was of secondary importance. Some of the patients improved while they scrubbed floors; others baked, made rugs, or drew pictures. We conclude that the physical material in the environment, while useful, was not the most important factor in producing the change. It was the nurses. And the most important thing about the nurses, and other people in the environment, is how they feel towards their patients. Our experiment has shown, we think, that the barrier between patients and staff is not erected solely by the patients but is a mutual construction. The removal of this barrier is a mutual activity.

This was an important step forward for Ronnie; he had made the point, in his mind at least, that patients really could be treated in ways other than those enshrined in established psychiatric practice. His ideas were now embedded in a respectable form. But what was the best move from there?

By late 1954 Fiona, Ronnie's first daughter, was two years old. Ronnie and Anne's second child, Susan, had been born in Nova Drive in September of 1954, and by early 1955 Anne was expecting another child. It was clear that larger premises would need to be found, so Ronnie and his young family moved into a larger flat in Ruskin Place in fashionable Hillhead, not far from the main Glasgow University campus.

Karen was born in Ruskin Place on November 1955. Ronnie was now the proud father of three daughters, all aged under three. Ronnie needed money to support his rapidly growing family and took a National Health job as a Senior Registrar at the Southern General Hospital working under Ferguson Rogers, who was the Professor of Psychological Medicine (Psychiatry).

The normal course would have been to follow the five-year medical course with three postgraduate years in psychiatric training. The two years spent in the Army between October 1951 and October 1953 counted as one year towards Ronnie's 'DPM' (Diploma in Psychiatric Medicine), and during the years 1954–5, Ronnie's psychiatric training was completed. On 1 January 1956 Dr Ronald David Laing's name was entered into the register of The Royal Medico-Psychological Association (the forerunner to the Royal College of Psychiatrists). Ronnie was thus formally qualified as a psychiatrist shortly after his twenty-eighth birthday. If he had had his way, he would have gone straight into mainstream research into the treatment of schizophrenics. However, there were other considerations closer to home.

The British psychiatric and psychoanalytical establishment in the mid-1950s was a small world. Professor Ferguson Rogers was a friend of a Dr Jock Sutherland, the Director of the Tavistock Clinic in London, a connection which was to prove extremely useful to Ronnie. Time was now ripe for the big move to London; for what Ronnie had in mind was a short-term four-year plan of high ambition: to qualify as a psychoanalyst at the British Psycho-Analytical Society; to work as a Psychiatric Registrar at the Tavistock Clinic; to persuade the Tavistock Institute of Human Relations to release funds for him to conduct research into schizophrenia; and to publish his first book, *The Divided Self*, which he believed would establish his name among the giants of psychiatry.

CHAPTER SIX

Psychiatrist to Psychoanalyst

In the latter part of 1956 Ronnie decided to move from Glasgow to London. The move was a complete and courageous break from his past. As the Senior Registrar at the Southern General in Glasgow, there was, if he so wished, a safe career in front of him as a Scottish psychiatrist and a future member of the Scottish medical establishment. The pressure to avoid risks, to take the safe path, to settle down and be content with his lot was heightened by his responsibilities towards his wife Anne and his three daughters: Fiona, aged four; Susie, aged two; and Karen, who had only just been born. However, having qualified as a doctor and psychiatrist, Ronnie needed to attain the elevated status of psychoanalyst, and the only place to do that was at the Institute of Psycho-Analysis based in New Cavendish Street, London.

He had a great deal to say. His heartfelt theories regarding those 'lost souls' in the wards of Gartnavel, Stobhill and the Southern General in Glasgow, and the Royal Victoria Hospital in Netley would amount to nothing unless he could gain professional respect. Becoming a psychoanalyst was, in Ronnie's mind, a necessary step towards the ultimate goal of credibility.

Although Ronnie's fundamental ambition lay in the pursuit of 'the truth', economic reality forced him to find a job. He was fortunate in the admiration with which Professor Ferguson Rogers at the Southern General, whom Ronnie regarded as a professional adversary, held him. Ronnie's antagonism towards Ferguson Rogers was based on Rogers's resistance to attempts by Ronnie to continue a 'Rumpus Room' type experiment at the Southern General. However, Professor Rogers had contacted Dr Jock Sutherland and put in a word on Ronnie's behalf. Jock Sutherland was not only a fellow Scot, but Director of the Tavistock Clinic and also Chairman of the Staff Committee of the Tavistock Institute of Human Relations. (The Tavistock Clinic and the Tavistock Institute of Human Relations were separate though affiliated bodies, the former having joined the National Health Service in 1948, the latter remaining independent.)

Setting up in London required secure employment through Ronnie's appointment at the Tavistock Clinic as a Senior Registrar. The £1,000 per annum wage was not much but would hold the fort. It was more tricky to have Ronnie enrolled as a training member of the British Psycho-Analytical Society and its administrative and financial arm – the Institute of Psycho-Analysis. Ronnie was accepted for training as a psychoanalyst under an experimental scheme through which promising young psychiatrists from the provinces could be trained by the Institute of Psychoanalysis while working within the National Health Service.

Ronnie's immediate strategy in 1956 encompassed three aims, the first being to publish *The Divided Self*. Ronnie was raw with jealousy over the publication in late May 1956 of Colin Wilson's book *The Outsider*; the author's precocity irked him even more. Ronnie had promised himself since his late teens that he would publish his first book by his thirtieth birthday. That book had been written but had not been published. He had already missed one boat.

Ronnie's second aim was to find accommodation within reasonable commuting distance to London. Anne found a modern house, large and inexpensive enough for the whole family to live in without being too cramped, in Harlow New Town, situated about twenty miles north of London. Although Harlow probably felt like a god-forsaken dystopia, it was the best that could be found in the circumstances. It would be two years and another two children before another move was made.

The third part of the strategy was to attain the authority of a psychoanalyst. Ronnie intended to challenge the psychoanalytical movement based at the Institute of Psycho-Analysis, and those involved in the therapeutic activities of the Tavistock Clinic and the Tavistock Institute of Human Relations. In order to make such a challenge it was necessary to qualify as a psychoanalyst, and this required the successful completion of a four-year training programme with three principal elements: fifty minutes' analysis five days a week, regular attendance of lectures at the Institute, and demonstrating over a two-year period with one's own patient, the ability to conduct analysis under the supervision of two senior members of the Institute. Of these three requirements, the most important to the training of a would-be psychoanalyst was the four-year period of analysis with a seasoned psychoanalyst. Who, taking everything into account, should be Ronnie's analyst? Jock Sutherland discussed this with his colleagues. Ronnie wanted Donald Winnicott, probably due to his relative fame. However, it was decided that Ronnie's analyst was to be Charles Rycroft; Marion Milner and Donald Winnicott were given the task of supervising what Charles Rycroft was later to describe as 'a special case'.

Ronald Laing and Charles Rycroft were a strange match for each other. In 1956, and for many years thereafter, Ronnie spoke with a thick Glaswegian accent which many people found difficult to understand. He felt like a working class lad who suddenly found himself in the comfortable, quasi-sophisticated, terribly nice world of the English upper-middle-class. Charles Rycroft was a natural member of the upper-class; not a snob, a very decent chap in fact. Charles Rycroft's father was well known in upper-middle-class circles as a Master of Fox Hounds, and the Rycroft forebears are 'country gentry of, as they say, good yeoman stock'. Worse still from Ronnie's ego-stance at that stage in 1956, Charles Rycroft was relatively unknown – it was not until the late 1960s that his psychoanalytical studies were published. Rycroft was appointed by the NHS as a part-time consultant in psychotherapy at the Tavistock Clinic for the specific purpose of being Ronnie's analyst.

Charles Rycroft does not accept that Ronnie would not 'submit' himself to analysis (although such resistance was not uncommon and Charles Rycroft quotes John Bowlby as a precedent). They went through the motions, with Ronnie duly lying on the couch ('part of the magic' as Rycroft puts it), for nearly one hour each working day for four years. However, it is difficult to determine or quantify any benefit of the analysis either from Ronnie's point of view or Rycroft's, except for the fact that for one hour during a busy day Ronnie could lie down, let out a big sigh, and relax.

If Ronnie had one particular emotional 'fault' it was the depression that lay buried in his heart all his life. Ronnie's depression was never expunged, and it accounted for much of his excessive and self-destructive behaviour. Throughout the whole of this psychoanalytical process it never came to light that Ronnie had lived the first years of his life in an atmosphere of deep and unremitting depression. At the time of his birth, Ronnie's mother was preparing herself emotionally and spiritually for the death of her father. Ronnie was two months old when Amelia's father died. The following year Ronnie's paternal grandmother died. Although the relevance of such external events to an individual between the time of birth and eighteen months old forms one part of the dividing line between psychiatrists and psychoanalysts, one needs no formal psychoanalytical training to imagine the effect of these events on the Laing household during the years 1927 and 1928. Ronnie himself thought of such factors as being crucial to the emotional and spiritual development of an individual, particularly at that age. The failure of these issues to emerge during four years of psychoanalysis (Ronnie to his dying day believed that his mother's father and his father's mother had died years before he was born) suggests that not only was the analysis unsuccessful but probably counterproductive.

Why Ronnie's analysis with Rycroft did not work out is a matter of speculation. Ronnie undoubtedly saw Rycroft as an intellectual inferior (as he did with everybody) and an Englishman to boot. He treated the whole time-consuming process as a necessary hassle in order to gain his badge as a psychoanalyst. Rycroft does not contradict this view and has written that the above interpretation is 'fair comment'. They both consciously acknowledged that Ronnie's depression was being avoided, but resolved to address the issue at that stage; there was a suggestion that they might delve into it at some time in the future.

Rycroft's overall impression of Ronnie's psyche was that he had 'an extremely effective schizoid defence mechanism against exhibiting signs of depression'. In a further attempt to shed some light on Ronnie's personality, Rycroft explained that only children tend to 'self-dramatize', especially when it comes to women. Only children tend to become author, actor and audience of their own internalized world. Moreover, they are more likely to be unable to express gratitude towards their parents. And so it was with Ronnie.

Ronnie felt his main task at the Institute of Psycho-Analysis, the Tavistock Clinic and the Tavistock Institute of Human Relations was to persuade his colleagues of the relevance of existentialism and phenomenology to psychology, psychiatry and psychoanalysis, with general and specific reference to the understanding and treatment of mentally disturbed patients. This was an uphill struggle. Ronnie's contemporaries included some of the best-known names in the enclosed world of psychoanalysis: W.D.R. Fairbairn, generally described as 'a very decent human being' and the author of many psychoanalytical books which challenged Freud's theories on instinct; Donald Winnicott, already an established senior figure in the psychoanalytical field; John Bowlby – a psychoanalyst who not only underwent analysis with a pupil of Freud, Joan Riviere, but was an acknowledged expert on child/parental bonding and the effects of parental loss and separation. Other psychoanalysts around at the time were: John O. Wisdom, an Irish analyst; Edmund Glover; Sylvia Payne (Charles Rycroft's analyst); Enid Bellett (author of *The Existential Core of Psychiatry*); and Marion Milner (author of *Hand of the Living God*). A most formidable, well-respected and famous psychoanalyst, Melanie Klein, was also very much part of this élite world until her death in 1960, as was Anna Freud, who had her own clinic in Hampstead. Finally, the less well-known Fanny Wride was in private practice as psychoanalyst. All these figures were considerably older and more experienced than Ronnie, who had commenced his training at the Institute of Psycho-Analysis shortly before his thirtieth birthday. He soon realized that he was up against an incredible wall of experience.

At the Tavistock Clinic were Russel Lee, an American; Herbert Phillipson, who was part of the army group; Wilfred Bion, a psychiatrist, psychotherapist and pioneer of group therapy; and Eric Trist, a philosopher working part-time who was later appointed Chairman of the Management Committee of the Tavistock Institute of Human Relations.

On the fringes of this group and in quite a different category was another important figure – Eric Graham Howe, who later wrote the immensely popular book *Cure or Heal?*. Howe was one of the few people around in the late fifties who shared Ronnie's growing passion for Eastern philosophy; he was also actively running an organization called The Open Way (later renamed The Langham Clinic for improved social effect) from 37 Queen Anne Street in London's West End, in close proximity to the centre of mainstream psychoanalysis: the Royal Society of Medicine in Wimpole Street, and the innumerable private medical practices in Harley Street. (The Tavistock Clinic had already moved many years previously from its original base in Tavistock Square to nearby Malet Place.) The proximity of The Open Way to these other establishments created the opportunity for an intellectual social circle whose common interests embraced philosophy (especially phenomenology), psychotherapy, mysticism and theology. The Open Way had a magnetic effect on the intellectuals around at the time, for here one could attend a talk and meet like-minded individuals. For those engaged in the art of therapy, The Open Way also became a source from which patients could be circulated from one therapist to another.

An important event occurred during Ronnie's analysis with Rycroft during 1959: the death of Douglas Hutchinson, whom Ronnie had regarded as his closest friend. They had been paired together throughout the clinical years at Glasgow University and had been on many memorable mountaineering expeditions together. Ronnie had persuaded Douglas not only to go into psychiatry but to join him at the Tavistock. Douglas had emotional problems of his own which he shared with Ronnie, as Ronnie did with Douglas. Douglas had decided to spend the Christmas and New Year vacation of 1959 in Glasgow. He also told Ronnie, with painful irony, that it would be his last mountaineering expedition. On Saturday, 3 January 1959, Douglas Hutchinson, aged 31, fell 1,000 feet from the snow-covered north-west ridge of Ben More to his death.

Ronnie was deeply shattered. It was his duty, as he saw it, to break the news to Douglas's wife, Gillian, who was expecting their first child. Ronnie was moved to write 'a private statement', in which he confided: 'In Douglas's death I have lost my brother.'

Ronnie felt responsible for Douglas's death. They were fellow spirits. They listened to each other. Indeed, so great was the effect of Douglas's death that Ronnie's analysand at the time, Sid Briskin, recalls Ronnie being unable to continue the session on the morning after Douglas's death: Ronnie broke down in tears, pouring his heart out. There is no doubt that this tragedy cut as deeply into Ronnie's life as any could. Ronnie's faith was shaken. Whether the subsequent path that he decided to take was already mapped out for him, or whether Douglas's death embittered him, is impossible to say. The fact is that when Douglas died, so too, did a part of Ronnie.

When Ronnie's impending graduation from the Institute of Psycho-Analysis became a live issue, two polarized schools of thought emerged.

Marion Milner and Donald Winnicott, Ronnie's supervisors, and Charles Rycroft, Ronnie's training analyst, together with John Bowlby and Jock Sutherland, were in favour of Ronnie's qualification. Fanny Wride and Ilse Hellman, the training committee of The British Psycho-Analytical Society and The Institute of Psycho-Analysis, were adamantly opposed to the idea that someone with Ronnie's temperament should be allowed to call himself a psychoanalyst. Ronnie and Fanny were never great mates. Indeed, during the first encounter between Fanny and Ronnie, Ronnie had to get through a formal interview, over which Fanny presided as chairman of the committee. Ronnie thought the whole thing had been sewn up between Ferguson Rogers, Jock Sutherland, Charles Rycroft, Donald Winnicott and Marion Milner. For whatever reason, during the initial interview four years earlier, Ronnie and Fanny had simultaneously embarked on a protracted and 'deeply personal' asthma attack. That had been four years earlier. But now Fanny had the knife out to prevent Ronnie graduating despite his having been on the course for four years. This was a serious battle. Correspondence flew between the parties. The matter was resolved only after Ronnie wrote three grovelling letters of apologies to Dr Rosenfeld, Dr Joseph and Dr Hellman for not attending their lectures with sufficient regularity. Things had got so bad that on 24 October 1960, Fanny wrote to Dr Charles Rycroft on behalf of the training committee:

Dear Dr Rycroft,

With reference to the correspondence about Dr Laing, the Training Committee has asked us to write to you.

Dr Laing was interviewed by Miss Hellman, as Training Secretary, and Dr Wride, as Chairman of the Training Committee.

So far as Dr Laing's actual knowledge and clinical work was concerned, the interviewers, so far as they were able to judge, thought that no useful purpose could be served by delaying Dr Laing's qualification. They were worried, however, by the fact that Dr Laing is apparently a very disturbed and ill person and wondered what the effect of this obvious disturbance would be on patients he would have to interview.

During Dr Laing's interview, a number of things transpired, which, if correct, show that he had been very ill-advised throughout his training. For example, with reference to his poor attendance at lectures and seminars, without mentioning names, he stated that after discussion of his difficulties over regular attendance with a 'responsible person' he had been advised to 'say nothing and hope he would not be missed'.

It is the wish of the Training Committee that the attention of all those who have been in a position to advise Dr Laing should be drawn to this statement and that they should be reminded of the note on the circular sent out each term which was originally for the attention of Dr Laing.

While recognizing the special circumstances which have led to Dr Laing's irregular participation in the training course throughout the years, the Training Committee considers that adherence to basic training procedure is essential. It is also felt as unsatisfactory that the Training Committee should be put into the position of qualifying candidates in an obviously disturbed condition.

Yours sincerely,

Fanny Wride (Chairman),

Ilse Hellman (Secretary), Training Committee.

It was true that Ronnie was ill. By late 1960 he found himself in a physical state the like of which he had not previously experienced. The doctors at Bolingbroke Hospital were not sure what the matter was. The symptoms were consistent with glandular fever, although cancer was not ruled out until a latter stage. He nearly died. But it was not his turn yet. His second book, *Self and Others*, was about to be published. There was much work to be done – including being a healer unto oneself, as the Hippocratic oath instructs.

It was no wonder that after Ronnie qualified he turned his back on the whole lot of 'them.'* He was a doctor, a psychiatrist, a psychoanalyst, a published author. It was like leaving school at thirty-three years of age and going straight into the fast lane. Now he could let them have it. Or so he thought. . . .

---

* Although contact with his former analyst was infrequent after 'graduation' from the Institute of Psycho-Analysis, it is clear that Ronnie did not feel any bitterness towards Charles Rycroft. As late as November 1985, Ronnie reviewed Rycroft's book *Psychoanalysis and Beyond* for the *New Scientists*, describing it as 'a breath of fresh air and a pleasure to read'.

CHAPTER SEVEN

The Divided Self of R.D. Laing

In 1960, the name R.D. Laing was unknown outside the cliquey professional circle of British psychiatrists and psychoanalysts. His publications amounted to a couple of student articles, 'The Ganser Syndrome' in 1953, 'The Rumpus Room' in 1955 and a paper with Aaron Esterson on Wilfred Bion's theories concerning group pairing in 1958.* But Ronnie was now ready with *The Divided Self*, which he hoped would put Colin Wilson and John Osborne in their places. The title of *The Divided Self*, dedicated to his parents, came from the eighth chapter of *The Varieties of Religious Experience* by William James. The concept of 'the false self' owed much – some would say more than was credited – to Søren Kierkegaard's *Sickness Unto Death*. The idea of a state of mind which Ronnie described as 'ontological insecurity' was based on *The Opposing Self* (1955) by Lionel Trilling, and the chapter on 'Self-consciousness' was rooted in an earlier paper by Ronnie entitled 'An Examination of Paul Tillich's Theory of Anxiety and Neurosis'.

The fundamental connection which Ronnie made between the philosophical disciplines of existentialism and phenomenology and psychosis was not an entirely novel idea, but the intense and persuasive manner in which the ideas were expressed was his and his alone. Many distinguished people regard *The Divided Self* as R.D. Laing's best and most original work; the basic purpose as stated in the preface, 'to make madness, and the process of going mad, comprehensible', being both ambitious and successful.

Although the manuscript was in a completed form by 1957, the

* 'The Collusive Function of Pairing in Analytical Groups', *British Journal of Medical Psychology*, 1958, pp. 117–23. volume 31.

book was not published by Tavistock Publications until 1960. Ronnie later boasted, in a spirit of both despair and achievement, that it was turned down by a dozen publishers none of which believed that such an esoteric work had any commercial value. John Bowlby thought it might sell 2,000 copies. By the time of Ronnie's death the book had sold over 700,000 copies in paperback in the United Kingdom alone. The book still sells well in this country and has been translated into nearly every language spoken throughout the world including Arabic, Hebrew and Japanese.

Throughout 1957 and 1958, Ronnie passed the manuscript around his colleagues at the 'Tavi' and the 'Institute' and recorded their reactions in writing. Jock Sutherland thought that Søren Kierkegaard's *Sickness Unto Death* (an important intellectual pillar of *The Divided Self*) was a very good example of early nineteenth century psychopathology, and hence his views were as predictable as they were depressing. John Bowlby liked *The Divided Self* but thought the first two chapters ('The existential-phenomenological foundations for a science of persons' and 'The existential-phenomenological foundations for the understanding of psychosis') contained 'too many long words'. Bowlby's view was that the book would be greatly improved by the deletion of the words 'existential' and 'phenomenology'. He was not sure of 'ontological'. Charles Rycroft thought it was very good but needlessly repetitive. Eric Graham Howe said he read it in an hour with great pleasure. Donald Winnicott disagreed over one word which turned out be a misprint. Donald Winnicott was also hurt but not reproachful that Ronnie had not given him more credit for the notion of 'the false self', which he called a good example of 'Winnicottism'. Ronnie's view was that this was a piece of cheek, considering that the relevant material had been written before he had even heard of Winnicott. Eric Trist is remembered for expressing the view: 'The trouble with you, Ronnie, is that you hate society too much.' Marion Milner, Ronnie's co-supervisor, in her book *The Hand of the Living God* (the story of a single-patient treatment lasting over twenty years), had this to say about *The Divided Self*:

> During the year 1958 I read the manuscript of Ronald Laing's first book, that phenomenological study of the schizophrenic experience that he calls The Divided Self. . . . I found the book contained vivid descriptions of some of Susan's main problems,

particularly the statement that the basic doubt, in this state, is about one's own existence, including the feeling that one only exists if seen by others.

The publication of *The Divided Self* prompted no fanfares heralding the arrival of a major new intellect. There was no sudden and immediate fame as experienced by Colin Wilson with *The Outsider* or by John Osborne with the stage adaptation of *Look Back In Anger*. No sudden rise in income. The book, as far as Ronnie was concerned, bombed. Maybe they would realize its importance in twenty, maybe thirty, years' time. In that respect Ronnie was quite right: the *British Journal of Psychiatry* finally reviewed *The Divided Self* in *1982*!*

Following the publication of *The Divided Self* in December of 1960, Ronnie delivered a long paper (thirty-five single-spaced A5 pages) to the Royal Medico-Psychological Association. Entitled 'The Development of Existential Analysis', the purpose of the paper was to inform the professionals around him of the intellectual background to his theories, particularly in the fields of existentialism and phenomenology:

> Existential analysis is not by any means the whole of
> psychiatry; it would be nonsense to claim this. But it is possible
> for psychiatry to become more totally existential. The existential
> tradition is beginning to emerge as the position of choice from
> which to orientate oneself in relation to psychiatry as a whole. It
> will almost certainly play an increasingly explicit and influential
> part in the psychiatry of the next century.
> But here, as elsewhere, only time will tell.

Shortly after Ronnie qualified from the Institute of Psycho-Analysis and published *The Divided Self*, he set up shop in 21 Wimpole Street as a practising psychoanalyst. Wimpole Street, which runs parallel to the more celebrated Harley Street, houses the base of The Royal Society of Medicine, and was Ronnie's first sanctuary for intense interpersonal encounter and extreme personal excess. There, for the first time in his life, he was in complete command of his own conduct and the method of psychoanalysis he wished to use with his fee-paying

* The *British Journal of Psychiatry*, 140, 1982, pp. 637–42.

clients. In Wimpole Street Ronnie could play out his personalized form of therapy using whatever props he wished. A small bed covered with a corduroy sheet was used not so much as a Freudian couch but as a space for someone to lie down if that was what they wanted. The consulting room was practically bare save for a desk positioned discreetly in the corner and a few chairs randomly scattered. Objects lay about to facilitate a feeling of knowledge and wisdom. A particular drawing, that of an ancient Druid symbol of three intertwining circles, for example, might be exhibited on the mantelpiece to generate a conversation. A print of 'The Death of Icarus' is well remembered by former visitors and overall, the general atmosphere was one of tranquillity. In this room his famous and not-so-famous patients poured out their deepest fears, regrets, hang-ups, childhood memories; they bared their very souls to this strange guy with a Glaswegian accent. As a psychoanalyst, Ronnie was never short of customers; his reputation as a liberal and sincere analyst soon spread.

Ronnie started taking drugs at an age when most people give them up. It was not until 1960 that Ronnie took his first acid trip, smoked his first joint and experienced the particular heights of the hallucinative drugs psilocybin and mescaline. He tried heroin, opium and amphetamines, but they were not to his liking. Cocaine was fine if you could afford it. LSD was a drug which intrigued Ronnie and for which he was given permission by the British Government, through the Home Office, to use in therapeutic context. LSD at that time was being manufactured in Czechoslovakia and, regarded as vintage stock, had been used in a medical context for many years. Ronnie fully realized that there was a degree of risk involved, particularly if the physical circumstances or the company were in any way threatening. Great tact and experience were needed to prevent someone 'flipping out'. Ronnie preferred to take a small amount of the LSD (administered in diluted form in a glass of water) with the patient, and for the session to last not less than six hours. These LSD sessions took place in Wimpole Street with various degrees of success.

Former patients have confided to the author that 'dropping acid' with R.D. Laing was both exhilarating and liberating; for some individuals a single six-hour LSD session could be more beneficial than years and years of orthodox psychoanalysis. For others the experience could prove too much too soon. One celebrated Irish novelist and short story writer, for example, has made it known that she did not have a pleasant experience. Besides, the political and social climate was changing. LSD was getting a bad press. Ronnie never advocated taking powerful hallucinogenics unsupervised or in circumstances where a patient or young person could well injure themselves or others, but this was the sort of reckless behaviour which gained attention. However, such a distinction between controlled and uncontrolled LSD experiences seemed academic to many influential people. The tide turned against LSD and consequently against its advocates. That was later. Throughout the early sixties, Ronnie's practice in Wimpole Street gained a reputation verging on the mythological, principally due to his use of LSD in therapy.

Dr Jock Wilson, Ronnie's colleague at the Tavistock Clinic during the early 1960s, remembers the excitement when confirmation of Ronnie's second application for funds to conduct research into schizophrenia and families was granted by the Tavistock Institute of Human Relations in 1961 (the first having been awarded back in 1958). By 1962 the Tavistock Clinic wanted Ronnie to stay on. Having spent five years as a senior registrar the next step was to be appointed Consultant Psychiatrist. Again, a big decision had to be made. Ronnie, always acutely aware of his age and his relative achievements or lack of them, was now thirty-five years old and had reached that half-way stage in life. He had quickly established a successful private psychoanalytical practice and with the publication of *Self and Others* (Tavistock Publications, 1961), hot on the heels of *The Divided Self*, business was thriving. In which direction should he go? Rightly or wrongly, Ronnie was already moving away from the idea of being part of the establishment, represented not so much by the Tavistock Clinic, which saw itself as marginal to the mainstream, as by the paid employee, with the consequential duties and responsibilities which accompany the regular pay cheque.

Ronnie's decision to go it alone in 1962 and do things his way was one that John Bowlby always felt was the beginning of the end for Ronnie. It was a question of tactics and strategy. If Ronnie wanted to 'change the world', Bowlby's view was that the best strategy was to do so from within the system itself. To start a one-man band, in Bowlby's mind, was a naïve method of achieving one's aims. However, Ronnie's mind was equally clear. Had he not tried from within to change things

– and all to no avail? The best minds at the Tavistock, with one or two exceptions, refused to see the relevance of metaphysical philosophy, as embodied in the existential and phenomenological traditions, to clinical practice in the field of psychiatry, or any potential intrinsic relevance to day-to-day psychoanalysis. Even the toilets were marked 'Staff' and 'Patients'. He felt that he was 'pissing in the wind'. It was time to move on.

Perhaps the straw that broke the camel's back was the Tavistock Clinic's reaction to a forty-four page paper that Ronnie slaved over, and in which he analysed the issues in the debate over the extent to which schizophrenia had its cause in genetic factors. Entitled 'A critique of the so-called genetic theory of schizophrenia in the work of Kallman and Slater',* this paper was submitted to the Tavistock in January of 1962. The philosophical and political issues raised in Ronnie's mind by the conclusions of Kallman and Slater were absolutely fundamental. They clearly saw a biological connection in the incidence of schizophrenia. Kallman was therefore inclined to believe 'that sterilization might be held in reserve for the eugenically dangerous cases of "incorrigibles"'. To Ronnie, this was the real 'hidden agenda': 'the eugenic campaign'. To the environmentally orientated theorist, this type of thinking is obscene, dangerous, misguided, élitist and, above all, frightening.

Ronnie mounted an all-out attack on Kallman and Slater, aligning their reasoning with that of 'Alice in Wonderland'. Bowlby, for one, was not impressed. He expected a more clinical approach: the paper should be toned down and the polemic and the rhetoric should give way to the scientific method of analysis. Ronnie clearly had had enough of this type of criticism. But there was still work to be done under the auspices of the Tavistock Institute of Human Relations.

In late 1962, Ronnie reported to the Tavistock on 'Work by R.D. LAING and Associates published, or in advanced stages towards publication, based on work of the last four years'. Each of these projects, and their subsequent development, tells much of the story of Ronnie's written works during the early 1960s: *Sanity, Madness and the Family*

* F.J. Kallman, 'The genetics of psychoses; analysis of 1,232 twin index families', Paris: Congrès International de Psychiatrie, 6:1–40, 1950. E. Slater, 'Psychotic and neurotic illnesses in twins', Medical Research Council, Special Report No. 278. This paper was reproduced in Richard Evans's book, *R.D. Laing: The Man and His Ideas*'.

with Aaron Esterson, *Interpersonal Perception*, written with Phillipson and Lee, two subsequent articles published under the titles 'Series and Nexus'* and 'Mystification, Confusion and Conflict',+ and the work on Sartre, entitled *Reason and Violence*, written with David Cooper.

An important project during 1962 was the 'development, especially with H. Phillipson and A. Russel Lee, of a Dyadic Perspective Test, which it is hoped will be ready for presentation in monograph form by the Spring of 1963'. This project subsequently resulted in *Interpersonal Perception – A Theory and Method of Research* by R.D. Laing, H. Phillipson and and A.R. Lee.

With hindsight, the spring of 1963 was optimistic, as *Interpersonal Perception* was not published until the early part of 1966. Perhaps because it was 'such a number', in Ronnie's terminology, that it is one his very best. This book is probably the least read of Ronnie's work, but one of the most enduring in its clinical application, particularly in the field of 'marital discord'. Thirty years later, the Tavistock Clinic is still using the principles outlined in the book.

Ronnie's co-authors of *Interpersonal Perception* were strange bedfellows. Herbert Phillipson was the chief clinical psychologist at the Tavistock Clinic, respected for his experience in Army selection. Russel Lee, an American, was on a research fellowship from the National Institute of Mental Health (NIMH) in Bethesda, Maryland.

> We worked together for two years, meeting biweekly to discuss our common interests and projects (including the *Interpersonal Perception* book).
>
> I brought a 'family systems' perspective to Ronnie and the group and he an 'existential' perspective to me.
>
> The original rudimentary idea for an algebra to describe interpersonal perceptions was [Ronnie's]. (He got the idea from one of Buber's essays). The idea to create a test from the algebra was mine.
>
> During the two years I was in London, we refined and elaborated the algebra and test into the form it finally took in the

---

* 'Series and Nexus' was published as an article in the May–June edition of the *New Left Review* in 1962.
+ The paper was published under the title 'Mystification, Confusion and Conflict', in *Intensive Family Therapy: Theoretical and Practical Aspects by 15 Authors*, edited by Ivan Boszormenyi-Nagy and James L. Framo.

book. For example, at one point I systematically and laboriously searched through a dictionary (from A to Z) in order to discover ideas for relevant questions.

Phillipson was involved in the couple testing only. He administered and scored and helped interpret the test, after I left England.

As to the book itself, Ronnie wrote the first draft, I wrote an extensive second draft and he married the two drafts.

NIMH was the institution that awarded me the grant to go to England originally and also partially funded me to work on the book once I left England. (Ronnie completed the first draft of the book after I had left England, and so we completed it via the mails).

Interpersonal Perception is a haunting book. Aspects of it appear in different forms throughout Ronnie's later work (for example, in *Knots*, which was published in 1969, only three years after *Interpersonal Perception*) and the main theme around which it so closely related − the analysis of interpersonal relationships − was not merely of academic, passing interest to Ronnie but a key component of his intellectual curiosity. The three years of 1962, 1963 and 1964 marked the most intense intellectual period of Ronnie's life, during which *Reason and Violence*, *Interpersonal Perception* and *Sanity, Madness and the Family* were written, in addition to scores of papers, lectures, articles and television appearances. The catalyst which catapulted R.D. Laing from obscurity to controversy was the implication, though not the thesis, of *Sanity, Madness and the Family*: that the very cause of madness lay in the family itself.

CHAPTER EIGHT

Sanity, Madness and the Family

In September of 1958, Ronnie was still living at 335 The Hides, Harlow New Town. By April of that year his first family was complete with the birth of his second son, Adrian (the author), his first son, Paul, having been born in January the previous year. Ronnie now had the financial and emotional responsibility of five children, the eldest of whom had not reached her sixth birthday. The strain between Anne and Ronnie was evident to all who knew them as a couple, including Aaron Esterson. In 1958 Aaron lived for a while with Ronnie's family in Harlow, during which time Ronnie and Aaron wrote a paper entitled 'The Collusive Function of Pairing in Analytical Groups'. This paper criticized Wilfred Bion, the recognized pioneer in group therapy, who, in 1949, had published the results of group interactions. Bion's conclusion was that the grouping was essentially sexual in nature, a view which Ronnie and Aaron challenged.

By October of 1958 Ronnie wanted to move closer to the action. Living in Harlow meant commuting daily to the centre of London to see his analyst, Charles Rycroft, sometimes as early as seven-thirty in the morning. A typical day involved Ronnie spending an hour in analysis with Rycroft, attending to his paid duties at the Tavistock Clinic, sitting through lectures at the nearby Institute of Psycho-Analysis, being available for weekly supervision sessions with both Marion Milner and Donald Winnicott and, most importantly of all, keeping up with his reading and writing. He would routinely rise at 5 a.m. and return home, exhausted, somewhere between 'half-cut and fully-loaded', usually around midnight. Too much time was being wasted getting from A to B.

If it was tough for Ronnie, it was even tougher for Anne who was expected, single-handedly, to look after the five children with very little money, no nanny, no washing machine, no disposable nappies, everything permanently on the blink (including the old banger of a motor car), and no sympathy. The relationship between Ronnie and Anne was under great pressure and a move of some kind had to be made. Financial restraint was still the dominant factor, but there was enough money to justify moving to Priory Court, a block of flats in an up-and-coming area of north-west London predominantly inhabited by the Irish working class – Kilburn. (Ronnie preferred to say he lived in the more fashionable 'West Hampstead'.) Now Ronnie and Anne could at least have people round and entertain the ever-growing crowd which Ronnie perpetually maintained in order to confront, cajole, argue with and, inevitably, dominate.

In the midst of all this activity another project was crystallizing. Although Aaron and Ronnie had put their energies together into the writing of the short critique of Bion, there was an opportunity to say a great deal more, particularly in the field of families and schizophrenics. Very little study had been done in the United Kingdom on the interrelation between schizophrenics and their immediate environment – the family. Gregory Bateson, based in Palo Alto, California, had already published a short but incredibly powerful paper expounding the theory of the double-bind two years previously,* but it seemed that no one had yet addressed the question of the extent to which schizophrenic behaviour had its context within the confines of the family itself.

In 1958, Ronnie and Aaron put a proposal to the grants committee of the Tavistock Institute of Human Relations, of which John Bowlby was a member. The basic plan was to investigate the interaction between family members and, in due course, produce two volumes of studies. The first was to be a study of the interaction between a small group of individuals who had been diagnosed as schizophrenic and their families. The second volume was intended to be complementary to the first; a study would be made of the interaction between families in which no one had been diagnosed as schizophrenic. The comparison between the two would, theoretically at least, support the theory that where a person had been diagnosed as schizophrenic, a certain

---

* 'Towards a Theory of Schizophrenia', by Gregory Bateson, Don D. Jackson, Jay Haley and John H. Weakland in *Behavioural Science*, volume 1, no. 4, 1956. Also published in 'Steps to an Ecology of Mind'.

78 • R.D. Laing

type of interaction – double-binding, mystification, confusion, people driving each other crazy, was always present. In 'normal' families (as defined by local general practitioners) this type of interaction was only *sometimes* present. This was Ronnie's original, tentative theory, but as events unfolded it was soon abandoned.* The first volume, *Sanity, Madness and the Family*, did, however, reach the printing presses of Tavistock Publications in early 1964.

The logistics of studying families in which one member had been diagnosed as schizophrenic was fraught with difficulties. Ideally, the full co-operation of the entire family would be required. This was not going to be easy. Aaron Esterson solved this particular problem at a stroke. At the time, Aaron was on the staff of two hospitals in London's East End, referred to for working purposes as the East and West Hospitals. In fact, Aaron was working at the Warlingham Park Hospital, which had two wings. Aaron, Ronnie, and others whose assistance was seconded, soon soaked themselves with the subject, to the extent of role-playing the various members of the families. Hundreds of hours of interviews in all the possible dyadic permutations were conducted by Aaron, tape-recorded in full view of the family members, and then transcribed with secretarial assistance provided from the Tavistock. Ronnie's involvement was relatively minor, sitting in on one session per family. According to Aaron Esterson, Ronnie's contribution to *Sanity, Madness and the Family* was merely 'literary'; the method of analysis was both devised and deployed by Aaron. Twenty-five families were initially selected for their paradigmatic value, although by the time the book was in manuscript form the field had narrowed to eleven, under the pseudonyms of the Abbots, Blairs, Churches, Danzigs, Edens, Fields, Golds, Heads, Irwins, Kings and Lawsons. The research lasted for five long years, from 1958 until August 1963, when the manuscript for *Sanity, Madness and the Family* was delivered to Tavistock Publications.

* This theory was later modified. In a paper to the grants committee of the Tavistock Institute of Human Relations in 1962, Ronnie advanced the hypothesis that where an individual had been diagnosed as schizophrenic 'mystification' was always present. Where there was no such interaction of the mystifying category there was no incidence of schizophrenia. However, if there was mystification, then only sometimes would schizophrenia follow. This projection was depicted in the application using the following formula, where X represented diagnosed schizophrenia and Y stood for mystification, or a failure to see another's point of view, accompanied by inconsistency, irrelevance and the individual finding himself in an 'untenable position': if X then always Y/or: if non-Y, never X/if Y then sometimes X'.

Although in his heart of hearts Ronnie felt there was no such thing as a 'disease' of schizophrenia, this was not thought to be an intellectual stumbling block to the study of a small group of people who had been diagnosed as schizophrenic and the relevance of the everyday interaction between the family members per se. Ronnie always believed that the proposition – 'there is a "disease" of schizophrenia' – was a valid theoretical position for which no evidence had been conclusively provided. Even to talk of a mental illness seemed a blatant confusion of the philosophical concept of the mind with the empirically verifiable scientific concept of a disease. The concept of mental illness, to Ronnie, was valid only as a metaphor. Aaron had his own views which were not, by any means, always the same as Ronnie's.

Aaron and Ronnie had been at Glasgow University together although Aaron, two years the elder, had been a year ahead. Although they had not been particularly good friends at University there was much common ground between these two very different personalities. What they shared was a view of the orthodox psychiatric world as being naïve, impersonal, heartless and, above all, ready to be taken on. More importantly, Aaron had had first-hand experience of a kibbutz-type community run entirely by the 'patients' in Israel, and was one of the few minds that Ronnie felt had any real understanding of the intellectual world outside mainstream psychiatry. (According to Aaron, Ronnie read *The Tibetan Book of the Dead* at his instigation). Ronnie and Aaron persuaded the Tavistock Institute of Human Relations (in particular, the amiable Jock Sutherland) to conduct research into schizophrenia and the family. Jock Sutherland was not concerned with the possible conclusions towards which they were heading. He had deep respect and admiration for Ronnie and his enthusiasm, and he knew the research would be conducted thoroughly and vigorously. The 'revolutionary' element would appear somehow, but this was, in fairness to Jock Sutherland's liberalism, not thought to be of concern to the Tavistock.

Both Aaron and Ronnie knew that they had a great opportunity. Published research into schizophrenia in the United Kingdom had, for some reason, shied away from any possible pathological connection with the family. It was as if it was too risky, too potentially controversial and too susceptible to misinterpretation. This was not the case in the United States, where Ronnie had discovered during his visit of 1962 that there were at least five centres of activity relating to families and schizophrenia: in New York under Nathan Ackerman; in Palo

Alto under Gregory Bateson; two centres in the Washington D.C. area, the government-funded NIMH and the private institution, Chestnut Lodge; and the Eastern Pennsylvania Psychiatric Research Institute (EPPI). Although these centres were spread from one side of the States to the other, there was much cross-fertilization of ideas, principally through the publication of articles and the delivery of papers at conferences.

In particular, the NIMH, under the control of Lyman Wynne, was well down the path of constructing a nexus of interconnecting theories bringing together the diagnosis of schizophrenia with the interaction of the family whose hapless member had been diagnosed as schizophrenic. Ronnie's first visit to the States in 1962 left a lasting impression upon him: not only did he realize that there was an incredible marketplace of ideas, but he came across some of the leading figures in the field of family therapy at that time – Lyman Wynne, Ross Speck, Roger Shapiro, Gregory Bateson, Murray Bowen and Raymond Birdwhistell.

The central idea that Ronnie adopted from the American scene was the theme of victimization. The candidate for schizophrenia, usually a girl in her late teens or early twenties, was being subjected to emotional brutality of such intensity by her own family (usually the mother), that s/he had become crazy. Gregory Bateson's theory of the 'double-bind' was the pivotal concept around which many of these new theorists worked. The idea was that a family member in a position of authority could give a series of contradictory commands or statements (directly or indirectly) to a family member of inferior status, and by so doing cause schizophrenic behaviour in the weaker family member. It was a powerful idea, especially when stated by qualified physicians and not the 'patient'. The 'victim' was the subject of an emotional game of chess resulting in an existential checkmate. The phrase Ronnie used to describe the loser's predicament was 'untenable position'. Neither Ronnie nor Aaron was intellectually naïve enough to believe that such great questions as 'the nature of madness' and 'the nature of schizophrenia' could be answered with a simplistic answer along the lines of 'blame it on mum' (as always). The point that they sought to address, through research, was the relation between a certain type of interaction within the family, and the diagnosis of one of the members as schizophrenic.

In November 1962 John Bowlby organized a meeting to discuss the progress of the developments in the schizophrenia and families project. The minutes show that Dr Bowlby chaired the meeting. Others present were Ronnie, Herbert Phillipson, Aaron Esterson, Sid Briskin and Joan Cunnold. It is clear from these minutes that Ronnie and Aaron's work on 'schizophrenic families' had gone on for many years, since 1958, and by 1962 they, and others assisting them, were now involved with 'normal families'. The meeting was informed that since April 1962, an investigation had been conducted into 'normal' families derived from General Practitioners associated with Tavistock Training Courses employing comparable procedures to those used in the study of schizophrenics and their families. The 'present position' was summarized as

1. Continued gathering of data on 'normal' families;
2. the administration of the Dyadic Perspective Test to 'normals' and dyads in schizophrenic families;
3. follow up of families in the schizophrenic series;
4. intensified analysis of existing data;
5. the filming (it is hoped) by J. Roberston of some of the schizophrenic and 'normal' families.

In addition to the five components relating to the 'present position', the 'future position', as recorded, centred on a plan to set up a small experimental model unit where 'the process of personal disintegration and reintegration can be more adequately studied'. The idea was to start the project in conjunction with the Richmond Fellowship under the chairmanship of Elly Jansen. A twelve-room house set in at least half an acre of grounds was envisaged. The purpose of the centre was 'for the in-patient treatment of acutely disturbed psychotic patients, in juxtaposition to a Half-Way House run by the Fellowship, to which disturbed patients will be able to be transferred as they get better'. Ronnie was trying to get money out of The Bollingen Foundation, Aaron was working on specific Trust Funds and Sid Briskin was making an application to the Charles Henry Foyle Trust for a personal grant to cover full-time work for a period of two to three years. All this was nearly three years prior to Kingsley Hall. In fact, no household formally materialized until 1964.

The possible collaboration between the Richmond Fellowship and The Tavistock eventually petered out, as did further work on 'normal' families. The difficulty in completing volume two of the study lay not only in the fact that other projects were crystallizing but also in the intrinsic problems of proving the central thesis behind volume one. Undeterred, Aaron had interviewed scores of families from the Warlingham East and West Hospitals where he was working. Sid Briskin, Ronnie's former analysand, assisted in the analysis of these interviews, as did a former University friend of Ronnie's – Dr David Sherrit, also working at the Tavistock Clinic during this period.

In April 1964 *Sanity, Madness and the Family* was finally published. Ronnie, for one, was not prepared for the public reaction; the subtle arguments were not the ones that gained public attention. The popular theory distilled from *Sanity, Madness and the Family* was that 'families cause schizophrenia'. In fact, Ronnie and Aaron were posing the question: 'to what extent is the experience and behaviour of that person who has already begun a career as a diagnosed "schizophrenic" patient, intelligible in the light of the praxis and process of his or her family nexus?' 'Praxis' and 'process' were key conceptual components adopted from Sartre. In the introduction to *Sanity, Madness and the Family*, the distinction between praxis and process is briefly explained:

> What is going on in any human group can be traced to what
> agents are doing, it will be termed praxis. What goes on in a
> group may not be intended by anyone. No one may even realize
> what is happening. But what happens in a group will be
> intelligible if one can retrace the steps from what is going on
> (process) to who is doing what (praxis).

The use of the concepts of process and praxis was a gamble. They are deceptive in their apparent simplicity and are quite alien to those neither versed in existentialism nor in Sartre's idiosyncratic use of the terms. Process and praxis were not only ambiguous terms but were part of a wider system of thought involving the concepts of 'series', 'nexus', 'mystification', 'confusion' and 'conflict'.

Ronnie's complex theories seemed to muddy the waters and, to this day, *Sanity, Madness and the Family* is often referred to as a book whose central thesis is that 'families cause madness'. Moreover, American family workers were keen to develop a pragmatism that could be applied on a daily basis to families in need of help. The last thing such a family would need or want would be a tortuous intellectual analysis of their 'process' and 'praxis', wrapped up in a 'series and nexus', which would indeed create even more 'mystification, confusion and conflict'. In any event, Ronnie had no real interest in practising as a family therapist. He had enough difficulty dealing with his own family, let alone trying to sort out others.

CHAPTER NINE

Opposition Is True Friendship

In 1961, after Ronnie completed his psychoanalytical training at the Institute of Psycho-Analysis, and his senior registrarship at the Tavistock Clinic, he was appointed senior researcher into schizophrenia at the Tavistock Institute of Human Relations. He was being paid to research and write *Interpersonal Perception* and *Sanity, Madness and the Family*, and these books should have taken precedence over his other, extra-curricular work, including *Reason and Violence*, of the last decade of the philosophy of J.P. Sartre, written with David Cooper. Ronnie and David were a fearsome, intellectual and competitive couple and it was out of that relationship that *Reason and Violence* came into being.

David Cooper, in the early 1960s, was in the middle of an early mid-life crisis. A qualified psychiatrist with a South African background who had moved to London in 1955, he realized that he had become just what he despised – a member of the professional middle-classes. To many aspiring medics he had 'made it'. David felt, and he articulated this to those around at the time, that he had created an 'anti-utopia' in which to 'un-live': his life was a meaningless waste of an existence, a complete sell-out; he was spirit-dead. He felt he was going over the edge, but he could see a way out. The Shenley Hospital in St Albans, where he worked as a psychiatrist (in addition to his private practice in Harley Street) was closing its insulin-coma ward. Cooper persuaded the authorities to allow him to take over the run-down ward along 'democratic' lines. The distinction between patients and doctors/nurses was to be avoided, superficially at least. The unit could be self-governing, giving responsibilities to the former 'patients', now 'visitors'. The experiment moved to one of the hospital out-houses, referred to as Villa 21; it was aptly described by Penelope Mortimer in a feature article for the *Sunday Times* in August 1965, as 'a cross between a provincial university and a crematorium'.

David Cooper was more of a political idealist than Ronnie, and his passion was firmly rooted in revolutionary romanticism. His true hero was Antonin Artaud, who spent nine years of his life in mental hospitals and committed suicide in 1948. Artaud was the originator of 'The Theatre of Cruelty' and in the early sixties, productions according to his principles were being staged in London.

David Cooper and Ronnie had met in late 1958 while David was working at the Belmont Hospital. Although *The Divided Self* was then unpublished, the manuscript was 'doing the rounds' among an élite corps of psychiatrists and psychoanalysts. Ronnie's reputation was rapidly growing within that small group. It was inevitable that Ronnie and David would, one way or another, cross paths.

Unlike cooperative work on *Interpersonal Perception* and *Sanity, Madness and the Family*, the collaboration between David and Ronnie was fairly clear-cut. Ronnie's chapter, 'Critique of Dialectical Reason', was a synopsis of Sartre's work, *Critique de la raison dialectique*; David concentrated on *Saint Genet, Comédien et Martyr* and *Questions de méthode*. The introduction was written as a double-act. Ronnie's version of events was that the book was finished in three solid and intensive weeks with virtually no sleep, the two of them surviving on little else other than nicotine and caffeine. David's recollection was that it took them 'years and years'. In one sense they were both right. Ronnie started his major piece early in 1961, and although the book was not published until 1964, it was fused together during a relatively short period of time during 1963.

Reason and Violence was never going to be a blockbuster. The task of condensing dense and difficult material to one-tenth its original length did not produce 'reading for weekend relaxation'. The purpose of the book was first and foremost to bring Sartre's work to a wider English speaking audience; it was also an act of friendship between David and Ronnie; but most importantly, it was intended to boost the intellectual credibility of Ronnie and David, who both knew that their way of thinking, in the orthodox psychiatric world at least, would provoke widespread controversy. The two were delighted when Sartre agreed to write a foreword to *Reason and Violence*. What better credential for the book than a favourable foreword from the man himself?

Ronnie went to Paris to meet Sartre. The encounter, relative to Ronnie's expectations, was not a success. Ronnie's understanding of written French was never more than competent and always a hard slog. Speaking in French was an art Ronnie never mastered, and despite his incredible intellect, Sartre did not speak English well. Ronnie's old flame from university, Marcelle Vincent, came along to help out. Although Sartre was in complete agreement with *Reason and Violence*, Ronnie was immensely disappointed that Sartre had read neither *The Divided Self* nor *Self and Others*. During a two-hour meeting, interlaced with French-sized measures of whisky, the conversation covered Andre Corz, mescaline, fantasy as a primary mode of experience, the concept of 'normality', Sartre's work on Flaubert, Sartre's plans for an autobiography, old age, *Being and Nothingness* (Ronnie recorded that Sartre 'took nothing back but the book was not a basis for ethics as he had thought'), alienation and Rachmaninov. They agreed to meet again, when Sartre would introduce Ronnie to Simone de Beauvoir. That meeting did not take place.

David Cooper and Ronnie were 'soul brothers'; Ronnie and Aaron Esterson were not. Neither were Aaron and David who, by all accounts, did not see eye to eye. David, even for a 'radical' such as Ronnie, was over the top. He was anti-everything: anti-apartheid, anti-hospitals, anti-universities, anti-schools, anti-prisons, anti-society, anti-families, anti-psychiatry. David and Ronnie shared a love of good music (particularly Eric Satie), they both felt they understood the language of madness, they detested the ignorance and arrogance of the psychiatric establishment, they both viewed the very concept of schizophrenia with contempt and they both felt that the diagnosis of schizophrenia was a *political* act. In setting up Villa 21, David had taken some of the initiative away from Ronnie. Ronnie's last radical experimentation had taken place back in 1955 in Glasgow. David was doing it now; he was 'doing' Villa 21.

The history of Villa 21 is well documented in David's book *Psychiatry and Anti-Psychiatry*, although it is clear from subsequent reports that the charge nurse, Frank Atkin, was not given as much credit for his role in Villa 21 as he deserved.* The project ran from early 1962 until late 1965. It would be unfair, even with hindsight, to say that Villa 21 was a failure. What David managed to achieve was quite extraordinary by any standards. His aim, achieved for a short time at least, was to eliminate the power structure between doctors, nurses and patients within the working confines of a state-run and state-financed institution. The constant pressure to resume institutional 'normality' was overwhelming. The nurses, in particular, were loath to put up with lazy male adolescents not accepting direct orders to get out of bed and help with the domestic chores.

To strip nurses and doctors of power was never going to be a popular idea. It was clear that in order to perpetuate the 'free-for-all, anything goes' philosophy, premises outside the direct control of the health service – a palace of wisdom – would have to be found. But where, and, more importantly, when?

By the end of 1962, Ronnie, a young man of thirty-five, was in a position of considerable authority. He was a qualified doctor, psychiatrist and psychoanalyst, principal researcher of schizophrenia at the Tavistock Institute of Human Relations, the author of two published books and numerous articles. *Interpersonal Perception*, *Sanity, Madness and the Family* and *Reason and Violence* were in the pipeline. Another feather was added to Ronnie's cap that year when he was appointed Director of The Langham Clinic based at 37 Queen Anne Street, near Wimpole and Harley Street. The Langham Clinic operated under the auspices of The Open Way Trust, run by Eric Graham Howe. Ronnie's appointment lasted from 1962 until 10 December 1965.

The Open Way was synonymous with Eric Graham Howe – the author of nine books, the most popular of which was *Cure or Heal?*. 'Graham', as he was known to his friends, was by all accounts an exceptional and distinguished man who is recorded as being on the professional staff of the original 'Tavi' as far back as the late 1920s as an educational tutor. The Open Way (the clinical activities of which were conducted under the name of The Langham Clinic) was a meet-

---

* Those who knew of Villa 21, including Aaron Esterson, Mary Garvey, Sid Briskin and Clancy Sigal, all testify to Frank Atkin being a very special individual who 'had a way' with extremely disturbed individuals. Their collective view is that Villa 21 would probably not have got off the ground without Frank's involvement.

ing place for many psychoanalysts, psychotherapists, phenomenologists and, in particular, intellectuals interested in Eastern philosophical disciplines. It was here that Ronnie first came across Paul Senft (a phenomenologist who had studied under Edmund Husserl in Prague and the founder and editor of *The Human Context*), John Heaton (who wrote The *Phenomenology of the Eye*; originally an eye surgeon and later one of the core members of the Philadelphia Association) and Alan Watts (whose many books, including *Psychotherapy East and West*, did much to popularize Eastern thought).

Howe had invited Ronnie to give a talk at The Open Way in late 1960 or early 1961, and by the end of 1961 Ronnie and Howe were very close, according to John Heaton, because of their intellectual rapport. In 1962, at Howe's instigation, Ronnie was appointed Director of the Langham Clinic. Perhaps there is some truth in Charles Rycroft's suggestion (in correspondence with the author) that the emotional vacuum following the termination of his analysis prompted Ronnie to establish a relationship with a father-figure.

Howe was one of the English 'old school' interested in Buddhism, meditation, mysticism, the occult, the paranormal and the like. His brother, Ellik, was an astrologer – the interest in the mystical seems very much to have run in the family. The Open Way was a training centre for therapists and analysts; there were lectures, training programmes, and people were seen in therapy. The American doctors Joe Berke and Leon Redler also worked for a while at The Langham Clinic. Howe did not like Americans, least of all loud and hairy ones.

The essence of the relationship between Howe and Ronnie becomes clear in the contrast between two passages in Howe's most popular book, *Cure or Heal? – A Study of Therapeutic Experience*. Ronnie's glowing foreword proclaimed Howe to be a 'master psychologist'. However, Howe quite openly airs his views concerning 'the modern existentialist' who has 'plunged himself into a self-destructive and irresponsible orgy of so-called experience. . . . So the hinge, which was man's great discovery, has already become, as truth has ever been, the latest object for everyman's debauched craze to find himself in it, instead of it in himself'.

This contrast between Ronnie's foreword and Howe's views on the 'modern existentialist' highlights one of the points of divergence between Howe and Ronnie – their attitudes towards the use of drugs.

Although the currently accepted wisdom[*] is that it was solely 'the drugs issue' that was behind Howe's decision to ask Ronnie to resign in 1965, there were other factors to be considered, including Ronnie's rather flippant attitude to the English 'ruling classes'. Moreover, Ronnie's association with the American doctors Joe Berke and Leon Redler, whom Howe had no time for, did not benefit their relationship.

[*] See Cooper, *Thresholds Between Philosophy and Psychoanalysis: Papers from the Philadelphia Association*, London, 1989.

CHAPTER TEN

The Fame Trip

By the spring of 1963 Ronnie, Anne and their five children were on the move once again. The small flat in Mazinod Avenue, Kilburn, had been vacated in 1961 for a six-roomed flat in Church Row in the heart of trendy Hampstead. As a family, they were not only large but extremely noisy. The rows between Anne and Ronnie took the form of uninhibited slanging matches, which often flowed over into a Chinese restaurant next to the Everyman Cinema, round the corner from Church Row. So vociferous were these encounters, which always concerned Ronnie's absence from home, that the neighbours in Church Row petitioned the landlord to have the Laings moved out. This time the family ended up at 23 Granville Road in North Finchley, which was slightly down-market from Hampstead, but at least the house was semi-detached, complete with staircases, separate bedrooms and a small garden. As with all previous homes, Granville Road lasted barely two years before being abandoned; it was subsequently taken over as a residential community of The Philadelphia Association during the latter part of 1966.

Ronnie and Anne hit a low point in 1963. Ronnie moved out to live with his lover, journalist Sally Vincent, much to the consternation and despair of his wife and children. Divorce papers were filed. However, Ronnie did eventually return. He seemed to be constantly changing. The Ronnie whom Anne had married – a dedicated if slightly wayward Army captain – had all but disappeared in the process of a metamorphosis into R.D. Laing. He was acquiring the air of a celebrity, heightened by his first television appearance on the *BBC* television programme, 'Viewpoint', on 27 July, which discussed the work of Elly Jansen and the Richmond Fellowship, a mental health after-care organization. Ronnie's contribution was minor but steady enough for another appearance to follow on commercial television on 9 December 1963. But by now he had forgotten that it was Fiona's eleventh birthday.

Ronnie's concerns during spring of 1963 were not with his family but with Sally Vincent, with whom he had been involved throughout 1962 and 1963. During that time they enjoyed vintage Saturday nights at the Establishment Club and the Hammersmith Odeon, where the best jazz musicians – Stan Getz, Herbie Hancock, Miles Davis and Dave Brubeck – might be found. They listened to the topical and satirical comedians around at that time, including the collective group which made up 'Beyond the Fringe', and the anarchic Morty Landis, whose flat at 2 Prince Albert Terrace Ronnie occasionally used for his extra-marital activities. Also part of this crowd was Ben Churchill, working in television at the time; he lays claim to the dubious distinction of giving Ronnie his first joint. The three of them – Ronnie, Sally and Ben – enjoyed a year or so of good times, although they were oblivious to the fact that this was at the expense of Ronnie's family, which, in his heart, he had already left.

Both David Cooper and Ronnie went through deep, personal, family traumas during 1963, and both felt that they had come out on 'the other side'. There was a feeling of a new dawn, the transcendence of the old. This feeling was personal to each of them but was very much part of the wider political climate: a process of 'quasi-spiritual de-shackling'; a type of declaration for freedom by virtue of the realization of freedom; a complete 'fuck-it', a declaration of war on the Establishment; the seeing of light, the way, the truth, the 'It'; the search for one's true self; the transcendence of the past; the debunking of negative feelings; the release of guilt; the abandonment of *la vie bourgeoise*, tune in turn on and drop out. . . .

It was a common belief during the sixties, perpetuated to this day, that Ronnie was a keen advocate of LSD. This was true in the limited sense that Ronnie used the drug in therapy sessions both at 21 Wimpole Street and, at a later stage, in Kingsley Hall. He was well aware of the powerful effects of LSD, especially if taken in a threatening environment without the presence of an individual who was accustomed to its effects. Ronnie's stance was therefore extremely remote, on one level at least, from that of Timothy Leary, the Harvard based Ph.D. who wrote *The Politics of Ecstasy* and *The Psychedelic Experience*. According to Leary, a hallucinogenic such as LSD 'opens the mind' and 'frees the nervous system of its ordinary patterns and structures'. Ideally, the drug would become available to anyone. This was not Ronnie's wish.

Ronnie recorded an episode that took place in Granville Road during the spring of 1963 in a rough and unpublished draft of a proposed second volume of his autobiography. Writing about his first visit to the States (in 1962), he says:

A few months later one of the self-appointed generalissimo-guru-high-priests of the acid revolution came over to see me.*

They were thinking of doing a similar experiment in London, but since this was my territory, if I said 'No' that would be the end of it no argument without question and if I said yes then it would be on.

What would be on was this. A number of people had arranged to distribute 300,000 304mgms units of acid (one serious trip) in the form of pills to the 17 to 20 year old especially in chosen sections of the Berkley-Bay [*sic*] area.

Could such a collective clarification of consciousness all at once all in the same territory possibly be a spark which might spread like wildfire once lit? . . . it was really changing America – how about it here?

I said 'No' and that was the end of it.

However, that was not the end of it. Ronnie's conscience would not leave him alone; it was 'action time':

Anyway, nevertheless – I thought I ought to let someone know the sort of thing that was now afoot, especially because I did not imagine that this sort of reality had yet knocked upon the minds of gentlemen in Whitehall, and because when it did, as I knew it must, soon, I hoped they would not react in too much haste through being too much caught in surprise.

So I tried to see the Home Secretary. He referred me to a Civil Servant. He kept me waiting an hour and then said through

---

* There is no suggestion that this was Timothy Leary.

his secretary that he was not aware we had an appointment. He had in fact made an appointment for me at another time and place with Chief Superintendent Jeffries of Scotland Yard who was in charge of such matters.

I went along and saw Chief Superintendent Jeffries and his Assistant Sergeant Bing, and we had a talk which they recorded and may still have.

Privately, Ronnie was proud of this story, although Scotland Yard cannot verify the names or the meeting. Understandably, Ronnie did not wish to promulgate this information to his critics, who were accusing him of irresponsibility towards the uncontrolled use of LSD. But Ronnie had made his point, albeit behind the scenes.

Although Ronnie's 'meteoric' rise to fame took many, many years, it was during 1964 that he finally achieved the recognition he so desperately sought. His raw ambition is remembered by many of his former colleagues – even Ross Speck, the tall American 'network therapist', recalls Ronnie talking about his 'fame trip' as early as 1962. A small entry in his diary also confirms the premeditation, written in February of 1964: 'I feel I am going to become famous, and receive recognition. Most of my work has not "hit" the public yet, eventually it will, like the light from a dead star.'

In 1964 Ronnie appeared on UK television on five occasions. Kingsley Hall was not yet operational nor had *The Politics of Experience and The Bird of Paradise* been published. However, it was that year that Ronnie wrote the vast majority of *The Politics of Experience*, which was not conceived as a book but was, in effect, a compilation of speeches and articles. These had been written during the course of 1964, and the first was delivered at the Institute of Contemporary Arts on 21 January under the title 'Violence and Love', and reprinted in the *American Journal of Existentialism* the following year. This milestone speech contained many of Ronnie's more celebrated and frequently quoted passages:

From the moment of birth, when the stone-age baby confronts the twentieth-century mother, the baby is subjected to forces of outrageous violence, called love, as its mother and father have been, and their parents and their parents etc., mainly concerned with destroying most of its potentialities. This enterprise is on the whole successful. By the time the new human being is 15 or so, we are left with a being like ourselves. A half-crazed creature, more or less adjusted to a mad world. This is normality in our present age.

Looking at the milestones during that year one sees how R.D. Laing exploded onto the British and American popular scene during those twelve months. Even at the beginning of 1964, despite the publication of *The Divided Self* and *Self and Others*, Ronnie was a virtually unknown writer and psychoanalyst, still engaged in his research projects at the Tavistock Institute of Human Relations.

On 16 April 1964, *Sanity, Madness and the Family* was published. On the same day, an article entitled 'Schizophrenia and the Family' appeared in the *New Society* magazine. (A similar article was published at around the same time in the *International Journal of Social Psychiatry* under the title 'Is Schizophrenia a Disease?'.) *Sanity, Madness and the Family* did not purport to provide a comprehensive theory or definition of schizophrenia. Both the *New Society* and the *International Journal of Social Psychiatry* papers kicked off with a conversation between two diagnosed schizophrenics taken from *Strategies of Psychotherapy*, recorded by the well-known American family therapist Jay Haley and published in the previous year. That conversation was a persuasive example supporting the proposition that schizophrenia was not a disease, but a form of communication in a coded, restructured form. There was method in this 'madness'. Although it is impossible to quantify the extent to which such material influenced psychiatrists and therapists, this idea was increasingly associated with the name R.D. Laing, and demonstrated a human interest in what those diagnosed as schizophrenic were actually saying.

With the publication of *Sanity, Madness and the Family*, Ronnie's following gained great momentum. The following week he delivered a paper on the same theme to the Welsh Psychiatric Society in Aberystwyth, and the next day he was on the BBC's 'Tonight' programme.

In May, Ronnie appeared on the BBC programme 'Short Circuit', and the same day he delivered a paper entitled 'Parental Crisis and Adolescent Identity' at the High Wycombe Conference on Families of Psychotic Children. In June, he made another BBC television appearance on the programme 'Way of Life. Priest or Psychiatrist'. In

August, at the First International Congress of Social Psychiatry, held over a period of three days at the Marlborough Hospital in London, Ronnie delivered two papers. 'Transcendental Experience in Relation to Religion and Psychosis' and 'What Is Schizophrenia?'; the latter was published in the *New Left Review* in the November/December issue of 1964. It was this *New Left Review* article more than any other that began the curious association in people's minds between Ronnie and 'politics'. Ronnie was never a 'political animal', but this was the most lucid and direct political statement he wrote.

The argument, influenced by the works of Erving Goffman and others, was that labelling an individual 'schizophrenic' is a political event:

I do not myself believe that there is any such 'condition' as 'schizophrenia'. Yet the label as social fact, is a *political event*. This political event, occurring in the civic order of society, imposes definitions and consequences on the labelled person. It is a social prescription that rationalizes a set of social actions whereby the labelled person is annexed by others, who are legally sanctioned, medically empowered, and morally obliged, to become responsible for the person labelled. The person labelled is inaugurated not only into a role, but the career of patient, by the concerted actions of numerous others who for some considerable time become the only ones with whom a sustained relationship is permitted. The 'committed' person labelled as patient, and specifically as 'schizophrenic', is degraded from full existential status as human agent and responsible person, no longer in possession of his own definition of himself, unable to retain his own possessions, precluded from the exercise of his discretion as to whom he meets, what he does. His time is no longer his own and the space he occupies no longer of his choosing. After being subjected to a degradation ceremonial known as psychiatric examination he is bereft of his civil liberties in being imprisoned in a total institution known as a 'mental hospital'. More completely, more radically than anywhere else in our society he is invalidated as a human being.

Ronnie's politics were those of the sixteenth-century French judge, Etienne de la Boétie, who wrote *The Politics of Obedience*, of Timothy Leary in *The Politics of Ecstasy*; and appeared in his own *Politics of Experience* and *The Politics of the Family*.

The events of national and international importance during 1962–3 – the independence of Algeria, the resurgence of Sir Oswald Mosley's right-wing extremism, the super-power confrontation after the Bay of Pigs, De Gaulle's rejection of the United Kingdom's proposed entry into the European Economic Community, the Profumo affair, and Martin Luther King's 'I have a dream' speech in Washington affected Ronnie deeply, but not to the extent of persuading him to make any political statement. Even the assassination of President Kennedy on 22 November 1963, which sent the British into deep mourning, did not prompt Ronnie into the political arena.

In October 1964 the Labour party returned to power under the leadership of Harold Wilson, after thirteen years of Tory rule. Being left was in. Being political was in. But political action was a very ambiguous concept. One need not join and become active in a political party. There was no need to work day to day within an unequivocal political context. These politics were almost surreal in nature: a black man sitting at the front of a bus in south Georgia was a political act. Refusing to accede to the authority of one's parents, smoking grass, playing truant, refusing to attend a lecture, – all were political acts. Any challenge to any form of authority was a political act. David Cooper lived and breathed this concept; Ronnie was a part-time politician by comparison.

The following year Ronnie delivered another speech at the First International Congress of Social Psychiatry conference, called 'Transcendental Experience In Relation to Religion and Psychosis'. It was published in the sixth issue of *Psychedelic Review* the following year. Perhaps here, for the first time, one comes across the would-be guru, the physician-as-priest, the prophet with an insight into the Higher Order of Things, the disseminator and promulgator of Wisdom, Truth and Light describing the madness encountered in 'patients' as

a mockery, a grotesque caricature of what the natural healing of that estranged integration we call sanity might be. True sanity entails in one way or another the dissolution of the normal ego, that false self competently adjusted to our alienated social reality; the emergence of the 'inner' archetypal mediators of divine power, and through this death a rebirth, and the eventual re-establishment of a new kind of ego-functioning, the ego now being the servant of the Divine, no longer its betrayer.

The Sixth International Congress for Psychotherapy followed immediately after the First International Congress of Social Psychiatry and Ronnie delivered another influential paper, 'Practice and Theory – The Present Situation', published as a front page article in *New Society* in October. This speech was later described by journalist Robert Shields, in a therapists' trade magazine, as a 'brilliant and forthright paper' delivered with 'almost Knoxian fervour', which 'tried to apply existential thinking to psychotherapy, concentrating attention on the significance of a meaningful relationship between two real persons within the clinical setting'. The ideas put forward in this speech were among Ronnie's most popular and enduring; psychotherapy was explained as the 'paring away of all that stands between us; all the props, all the masks, the roles, the lies, the defences, anxieties, the projections, in short all the carry-overs from the past, the transference and the counter-transference, that we use wittingly or unwittingly as our media for relationships'. The polemic was deeply persuasive at the time, mainly due to Ronnie's knack for being able to bring the concept of existential analysis into the field of psychotherapy. He concluded:

Existential thought is a flame which constantly melts and recasts its own verbal objectifications. It offers no security, no home for the homeless. It addresses no one except you and me. It finds its validation when, across the gulf of our idioms and styles, our mistakes, errings and perversities, we recognize in the other's communication a certain common experience of relationship that we are seeking to convey, knowing that we shall never entirely succeed.

Still in August of 1964, Ronnie published an article called 'Them' in the trendy *Queen* magazine. It was an overview of pieces written by the American author and critic Clancy Sigal, seventeen-year-old Polly Toynbee, the novelist and playwright Elaine Dundy, Kingsley Amis, Caroline Wedgwood Benn and Ruth Fainlight, on the subject of 'Woman: A Special Kind of Hell'. Before the month was out Ronnie put in his fourth television appearance of the year on Southern Television's programme, 'Home at 4.30'.

During the latter part of September and early October, Ronnie embarked on a 'mini-tour' of the United States, lecturing at the Veterans Administration Hospital in Lexington, Kentucky, and then at the Department of Health, Education and Welfare in Bethesda (also the base for the NIMH), the Philadelphia Psychiatric Centre and the EPPI, during a conference on Family Process and Psychopathology. Although Ronnie's fame was rapidly spreading on this side of the Atlantic, in the States he was, by American standards, a 'nobody'. Ronnie realized this but knew it would not be too long that he would make it in the States, initially through the New York radio broadcast of the 'Violence and Love' speech on KPFK and WBAI-FM in December and the publication of *Sanity, Madness and the Family* by Basic Books (run by Arthur Rosenthal) later in 1965. The primary purpose of visiting the States was still to do with family research under the auspices of the Tavistock Institute. However, it was during this particular visit that Ronnie made another layer of contacts, this time with the radical element: those personalities and their writings which formed the core components of the 'counter-culture'. Ronnie moved about these two worlds, one mainstream and the other marginal, with equal ease.

On 1 October 1964, Ronnie flew from Lexington to Washington and, after attending to his official duties at the NIMH, travelled the next day to New York, where he met the young doctor Joe Berke (whom he had previously met in London the previous year), an equally young Dr Leon Redler, and Dr John Thompson, a Scottish existentialist who held the position of Professor of Psychiatry at the Albert Einstein Medical Centre in New York. On the Sunday, he met with the American poet Allen Ginsberg and his lover Peter Orlovsky, and throughout the next two days mixed and partied with New York radicals and poets including Timothy Leary, Claudiet Mitchell, Joe Oranos and Harry Fainwright. On the Wednesday (no doubt completely shattered), Ronnie flew back to Lexington to attend a lecture, and then back to Washington on the Thursday to the NIMH for further meetings with Roger Shapiro and Lyman Wynne. By the weekend he was at the family conference unit at the EPPI to attend a discussion between Lidz, Don Jackson, Lyman Wynne and Raymond Birdwhistell. The evening was spent at Ross Speck's house where Ross gave a talk; the next day was kept free for a low-key recovery patch at Benjamin

Franklin's house. The trip had only lasted for a few days but must have seemed like a lifetime. During the course of those early days in October 1964, Ronnie must have become acutely aware of how much more he enjoyed the 'marginal element' as opposed to the mainstream. The next time he would visit the States he would no longer be a 'nobody', he would be R.D. Laing.

Returning to home territory, Ronnie only had to wait until the following month before he was in front of the cameras again, this time on Associated Rediffusion Television in a programme entitled 'The Meaning of Love'.

This furious pace continued unabated throughout the whole of 1964; on the first day of December, Ronnie delivered a lecture entitled 'Psychiatry and Medicine' at the Osler Medical Society in Oxford, and the next day, an article for *Queen* magazine under the title 'A Happy Hypomania to You All' was let loose on an unsuspecting readership. Ronnie was taking the opportunity to release his venom against the commercialization of Christmas and its transformation into 'Xmas'.

Ronnie delivered his speech, 'On Nothing', at the St Martin's School of Art. He also published two reviews, one of Herbert Marcuse's *One-Dimensional Man* in the *New Left Review*, the other of Karl Jaspers's *General Psychopathology* in the *International Journal of Psycho-Analysis*. *Reason and Violence* was also published before the end of 1964. R.D. Laing seemed to be everywhere.*

It was also during October 1964 that for the first time in his life Ronnie began rubbing shoulders with London-based writers and poets through an established acquaintance with Alan Sillitoe (already famous for his play *Loneliness of a Long Distance Runner*) and his wife, the American poet Ruth Fainlight. It was at their house that he met the author Robert Graves and the poet Ted Hughes (later appointed Poet Laureate), husband to the equally well-known poet and novelist Sylvia Plath. Of this encounter with Robert Graves, all Ronnie recorded was:

* It was no wonder that an article by Joseph Schorstein, FRCS in the *Philosophical Journal*, vol. 1, no. 1, 1964 under the title 'The Metaphysics of The Atom Bomb' (the reprint of a lecture delivered to the Philosophical Society on 5 December 1962), was deeply buried under an avalanche of R.D. Laing material. In the course of this speech, Schorstein reminded his audience that in 1950, Heidegger had delivered a lecture entitled 'The Thing', during which he said 'Since the dreadful has already happened for what waits this helpless fear'. The phrase 'the dreadful has already happened' became a catch-phrase between Ronnie and David Cooper.

'A noticeable lack of sympathy between Graves and self., Unfortunate. At least politeness and courtesy persevered.'

Through an Eastern European aristocratic lady-friend, Beba Lavrin, Ronnie also came into contact with the celebrated playwright Harold Pinter. He was now lunching with the likes of the writer, broadcaster and biologist Sir Julian Huxley, with whom he had much to discuss. Sir Julian's more famous brother, Aldous, had recently died, in 1963. Aldous Huxley was not only celebrated for his writings (including *Brave New World* and *The Doors of Perception*), but also for having taken LSD on his deathbed. By late 1964, Ronnie was part of a growing network of intellectuals who were based not only in London, but across the whole of the United States.

1964 was a landmark year for Ronnie. Through the extraordinary diversity and range of papers, articles, speeches and television appearances in conjunction with the publication of *Sanity, Madness and the Family* and *Reason and Violence*, R.D. Laing 'suddenly' became the most well-known psychologist (at least in the United Kingdom) since Freud and Jung. There was a message being put across at every available opportunity, whether to psychoanalysts, psychiatrists, psychologists, family social workers, psychotherapists, radicals, students and 'trendies', which embraced and integrated madness, alienation, love, violence, families, politics and religion. Ronnie was becoming accepted as a new age prophet at breath-taking speed. Some may have thought that he had overstepped himself, burnt out, dried up − but he was only getting into his stride. The 'palace of wisdom' was about to open its doors to those in search of their true selves − Kingsley Hall was on the horizon.

CHAPTER ELEVEN

Early Days of Kingsley Hall

The search for 'the place' had been going on for years and years, for as long as anyone could remember. During 1963, regular Friday night meetings started to take place at Ronnie's home in 23 Granville Road where 'the place' would be discussed amongst a core group of people. This core group, by late 1963, consisted of Ronnie, Aaron Esterson, David Cooper, Sidney Briskin and the American author–critic Clancy Sigal – 'the brothers', as Clancy called them. On the fringe of this particular group was a lady called Joan Cunnold, and later Raymond Blake (known in those days as Raymond Wilkinson), who between them made up the seven people behind the original Philadelphia Association, commonly referred to as the PA.

Partly due to the shock wave of the Cuban missile crisis in 1962, talk about 'the place' intensified during 1963. Clancy had written a short written piece about 'The Place' in November of 1963, setting out his ideals to 'the brothers', which were along the lines of a refuge for meditation, healing and education. Clancy's idea was that there should be three places: one for 'the brothers', one for families and friends, and a third place for meeting the outside world. Ideally 'the place' would be on the outskirts of London, but many options were discussed during these Friday night 'mush meetings' (a term also coined by Clancy) at Granville Road.

In October 1964 a young idealistic student called Philip Cohen was living in a settlement-type house in the East End of London, known as Kingsley Hall. Philip knew Ronnie's secretary Joan Westcott and had heard of the search for 'the place', and to that end he wrote an informal paper under the title 'The Future of Kingsley Hall', which was circulated among 'the brothers'. Sid was instructed to inspect Kingsley Hall, and he passed the message back that he thought the premises suitable. The great excitement was tempered by severe misgivings, not least because not everyone had the same idea about 'the place'.

In David Cooper's mind there was Villa 21, which was not only functioning but receiving widespread public attention.* David, in those days, was not prone to saying very much. His favoured means of communication was a nod of the head. His nods were understood, depending on the particular circumstances, to mean either 'I agree', 'I disagree' or 'I don't give a shit'. David was a much loved 'brother' whose nods had great weight with the other 'brothers'.

For Ronnie, there was 'The Rumpus Room' (Gartnavel Royal Mental Hospital in 1955) and the days with 'Hamlet' in the padded cells in Netley in 1951. He remembered the community run by George MacLeod in Iona, a small island in the Scottish Hebrides, which he had visited in the early 1950s. The principles of the Iona Community – a requirement that time should be spent each day in study and prayer, the willingness to make personal economic and emotional sacrifices for the sake of the well-being of the community, acceptance of the need to spend time in recreation and with one's family, the need for regular meetings, and the pledge to work for peace at national and international levels – had parallels with Ronnie's idea of the empathetic suffering (Ronnie's term for this was pathos) in which a community should operate in theory but not necessarily in practice. The serious idea that Ronnie wanted to put into practice was the testing of what he believed to be his own original theory: that 'madness' is a natural healing process with an identifiable beginning, middle and end, if allowed to take its natural course, without intervention.

Aaron Esterson had had firsthand experience in Israel of a democratically-run and well-organized kibbutz-type community where the patients ran everything from the administration to the ambulance service. Aaron had learned that a place of quiet decency could be run with no apparent internal corporate structure, no recognized distinction between patients and doctors, and without an individual who held the position of 'Medical Director' or similar title. Aaron wanted Kingsley Hall to approximate as closely as possible to his ideal of 'the place': 'to pro-

* See, for example, the front-page article 'Anti-hospital' in *New Society*, 11, March 1965.

vide for people going through the terrifying experience of personal disintegration a tranquil social setting, with no more structure than was needed to keep people warm and fed (if that was what they wanted) and safe, without intrusion upon them, neither the intrusion of structure, nor the intrusion of other people's chaos'.*

Sid Briskin felt that 'the place' would require coherence in administrative and economic terms, with very specific ground rules. He was raising pertinent issues. The idea of opening one's own house to those in need had already been put into effect, for a short while at least, by Ronnie himself, despite the natural objections raised by Anne. The morale of those attending the 'mush meetings' at Granville Road during 1964 was very low. For nearly a year, charities had been written to, enquiries made, premises visited – but all to no avail. Everyone was very down-hearted.

During one of the Friday night 'mush meetings' in early summer of 1964, Sid suggested that his own house could be used as a residential community, as a result of which Sid went to visit Villa 21 at David Cooper's instigation. Sid met the chief nurse, Frank Atkin, sat down with the patients, and had a chat over a cup of tea with some of the residents. His informality and composure upset some of the staff (even at that stage it was thought rather bizarre to sit and chat with patients), but by so doing he further established his credentials as one of 'the brothers'. In October Sid agreed to have his own house used as a household on four conditions: he did not want to know about the residents' mental histories, there would be a process of mutual self-selection, Sid was to do nothing for them as patients and the residents would have to respect Sid's rights as a person.

During the autumn of 1964 Sid was also working as a staff consultant at Richmond Fellowship. He worked eighteen hours a week and, following the first weekend, when three young male residents from Villa 21 moved in to Sid's house on Saturday 10 October, Sid was away from Monday afternoon until Wednesday afternoon. There were real fears as to what Sid would find on his return – would the place be smashed up, would they still be there unharmed, would the neighbours have called the police? In fact, the only consequence was that the inside of Sid's house had been rearranged to look like the interior of Villa 21. On the evening of the fifth day the former residents of

* Aaron Esterson, letter to the author, 28 November 1992.

Villa 21 cleaned up the house, made a meal, brought in some drinks and invited Sid to join them in a celebration. One of them had found a full-time job — his first for over two years — and was due to start the following Monday. Within two weeks, all three of the young men were in gainful employment and, in due course, left to live their own lives. A serious lesson had been learned, which gave 'the brothers' further confidence in their vision of non-authoritarian care. In effect, Sid's own house was the first 'household' of this group and it operated from October 1964 until September 1968.

There was much local, national and international kudos attached to Kingsley Hall. That Gandhi had stayed there in the thirties was well known. But why did Gandhi stay in Kingsley Hall, of all places?

In 1964, Kingsley Hall was situated in Powis Road in London's East End, where it still is today. In October it was occupied by a paid warden, Janet Shepherd, and her husband Jack. Also in residence were doctors, probation officers and social workers. Kingsley Hall was at that stage what used to be called a settlement-house; these had existed throughout the country for many generations. The house boasted a fine history, having been opened originally in 1923 as 'London's First Children's House' by H.G. Wells, and in September of 1928 a 'new' Kingsley Hall was ceremoniously opened by Lord Knebworth.

The original Kingsley Hall was a work of high craftsmanship and beauty; the floor was made of the best Austrian oak polished to the point of perfection; George Lansbury, leader of the Labour party prior to Clement Attlee, had donated the stained glass windows. In her book, *It Occurred to Me*, Muriel Lester describes the imagery inside the Hall with great love and affection:

The polished oak floor was laid in such a manner as to break up the reflection of light from window or electricity into scores of patterns. It reminded us of the sunset glow reflected on wet patches of seashore sand as the sea recedes. The arches over the windows, the curves between wall and ceiling, and the semicircular chancel were so designed as to prevent the worshipper from noticing that the ceiling of this church was flat, and high above it were club rooms, kitchens, bedrooms, and a garden.

The exterior of Kingsley Hall gave the impression of a church that had been converted for private use. A blue plaque informed the passer-by that Gandhi had lived there during the 1930s, and inside the building there were three floors, on the first of which was a dining area and billiard table. Inside the main hall was a little room hidden away, called 'the Sanctuary', previously the home for all types of runaways. The general atmosphere was one of peace.

Muriel and Dorothy Lester had lived at Kingsley Hall and were among the first people to start up activities later called 'child care facilities' for the deprived children of the East End, and it was they who named the place 'Kingsley Hall' after their brother who, in turn, was named after the philanthropist-writer Charles Kingsley. Muriel and Dorothy were now two of the all-powerful trustees. Clement Attlee had been a local alderman and the Christian Socialist League also had a presence in the area. Kingsley Hall itself had been built with local pennies from the generosity inspired by Christian-socialism, as advocated by a well-known exponent of this philosophy at the time – Sidney Russel.

Those involved in the day-to-day running of Kingsley Hall had to be consulted before the premises could be taken over by the Philadelphia Association. Janet Shepherd was ambivalent and Muriel Lester, a friend of Gandhi and Mao Tse-tung, had to be persuaded, as did the other trustees. A preliminary meeting with Ronnie, Sid and Muriel Lester was arranged. Ronnie and Muriel hit it off straight away. Muriel was a lady of great learning and dignity – a rare and dying breed. Her method of greeting her guests (distinguished or otherwise) was to fall to her knees with clasped hands. Ronnie was impressed.

Sid had to meet Sidney Russel and report back to 'the brothers' who were now formally incorporated with Memorandum and Articles of Association, and registered as a charity under the name The Philadelphia Association – a term denoting 'brotherly love'. Sid and Ronnie met formally with the trustees. At stake were Sid and Ronnie's 'working-class credentials'. Sid came from Bethnal Green in the heart of the East End, and was therefore 'safe'. Ronnie emphasized his Glasgow working-class background although he nearly blew it by wearing his best black leather shoes, the debate over which threatened to turn the meeting the wrong way. However, Ronnie and Sid 'passed', and they went out to celebrate over a few quiet drinks at the London Hotel and to think through their immediate strategy. The most difficult task had now been overcome: the obtaining of premises without the need for raising capital, and at a peppercorn rent. Following one more meeting with Muriel Lester at her cottage in Loughton, Essex, all the required consents had been obtained and the green light was given.

The 'PA' moved into Kingsley Hall in the beginning of June 1965. Within four weeks, a qualified staff sister named Mary Barnes moved in before the previous residents found new accommodation. About four people stayed on to help out, two of whom remained until the end of the year. But Mary Barnes had not moved in with the aim of nursing others. She had met Ronnie in 1963 at Wimpole Street at the suggestion of James Robertson, a child care worker employed by the Tavistock. Mary Barnes had shown Robertson's films on the effect of the separation of children from their mothers during her teaching days. She had waited patiently for over a year in order to move into 'the place' and, in the meantime, was seeing Aaron Esterson in therapy; his offices were directly above Ronnie's at 21 Wimpole Street. Ronnie had told Mary Barnes that she needed therapy 'twenty fours hours out of twenty four' and, upon her arrival, she immediately regressed into a state that commanded the attention given to a new born baby. Mary became a showpiece for Ronnie's central theory of the potential healing function of extremely disturbed forms of behaviour. Almost accidentally, Kingsley Hall rapidly gained the reputation as part of an underground movement with allegiance to the New Left. David Cooper might have called it an 'anti-establishment' − part of what was being called the 'counter-culture'.

Disagreement among 'the brothers' as to how 'the place' should be run intensified. Aaron Esterson was advocating the appointment of a medical director not unlike the position held by Dr Maxwell-Jones at the Dingleton Hospital near Galashiels in Scotland. Ronnie wanted a type of spiritual free-for-all, with no rules except for those that evolved through the experience of people actually living there. Much of the history of Kingsley Hall is the story of the personal conflict between Aaron and Ronnie.

The main difficulty was that Kingsley Hall began fulfilling its own prophecy. The distinction between those who were 'together', in the sense of being responsible and financially independent people and those who were not, began to become very blurred, mainly because the majority of people at Kingsley Hall were not 'together'. David Cooper was beginning to crack up, as was his marriage. There was concern that Clancy Sigal was cracking up. Aaron Esterson and many others thought Ronnie was cracking up. In fact, Ronnie *knew* he was cracking up, along with his marriage and his relationships with each of his five kids, now aged between seven and thirteen. Ronnie thought Aaron's problem was that he was unable to crack up.

In the meantime, they were there and Kingsley Hall began to happen around them. Mary Garvey, a social therapist from Villa 21, moved in and Kingsley Hall started functioning in a roller-coaster manner.

Towards the end of 1965 Mary Barnes was causing great concern. She refused to eat and was generally to be found in the basement room naked, smeared in her excreta, and covered with a dirty blanket — or nothing. There was an openly expressed fear that she might not pull through. For a death to occur so soon after Kingsley Hall opened, would be fatal to the reputation of the PA. Mary's predicament forced one issue out into the open: Who was the boss? Who could see the way most clearly?

The dilemma was this: Mary was risking death. Should she be forcibly fed and, if necessary, detained against her will if her reaction was to leave? Or should she be taken to hospital, which action would betray the whole ethos of Kingsley Hall? Mary's refusal to eat became a bone of contention between 'the brothers' and, following a crisis meeting which lasted through the night, it was decided that Ronnie should speak with her and explain what the options were. Ronnie put it to her that the matter rested in her hands and that she must decide what to do. Some food was put outside her door and, of her own accord, she ate. Everyone could breathe a sigh of relief.

An unintended consequence of Mary's behaviour was that it became a role model for others. Mary was the centre of attention and, as such, generated much jealousy among the others who had moved in. The voyage upon which she had embarked seemed to bring into focus the central themes of Ronnie's theories of schizophrenia, and was therefore rewarded with attention. She objectified Ronnie's theories of regression, existential death and rebirth, and the self-healing process of madness; she was the embodiment of Ronnie's ideas. She had been told that she needed therapy twenty-four hours out of twenty-four and she therefore expected therapy twenty-four hours a day. But the question still remained — who was to deal with the excreta, engage in the endless and incredibly draining shouting and screaming matches, persuade her daily to take a little food — who was going to *care* for her?

The reputation of Kingsley Hall spread with enormous energy. This was a place were one might find R.D. Laing, Aaron Esterson, David Cooper on rare occasions, and definitely Mary Barnes – all under the same roof. There were no 'patients', there were no 'doctors', no white coats, there was no 'mental illness', there was no 'schizophrenia', and therefore no 'schizophrenics' – just people living together. The visitors became increasingly frequent and celebrated: Kenneth Tynan dropped in, as did David Mercer, Timothy Leary and Sean Connery. It was not uncommon for psychiatrists from all corners of the world to turn up including Dr Maxwell Jones and the much-loved Italian, Dr Franco Basaglia, who had been running the state hospital of Gorizia in northern Italy since 1961. Basaglia, who had also visited Maxwell Jones in Scotland, became a prolific and widely read writer, tireless law reformer in his home country and founder of *Psichiatria Democratica* (The Society for Democratic Psychiatry) in 1973.*

There was a feeling of revolution about Kingsley Hall. The ideas and the people were so radical that the focal issues created the feeling that Kingsley Hall was the paradigm of psychiatric revolt, itself part of a wider, greater revolt, against the 'old order'. It was all terribly exciting. The philosophy was to find one's true and authentic self, to let go of the preconceived ideas of one's false self as imposed by the family and society at large. To further this 'letting-go', a plethora of mind-altering substances were floating around. Most popular of all was LSD–25. There was nothing illegal about this. Under the Misuse of Drugs Act 1964 a qualified doctor was entitled to prescribe LSD to patients. Invariably this led to a sharp distinction as to what sort of doctor one was – liberal/hip or conservative/square. There were no squares at Kingsley Hall. The actual effects of LSD mimicked a psychotic breakdown. One's view of the world changed dramatically. The trip had a beginning, middle and an end. Experiences likened to religious awakenings, during which an affinity with the 'one-ness of the universe' and with the eternal true and never-ending light, were not uncommon.

---

* Loren Mosher, an American psychiatrist and an associate director of the Department of Addiction, Victim and Mental Health Services in Bethesda, Maryland, also spent time at Kingsley Hall. In addition to creating his own 'Kingsley Hall-style' communities in the States, he has co-authored with Dr Lorenzo Burti a detailed account of the work of Basaglia and his colleagues in *Community Health Care: Principles and Practice*, 1989.

Despite the availability of LSD, Ronnie's view towards its use was more responsible than most people either believed or understood.* He believed that there should be an 'active presence' around, i.e., someone familiar with the effects of the drug should be on-hand to deal with the possibility of someone 'freaking out'. But there was, and still is, a very thin line between self-indulgence and self-awareness. Ronnie's detailed views on drugs and drug-taking were usually reserved for his inner-circle of friends and colleagues. Those hanging around Kingsley Hall might, if they were lucky, be privy to his deeper rationale of consciousness-awakening and of new realms of inner experience. James Greene, the son of the then Director–General of the BBC, persuaded Ronnie to give an interview for Loveday Drugs Books on the theme of drugs. During this long, unpublished and uncorrected interview, Ronnie extolled the virtues of lysergic acid, mescaline, psilocybin and hashish, and he told the story of how he first became imbued with the idea of using drugs for therapeutic purposes:

I was interested maybe 15 years ago in, as far as I knew, mescaline and lysergic acid, these had been discovered not long before that. Well, mainly because they seemed to open out very unusual states of consciousness and I was very curious about what relevance these might have to anyone's life or to my own life in particular when some people suggested that they produce model psychosis, that they could project people into experiences that were identical with or extremely comparable to the experiences of schizophrenics, because I'd already got interested in what madness was regarded as being in our society. But I never got round to the question of taking any of these compounds until 6 years ago. The person who turned me on to LSD first of all did so in rather a curious way in that he suggested that taking this drug I was very likely to go psychotic, and so I took it with a certain amount of anxiety but this first experience was both very remarkable, and it had, it was an experience of extra-ordinary familiarity, as though my ordinary experience was transitory and alienation or estrangement from more radical, more primary sort of experience which it seemed that I had

* Ronnie went so far as to give evidence to the Home Office on the issue of cannabis. The fact, though not the detail of his contribution is recorded in 'Cannabis: Report by the Advisory Committee on Drug Dependence', HMSO, 1968.

probably been in as a very young baby, a very young child which I had lost in adjusting to other peoples social reality I'd lost touch with this. And it was remarkable in all sorts of ways which have been described by all sorts of people: enhancement of multi-levels of association that one can simultaneously bring to bear in a way that one only glimpse in a usual state of consciousness. The experience of being able to travel through time in a way that the past wasn't simply something at a distance but parts of this present experience were co-present to one, one could move from one to the other and any nook and cranny to the side was opened out etc. I needed to go over all that: I covered the ground that other people have covered, one talks about it very glibly, but of course it's extra-ordinary no matter who experiences it.

During the course of 1965 Kingsley Hall became one of the 'in' places of London — a refuge for left-wingers, radicals, poets, philosophers and people who fell under the all-embracing term 'artists'. Self-awareness and self-discovery was all. There was an informal pressure to be creative, to find one's true self through uninhibited self-expression. Martin Buber's *I – Thou* was hip, as was Groddeck's *Book of the It*. The intellectual discipline provided by Ronnie, Aaron and David Cooper did not deter a lot of people having an enormous amount of fun. Painting was encouraged as were poetry, singing, dancing (particularly Indian dancing, organized by Sid Briskin) and — most important of all — 'letting yourself go'.

The popularity of Kingsley Hall created its own problems. A healthy amount of paranoia pervaded the atmosphere when strangers were about. Everyone was acutely aware that 'straight' people would find a hundred and one excuses to close the place. But the visitors kept coming. By November of 1965, Ronnie thought there were as many as one hundred people a week passing through the doors.

The highlight of a 'normal' day in the life of Kingsley Hall was undoubtedly the evening supper. Ronnie presided over a grand old wooden table, and he dominated the proceedings with impromptu lectures, dirty jokes, irreverent stories from the Army, medical student horror stories, pearls of wisdom and insight, critiques of the social order and psychoanalytical theories. Ian Spurling (a former patient at

Horton Hospital in Epsom and later an award-winning costume-designer much favoured by the late Sir Kenneth MacMillan and the late pop star Freddie Mercury) stayed at Kingsley Hall during its vintage period. Ian was best remembered for the white pigeon, affectionately called Madam Coup-de-Bec, which had been his closest companion for many years, though thick and thin, mental hospitals and all. Indeed, the first night Ian turned up, the resident Kingsley Hall cat tried − almost successfully − to eat Ian's 'Madam', creating a drama that moved from Kingsley to the nearest hospital, where a surgeon was persuaded to perform emergency treatment on the bird. An all-night vigil was maintained, prayers were offered, and 'Madam' lived to see the dawn. She became an overnight Kingsley Hall miracle. On occasions, Ian Spurling would release his creativity by hanging some netting material on which all manner of objects were hung over the dining table. The combination of these props and Mary Barnes's wall-paintings, faintly lit by candle-light, provided an almost magical scenery for Ronnie and the others to share their food, wine and the occasional joint.

Kingsley Hall was the centre of the world to those who lived there. To Ronnie, however, it was merely part of his own life, which was becoming increasingly complex. By the time Kingsley Hall was fully operational (July 1965) his name was associated with an extraordinary number of subjects across an incredibly wide field. *The Divided Self*, nearly five years after its original publication, was beginning to be read widely, and Ronnie was soon associated with psychoanalysis, existentialism and phenomenology in addition to Kingsley Hall itself. The name R.D. Laing was becoming synonymous with radical psychotherapy and the New Left.

Sanity, Madness and the Family cemented the association between Ronnie, schizophrenia and the family. *Reason and Violence*, although not as widely read as his other works, none the less connected Ronnie not only to David Cooper but also to the works of Sartre. Ronnie's status in the world provided a strange paradox for the clearer minds at Kingsley Hall. Inside this building was talk of revolution, a world revolution, the mother of all dialectics. Outside Kingsley Hall the R.D. Laing story continued: lectures, papers, conferences, television and radio appearances − all of which were an intrinsic part of Ronnie's life. Inevitably, the likes of Clancy Sigal saw this dual-life as a contradiction, a hypocrisy, a sell-out. Ronnie on the other hand still had a great deal to say as a professional doctor, psychiatrist and psychoanalyst, and refused to accept any accusations of perpetuating the world order by playing into the hands of the corrupt capitalist system. To him such self-restraint was naïve bullshit.

Indeed a cursory look at a retrospective reconstruction of Ronnie's schedule throughout 1965 reveals an incredible demand for personal appearances on an equally breath-taking variety of subjects:

January/February – a television appearance on the Associated Rediffusion programme 'The Explorers'; a lecture on 'A Marxist Theory of the Modern Family' at the London School of Economics, followed the next day by a caseworkers' study-weekend in Swanswick, Derby, on the theme of 'The Family and the Individual'.

March – a paper, 'Problems in Treatment of Outpatient Schizophrenics', given at the Association of Psychotherapists' seminar; followed the next day by a television appearance on the BBC's 'Syanon' programme; later in the month, a lecture on psychotherapy at Bristol University.

April – a lecture, 'The True Function of Psychology', at Keele University.

May/June* – 'Time Lost and Regained', delivered at the Open Way; a seven-day United Nations Conference in Holland, under the auspices of Field Family Workers, including a lecture on 'Family and Individual Structure'[+] and 'Mystification, Confusion and Conflict'; a lecture, 'Ritualisation in Abnormal Human Behaviour', given at The Royal Society.

June/July – a three-day conference on family dynamics at The Tavistock Institute of Human Relations; a lecture at The London School of Economics – 'The Study of Inter-experience'; three lectures on the family at the Davidson Clinic Summer School in Edinburgh.

October – a lecture on interpersonal perception at a scientific meeting of the Tavistock Institute of Human Relations.

---

* During May/June 1965 Ronnie also attended a weekend in Oxford concerned with Alex Trocchi's 'Sigma' project, details of which were recorded by Jeff Nuttall in *Bomb Culture*, 1970.

[+] Published in 'The Predicament of the Family' edited by Peter Lomas, 1967.

November – a lecture at a conference of The Society for Psychosomatic Research, on the subject of 'Invalidation as a stress variable in interpersonal relations'; a lecture at the Cambridge University Psychological Society under the title of 'The Politics of Experience'; a television appearance on 'Scene at 6.30', Granada Television.

Fame, for Ronnie, was not an overnight phenomenon.

By July of 1965 Ronnie's fame was beginning to take on a life of its own, of which Kingsley Hall was only one component. An article by Marion Magrid, 'The Death of Hip', had appeared in the June issue of *Esquire* magazine. Marion toured the 'hip joints' of Paris, Amsterdam, East Berlin and Copenhagen, returning to London to 'check out' R.D. Laing before going off to the States. This article, in addition to capturing the immediacy and excitement of the times, provides a rare insight into 21 Wimpole Street and the public perception of R.D. Laing in the early part of 1965, and evokes the soul-searching mood of the sixties. It was a long piece and, no doubt, further established R.D. Laing as a New Wave psychoanalyst.

During the course of 1966 another story was coming to a climax. Running parallel to Ronnie's growing fame was the final disintegration of his relationship with his wife, Anne. Although attempts had been made to patch things up following the traumas of 1963, by late spring of 1965, Ronnie was effectively living where he wanted. There was the family home at 23 Granville Road, the rooms of his private practice at Wimpole Street, Kingsley Hall, Sid's house (if need be) and the spacious Earls Court flat of his young German girlfriend Jutta Werner, whom he had first met in March 1965 through Timothy Leary's colleague, Ralph Metzner. Considering the instability in his private life it is quite an achievement that he managed to keep such a high-flying professional life together. However, Anne had had enough. Ronnie was rarely home and when he did make an appearance, ferocious arguments soon followed. The less time he spent at home the more unpleasant were the times when he was there. Anne decided she could take no more of Ronnie's lifestyle and in the spring of 1966 decided to take the five children to start a new life near La Gourra in the South of France where the entire family, (Ronnie included), had been on holiday the previous summer.

However, the dream life Anne had imagined soon turned into the nightmare of living day to day with no money, no schools willing to take the children, no friends, nothing. Ronnie came over for a last ditch attempt to patch things up, but was unsuccessful. Following a long attempt at 'local integration', defeat was finally conceded, and the French Government provided Anne with enough funds for the family to return to England.

Anne's parents were living in Devon and there was hope that the family might settle there. But the sight of five unruly children with no father around proved too much for Anne's deeply respectable and moral parents, so the family headed back to London to see what was left of the life they had left some months before.

Granville Road had taken a serious decline. There was irreversible rising damp and the premises had an abandoned and cold feeling. Whatever had been there before was no longer there. Ronnie made no effort to assist Anne in getting back into the swing of things. She took us to pay a cursory visit to Kingsley Hall one Sunday lunchtime, and we saw not the old Ronnie but the famous R.D. Laing, now paired up with Jutta, who was pretending to be Joe Berke's girlfriend. There was no possibility of us children returning to private fee-paying schools. The days when the girls attended the Aida Foster theatrical school and Paul and I the fee-paying primary school, Comrie House, were long since gone. There was no way Anne could suffer the constant and intense humiliation of the open secret that Ronnie had found another woman. It was time for 'the first lot' to leave, and this time for good.

Anne packed the car and we said our goodbyes to Granville Road, expecting never to see it again. When Anne asked for a show of hands as to where we should go, 'Scotland!' was the cry. And we were off. It was September 1966. Ronnie came to see his first family in Glasgow two years later, by which time I had forgotten what he looked like.

Ronnie moved into Kingsley Hall on a permanent basis in December 1965 and stayed there for a year before moving into a four-roomed flat with Jutta at 65a Belsize Park Gardens in north-west London, where the couple lived for almost ten years. Kingsley Hall was never the one place. The atmosphere and ethos changed depending on who was living there and who was effectively in charge. The year Ronnie stayed there is remembered by all and sundry as the vintage period. There was a shortage of 'staff', not least because the concept of 'staff' was not recognized. However, this was soon remedied with a surge of new blood from New York – 'The American Invasion' as it was later termed.

El Castillo Feliz set sail from Manhattan in early September 1965. On board was a vibrant group of crazy (i.e., wild, untamed) Americans heading towards a new and uncharted life in the centre of the modern world – the London of the swinging sixties. The group included Doctor Joseph Berke – a twenty-six year old medical graduate from the Albert Einstein University in Brooklyn. Joe had already met Ronnie two years previously, and had stayed at Dingleton Hospital run by Maxwell-Jones. Joe had also provided some assistance to Ronnie in the proposed second volume of studies of 'normal' families. With Joe was his friend, the young poet John Keys, and John's girlfriend, Helen. Calvin Hernton, an extremely engaging and cultured black American from East Village in Manhattan, already known for his book *Sex and Racism*, attended on a whim. All of these characters descended on Kingsley Hall on the evening of 18 September 1965. It was a great night in the annals of Kingsley Hall, and Ronnie was truly on form. But the wind of change was blowing, and Sid Briskin cried that night, knowing that Kingsley Hall would never be the same again.

Joe Berke had been aware for over two years that some revolutionary place would be established by the equally revolutionary R.D. Laing. To Joe, this was a chance of a lifetime. This was where it was at: Kingsley Hall, London in the sixties, around R.D. Laing. By the time Joe moved into Kingsley Hall, many changes had already taken place. Aaron's fight to have Kingsley Hall set up on a more established basis had been lost to Ronnie's charisma. David Cooper was becoming more and more reclusive. It was clear that Mary Barnes was going to stay and get the twenty-four-hours-a-day attention that she had been promised. Against that background, Joe and Mary established a relationship, which is one of the truly remarkable stories of Kingsley Hall immortalized in later years by their book *Mary Barnes – Two Accounts of a Journey Through Madness* and later adapted for the stage by David Edgar.

Ronnie had much to thank Joe Berke for. However, Joe's relationship with Mary was the beginning of the end of Joe's relationship with Ronnie and the Philadelphia Association. Ronnie thought Joe was the ideal candidate for someone such as Mary. He also thought of himself as giving Mary to Joe as a means of initiation into the 'pathos' of 'the brothers'. The expression he sometimes used was that Mary was Joe's 'spurs'. Joe, although relatively young and undoubtedly in awe of Ronnie in the early days, came to realize over the passage of time that Ronnie had serious defects in his dealings with 'patients'. Ronnie could wind someone up, make them feel as if they had seen the light, inspire them with revolutionary ideals – but then he was off on some other venture, leaving the individual with nowhere to go, stranded. It was Joe who looked after Mary more than anyone else. It was Joe who put up with her incessant demands, the smell of her excreta and the exhausting physical encounters.

What Ronnie had not foreseen was that as his own popularity declined, so too would his charismatic power. Ronnie's 'stuff' was brilliant and exciting the first time round; listening to his views more than once made them seem platitudinous, bordering on the self-indulgent. Only the die-hards stuck with Ronnie through the sixties and seventies. But to stick with Ronnie meant sticking to someone else's dream and ambitions. It was as natural for Joe and Ronnie to end up going their own ways as it is for a child to leave home. Unfortunately, Ronnie managed to live a personal philosophy which equated disagreement with betrayal, and to put up with that needed devotion bordering on love, which was beyond the bounds of the relationship between Joe and Ronnie. However the parting of their ways was a process which took many years to come to a head. In the meantime, Kingsley Hall, throughout 1966, 1967, 1968 and 1969, staggered on its perilous course.

In the mid-sixties Aaron Esterson, Ronnie and David Cooper were the high command of the Philadelphia Association. It was they who held the professional medical qualifications and it was they who took on all-comers in private and in public. Villa 21 had provided an invaluable source of practical experience which could be put to good effect by the PA. It was felt, however, that as the great debate was now getting white-hot and, consequentially, the views of the brothers were receiving greater attention and scrutiny, a serious card should be played. To that end Ronnie, David and Aaron wrote the only paper that appeared under their collective names – 'Results of Family-orientated

Therapy with Hospitalised Schizophrenics'.* This article was clearly intended to address the growing criticism from the 'establishment' that Ronnie's, Aaron's and David's views and their published works (especially *Sanity, Madness and the Family*) were too polemical, too subjective and altogether lacking in sufficient clinical discipline expected from the medical world. The paper concluded:

> Twenty male and 22 female schizophrenics were treated by conjoint family and milieu therapy in two mental hospitals with reduced use of tranquillizers. No individual psychotherapy was given. None of the so-called shock treatments were used, nor was leucotomy. All patients were discharged within one year of admission. The average length of stay was three months. Seventeen per cent. were readmitted within a year of discharge. Seventy per cent. of the others were sufficiently well adjusted socially to be able to earn their living for the whole of the year after discharge. These results are the first to be reported on the outcome of purely family and milieu therapy schizophrenics, and they appear to us to establish at least a prima facie case for radical revision of the therapeutic strategy employed in most psychiatric units in relation to the schizophrenic and his family. This revision is in line with current developments in social psychiatry in this country.

The reaction for and against this paper was quite extraordinary. Professor Morris Carstairs (himself a closet guru) wrote an article in the same edition of the journal rejecting the authors' claims, and the debate rumbled on in the correspondence section of the *British Medical Journal* until late January 1966. However, the point had been made – Laing *et al* were out to take on the medical world head-on. It seemed at this stage as if nothing was going to stand in their way – the great battle, as far as they were concerned, was turning a corner. The 'establishment' was on the run, the growing tide of positive public feeling for 'the cause' was gaining ground by the day. How long would it be before the social revolution saw its finest hour?

---

* Published in The *British Medical Journal*, December 1965.

CHAPTER TWELVE

'66 and All That

By late 1966 Ronnie's life was going in several directions. On the therapeutic community front, three households were fully operational: Kingsley Hall, Granville Road and Sid Briskin's own home – all of which were being fully utilized as residential communities. Kingsley Hall was housing a floating population of about twenty people in a space adequate for maybe fourteen. Each of these premises was functioning outside 'the system' in the sense of not being registered with its respective local authority, unconventional in its methodology and, in a commercial context, non-profitable. The fact that the 'therapists' were unpaid was often forgotten. Were it not for Ronnie's personal charisma, this arrangement would never have lasted for any significant period of time. However, people were willing to make great personal sacrifices to be part of the Philadelphia Association. Living on the breadline was a small price to pay.

Ronnie's personal fame was continuing to grow daily. Although the only book to be published in 1966 that bore his name, *Interpersonal Perception*, was never going to reach as wide an audience as *Sanity, Madness and the Family* or *The Divided Self*, the reputation of this 'New Wave' psychoanalyst was now feeding on itself. However, as far as Ronnie was concerned, the principal area into which he felt the need to expand during 1966 was drugs and, in particular, LSD, hashish and mescaline.

From 1960 till 1967 Ronnie's intake of substances, legal and otherwise, increased considerably, and there was clearly a steady increase in his personal consumption during 1965 and 1966, which coincided with his living at Kingsley Hall. Ronnie had come across the three self-appointed high-priests of mind-altering substances – Timothy Leary, Ralph Metzner and Richard Alpert (who subsequently changed into his Buddhist-self, 'Ram Dass'), primarily due to Ronnie's personal contact with Leary in late 1964, and partly due to their successful adaptation of *The Tibetan Book of the Dead* into *The Psychedelic Experience*, first published in the States during the same year. These three characters were uninhibited advocates of the use of LSD and published a periodical, *The Psychedelic Review*, which sought to gain the high ground on the drug culture. An example of where these 'heavy dudes' were at can be taken from the introduction to *The Psychedelic Experience*:

Here then is the key to a mystery which has been passed down for over 2,500 years – the consciousness-expansion experience – the pre-mortem death and rebirth rite. The Vedic sages knew the secret; the Eleusinian initiates knew it; the Tantrics knew it. In all their esoteric writings they whisper the message: it is possible to cut beyond ego-consciousness, to tune in on neurological processes which flash by at the speed of light, and to become aware of the enormous treasury of ancient racial knowledge welded into the nucleus of every cell in your body.

Despite Ronnie's slightly more responsible attitude to drugs, there were considerable overlaps in his and Leary's thinking, particularly regarding the idea of the mind-expanding capacity of certain hallucinogens.

In the last week of February 1966 Ronnie attended the Annual Conference of the National Association for Mental Health at Church House in Westminster. Among the great and good brought together to discuss 'The Heart of the Matter' were Lord Balniel, MP (Chairman of the Council), Sir George Godber, KCB, DM, FRCP, DPH (Chief Medical Officer, Ministry of Health), Evelyn de Rothschild, the Rt Hon. Lord Segal, MA, MRCS, LRCP, and R.D. Laing, MB, Ch.B. DPM, Principal Investigator, Schizophrenia and Family Research Unit, Tavistock Institute of Human Relations; Fellow, Foundation Fund for Research in Psychiatry. This conference was more like a two-day summit on all matters relating to the well-being of society, covering senile diseases and subnormality on the first day, followed by a discussion on schizophrenia during the course of the second.

120 • *R.D. Laing*

Ironically, to some members of Ronnie's growing entourage, his participation in 'Establishment events' contradicted his outspokenness and radical opinions, and he seemed to have become part of that very system that his ideas militated against. Ronnie was more complicated than that. Despite his outward radicalism, he found something intrinsically enjoyable about formality and ritual, especially if done well and in the right spirit. On the occasion of this conference, the gathering cut no corners. Schizophrenia was on the agenda for the whole of the second-day session, as a prelude to which Mass was said in Westminster Cathedral for members of the conference, followed by a service in the chapel of Church House.

On the day of Ronnie's active participation Evelyn de Rothschild was in the chair and the panel consisted of J.R. Smythies, a senior lecturer from the Department of Psychiatry, University of Edinburgh, and Elizabeth Shoenberg, a consultant psychiatrist based at Claybury Hospital in Essex.

The established world was capable of bringing out the worst in Ronnie. It was as if he thought that by behaving in a socially acceptable manner he had somehow betrayed his true self. Indeed, a pattern of confrontation emerges right through his life, beginning with the 'Health and Society' speech delivered as an undergraduate, in which he spoke of 'the syphilisation of society' in the midst and under the gaze of his superiors. Sometimes he got away with it, sometimes he did not. On this occasion, Ronnie could not resist the challenge to blow what he perceived as tiny, ordered, disciplined, puritanical, paternalistic minds, into as many fragments as he could. As his colleagues observed at the Tavistock, for some reason Ronnie spat not on the middle classes, but on the middle-class mind.

In this spirit Ronnie delivered a memorable mini-speech, which was in all likelihood completely unrehearsed. Not for him a long list of self-serving statistics wrapped up in a detailed case study. He came to the conclusion that his twenty minutes would best be served by informing the assembled throng of the therapeutic benefits of LSD and mescaline, of the non-existence of schizophrenia, of the necessity of healing oneself before attempting to treat others, and that schizophrenia 'remains one of the greatest challenges and scandals of our time'. Indeed, he went so far as to say midway through this blasting:

An LSD or mescaline session in one person, with one set in one setting may occasion a psychotic experience. Another person, with a different set and different setting, may experience a period of super-sanity.... The aim of therapy will be to enhance consciousness rather than to diminish it. Drugs of choice, if any are to be used, will be predominantly consciousness expanding drugs, rather than consciousness constrictors – the psychic energisers, not the tranquillisers.

It seemed as though Ronnie was becoming increasingly aware of the fact that he had a choice to make – and increasingly unwilling to make it. He had to declare himself either 'anti-establishment', part of the 'counter-culture', or otherwise. But his heart was in both camps. He came from a good school in Glasgow, followed by the highly respected Glasgow University; he was an established and successful writer; a paid-up member of the Royal College of Psychiatrists; a trained, qualified and practising psychoanalyst. But he had already burned his bridges with part of the establishment by refusing to pursue the position of consultant psychiatrist at the Tavistock Clinic.

Ronnie's alternative to the established order seemed potentially all-embracing – he was in charge of several households, he was very much in demand as a speaker at conferences and in the television world, his private practice in Wimpole Street was flourishing, his books were selling like hot-cakes and – most important of all – the revolutionary social climate was creating an atmosphere in which his utterances could be taken with the utmost seriousness. His time had come. R.D. Laing the guru was coming to life.

Much of Ronnie's writing was done while most people were asleep, often between the hours of midnight and 5 a.m. During these 'wee, small hours' Ronnie found his inspiration and strength to commit to writing his personal thoughts, some of which would later appear as part of a speech, and then perhaps as an article. One small piece that did not see the light of day goes some way towards explaining the growing influence of his works. He had already publicly stated his views on drugs and found the effect was extremely powerful. People wanted to know more about mysticism, more about their true selves, more about the meaning of life. This type of enquiry Ronnie privately called the 'Lost and Found Department'. As if he were defining and polishing his guru role, he wrote the following in a personal diary during the early part of 1966, while living at Kingsley Hall:

> You can never find what you are looking for because you are
> what you are looking for and since you are the self you have
> lost – who else – the self you are trying to find is the you that
> is trying to find the self that is trying to find you. So since you
> have never been lost you can never be found.

Another version followed:

> The self you are trying to find is the you that is trying to find
> the self you are trying to find so you will never find yourself
> since you have never been lost yourself since the self you have
> lost is the you that has lost it.

Despite this growing guru element in Ronnie's own thinking, to the
outside world he was still riding two horses. His establishment side
was not yet completely abandoned. When it proved necessary he would
give a relatively straight talk in formal circumstances. For example,
in March 1966 he gave a lecture at the Students' Conference at the
University of London Psychological Society on the subject of 'The
Function and Nature of Psychotherapy'. In July, it was 'Research into
Schizophrenia' at the Staff College for Ward Sisters at King Edward's
Hospital Fund for London. 'Personal Problems in Adult Students' was
delivered later that year at a conference on 'Personal Relationships' at
the London Institute of Education. He even lectured at the Royal Society
of London at the request of Sir Julian Huxley, on 'Ritualisation and
Abnormal Behaviour'. But increasingly throughout 1966, the subject
addressed had to do with drugs. In January he spoke to the Department
of Psychiatry at the London Hospital in Whitechapel on the 'Phenomenology of Hashish, Mescaline and LSD'. At the Institute of Contemporary Arts in June there was no mistaking what was in store with a
talk on 'The Experience of LSD'. There seems no doubt that by any
standards, Ronnie was taking a lot of drugs himself during 1966. The
combination of living at Kingsley Hall (where being out of your head
was thought to be part of the process of self-realization), Ronnie's
own personal economic freedom, and a life where taking LSD could
be put down to 'work', provided Ronnie with the opportunity to rationalize to himself that his world was the centre of a higher order.

Others were not so impressed. Aaron Esterson was coming to the end of his patience. Kingsley Hall was, as far as Aaron was concerned, a complete disaster. The relationship between Ronnie and Aaron was heading for the climax that had been brewing for years.

Aaron and Ronnie fell out quite spectacularly. Before 1966 was over, there came a night when Ronnie 'let Aaron have it' at the home of Ben Churchill, who was running Granville Road. Ronnie refused to continue their friendship unless Aaron 'took Jesus Christ into his heart'. Aaron took the view that this was a piece of unadulterated cheek. Ronnie asked Aaron to stand up. Aaron, acclimatized to bizarre requests, stood up in front of Ronnie. Ronnie very carefully removed Aaron's glasses, Aaron thinking that Ronnie had noticed something on them. Ronnie put the glasses down on a table as carefully as he had taken them off and, quite out of the blue, delivered a full blow to Aaron's jaw. This was the moment they had waited years and years for. Aaron and Ronnie battled it out around the room, ending up on the floor, where they were eventually separated, both, by this stage, in uncontrollable laughter. However, that episode more or less marked the end of their relationship as far as Aaron was concerned. Things were never quite the same.

Aaron was not the only one to become completely disillusioned with Ronnie and the goings-on of Kingsley Hall. An episode written up as fiction in Clancy Sigal's hilarious book, *Zone of the Interior*, brought Sigal's involvement with Ronnie, Kingsley Hall, the PA in general and 'the brothers' in particular, to a rapid halt.

One night at Kingsley Hall 'the brothers' became concerned about Clancy, whose behaviour, to them, seemed potentially suicidal. Clancy made a break from the confines of Kingsley Hall to his flat in Bayswater. 'The brothers' (Ronnie, Joe Berke, Aaron Esterson, David Cooper and Raymond Blake) followed him. Just before Clancy reached his door they pounced. A serious scuffle ensued, during which Clancy received numerous heavy blows. A heavy dose of a tranquillizer was none too precisely stuck into Clancy's thigh by Aaron. Although the prevailing view was that 'brother Clancy' might have committed suicide had this course of action not been taken, this was not how Clancy himself saw it. To him, the ethos of Kingsley Hall was to let someone go through their craziness without forcible intervention. He felt deeply betrayed and in a letter to the author, stated that he believes to this day, and without reservation, that Ronnie and the others 'tried to kill me and almost succeeded'. After sitting tight for two days (having been carried back to Kingsley Hall) he made a run for it, never to show his face round Kingsley Hall again, despite requests from Ronnie.

The book Clancy wrote about Kingsley Hall was never published in this country, party because Ronnie took steps to prevent it. The portrayal of Kingsley Hall as 'Meditation Manor' under the control of a crazy Scottish doctor (Doctor Willie Last) and his cronies was too much for Ronnie, who felt that Clancy had not realized that 'the brothers' had made a great exception to their norm, not out of malice but out of love. Ronnie believed Clancy would, eventually, understand. Perhaps even have an acid trip for old time's sake. As it was, the residual bitterness persisted for many years, unresolved. As late as 1989 Ronnie was still actively resisting the publication of *Zone of the Interior* in the United Kingdom, and the rights and wrongs of the 'Clancy episode' still occupy the minds of those who were there on that night. In fairness to Clancy, one might have had greater sympathy for Ronnie's stance had he ever bothered to read the book. In June 1989, just weeks before his death, Ronnie wrote to Joe Berke: 'The Free Association Press wrote me about the Sigal book. I said I would have to consult the Medical Defence Union. I haven't read it, but I've been told it's fairly malicious.'

To the outside world, Kingsley Hall continued to represent a brave experiment in new thinking about schizophrenia, with a recent precedent – Villa 21 – and an exciting present – Mary Barnes. In an article in the *Guardian* newspaper on 4 October 1966 journalist Ruth Abel painted a very rosy picture of Kingsley Hall. Abel had spoken with Sid Briskin, and her article informed the liberal readers of the day-to-day running of Kingsley Hall, its short history, and its beneficial effects, quoting the example of 'George', who had arrived in a completely mute state but was now able to speak and even participate in the singing and dancing.

This was the popular front of Kingsley Hall; a commercial company does not inform its shareholders of the boardroom back-stabbing unless absolutely necessary. And so with Kingsley Hall – the image of a radical but functioning community was deliberately espoused as the party-line. Ronnie had much to thank Sid Briskin for.

Ronnie's American contacts were proving useful. Ross Speck, the tall American psychiatrist with whom Ronnie had forged a friendship back in 1962, wrote to Ronnie inviting him to participate in a two-day conference to be held in Philadelphia over 14–15 October 1966 at the Bellevue Stratford Hotel, under the auspices of the Hahnemann Medical College. Of the many conferences Ronnie attended, this one was of notable influence. The conference, 'Society and Psychosis', was, in Ross Speck's view, the catalyst for the Round House meeting organized by Ronnie, David Cooper, Joe Berke and Leon Redler the following year. (This view is not endorsed by Joe Berke, who points out that the organization for the 1967 Round House Conference was already well underway by the summer of 1966.) The cream of the American intellectual heavyweights – those one might loosely call 'communication/environmental/family interactionists' – attended the conference: Jules Henry, Gregory Bateson, Murray Bowen and Ross Speck. Nathan Ackerman and Erving Goffman had agreed to attend but stood down at the last minute due to family commitments.

There was a great deal of common ground between Ronnie and these characters. Jules Henry was advocating the 'sham' theories put forward in his popular book *Culture Against Man*; Gregory Bateson was already renowned for his double-bind theory, which was becoming increasingly widely accepted, in one form or another, since its publication in 1956. Ross Speck's reputation in the American psychiatric world was due in part to his family network approach to schizophrenia, which involved bringing together as many people associated with a person labelled 'schizophrenic' as was practically possible. On each and every occasion when Ross had managed to bring the relatives and friends together, something had happened to resolve the crisis. Murray Bowen believed that a person's disintegration into schizophrenia was comprehensible only in the historical context of the family – not just the immediate family, but previous generations. The further back one went the more developed the context of an individual's behaviour. Murray insisted, for example, that anyone who wished to practise as a family therapist should actively investigate their own family history, going back at least three generations.

All of these individuals were at the forefront of their profession. Ronnie was in good company and on form. He planned to tell them a thing or two about 'society and psychosis'. His unpublished speech, delivered at 9.30 a.m., makes one feel the remaining company were, by comparison, inhibited conservatives:

First of all I would say that 'normal adjustment' including mature genital sexual functioning is a social lobotomy, and if that doesn't succeed, then a therapeutic lobotomy is initiated; if that blunders, a chemical lobotomy is attempted and when all else fails a physical lobotomy is undertaken. Middle class society in dealing with its children lobotomizes them instead of shooting them. And the schizophrenic can be regarded as someone on whom the *social* lobotomy has not succeeded; therefore, rather more intensive and specific measures should be brought to bear on this deviant. We can shoot others but we lobotomize ourselves. We must do this long before we rationalize the conflicts in which we engage and our image of ourselves as God's gift to the world, the majority of whose inhabitants subsist in a semi-starved condition. We must extirpate the experience of our early years and finally, as Jules Henry has observed, we must cultivate a patina of false consciousness inured to its own deceit. And once you've done that, which means having a good ego, then you're in!

As a result of this conference, Gregory Bateson told Ronnie that Ronnie 'had 10 per cent more' (in overall intellectual terms) than Bateson himself– a fact remembered not only by Ronnie but Ross Speck. His reputation was, in the States at least, not only intact but strengthened. The next American visit – a major invitation from the William Alanson White Institute in New York to deliver a series of lectures by their very 'first Visiting Distinguished Psychoanalyst' – would soon follow.

In the meantime Ronnie returned to London and delivered a lecture at Kingsley Hall under the title 'Psychosis, Porpoises and Society', telling wondrous tales of his amazing visit to the States. (Gregory Bateson had now turned his attention to the communication between dolphins.) It was soon time to start organizing the main event of 1967 – The Congress of the Dialectics of Liberation.

By the end of 1966 Ronnie was getting tired of Kingsley Hall. Having lived there full-time for nearly twelve months during the latter part of 1965 and late 1966 (and for a good deal of time thereafter on an *ad hoc* basis), he had had enough. It was time to hand over the baton.

There was no shortage of people to look after the running of the place in Ronnie's absence. Joe Berke was around, as were two other American doctors, Leon Redler and Morton Schatzman. However, with Ronnie's visits restricted to Friday nights, the Kingsley Hall of old vanished. It was no longer the palace of wisdom it had once been.

CHAPTER THIRTEEN

The Politics of Experience

With hindsight one can see that Ronnie himself went through his own personal metanoia while living at Kingsley Hall. He was now freer, could breathe better, felt better, was able to live better. His first child from his union with Jutta was due in September. He was a new man with a new life and a busy schedule.

The year 1967 promised another gruelling but challenging year of lectures, television appearances, the publication of another major book, the start of a new family and the co-ordination of Kingsley Hall, Granville Road and Sid's house – all of this while keeping together his 'day job' as a practising psychoanalyst and LSD therapist in Wimpole Street.

Ronnie's attendance at a lecture was, by now, a major event. No longer confined to 'the ranks', the name R.D. Laing by 1967 had enormous pulling power. It was not long into the year before Ronnie attended the first of several major conferences at which he spoke. During the period 9–21 January 1967 Ronnie was resident at the William Alanson White Institute of Psychiatry, Psychoanalysis and Psychology in New York, a non-profit psychoanalytical training organization. Their first ever newsletter, published in the fall of 1966, heralded the arrival of Ronald David Laing, MB, Ch.B., DPM on its front cover, complete with a photograph of the young, handsome Scottish high-flyer with piercing dark eyes. This was a very prestigious occasion for Ronnie. He was invited not merely as a guest speaker but as the institute's 'first Visiting Distinguished Psychoanalyst'. This was praise indeed, considering the celebrated doyens of the historical American psychoanalytical scene, including Harry Stack Sullivan and Frieda Fromm-Reichmann.

Ronnie's work and the research of the White Institute were both focused on the inter-personal aspects of the understanding and treatment of schizophrenia, the family context, and the use of LSD in a formal therapeutic setting. While at the institute, Ronnie delivered five important lectures, in addition to participating in workshops and seminars. The director of the institute, Carl Wittenberg, remembers Ronnie very well. Perhaps the most remembered aspect of these talks was Ronnie's soft-spoken delivery – his quiet Scottish accent, his intellectual intensity and his profound dedication to his chosen subject. He did not disappoint his audience. Not surprisingly, he relied on Kingsley Hall as one of the main components of his talks.

Although the institute was fascinated to hear Ronnie's account of LSD therapy in the UK, the clinical use of LSD was nothing new to this audience. A Dr Hanscari Leuner, Professor at the University of Göttingen, West Germany, and Visiting Professor of Psychiatry at Yale, had already addressed the institute in May 1966 on what was being called 'psycholitic therapy' (as opposed to 'pharmaco-therapy'), and had investigated all the LSD research being conducted under the auspices of the American National Institute of Mental Health. Dr Leuner was giving LSD to those with severe, long-standing neuroses, including those diagnosed as psychopathic personality, juvenile delinquency, regressive reactions and borderline cases. He had already reported that 'the best results are achieved with sociopaths and patients with anxiety neuroses or reactive depressions'.

There was nothing new about the family context. The Americans were way ahead of the UK in the study of the family context of schizophrenia. There was nothing new about the 'inter-personal' method espoused by Ronnie. Indeed, the idea of psychoanalysis as a personal encounter between two people, one of whom, to coin a phrase from *The Divided Self*, was sane by mutual consent, had reached mythological proportions through stories of the female psychoanalyst, Frieda Fromm-Reichmann. This lady had already shocked the therapeutic community by relating an account of a young man she had encouraged to masturbate in front of her during a 'routine' psychoanalytical session. This crowd would take a lot to rattle.

Perhaps it was because Ronnie was in front of such seasoned characters that his talks were relatively passive. There was no desire to shock, no intention to rock the boat. It was, as much as anything else, a lesson for Ronnie to realize that in this context, his ideas were already part of the accepted cutting edge. The early part of his second lecture shows a distinct indication that he was groping in the dark for a new, unfamiliar angle:

> I'm going to attempt what is literally impossible, to try to use words and syntax to speak about modes of experience where the distinctions enshrined by language haven't yet been formed. Since language proceeds by the delineation of contours, we can't use it directly or in an unequivocal way to describe a state of affairs before contours have been formed. Yet at the same time, if I'm not going to whistle it or dance it, I've got to use language, in a sense, against itself to convey that it's not conveying what it's purporting to convey. And I've got to do this in such a way that isn't what's usually regarded as total schizophrenese. I'm trying to talk about what some people talk about more directly, hence are regarded as psychotic for doing so. I might not succeed in this. I'm not without my own anxieties on both sides, that if I say too directly what I'm trying to say, then you'll regard me as mad but interesting; on the other hand, if I say what I'm trying to say too deviously, you will regard me as sane and dull. As long as you don't think I'm being clever...

Ronnie conducted himself impeccably throughout his stay in New York. He had been faced with a tough and demanding schedule and an equally tough and demanding audience. It was now time to return to London, to Belsize Park Gardens and Kingsley Hall. It was time to prepare for another series of key-note speeches, television appearances and patients.

Kingsley Hall was becoming the object of increasing public attention. There was a natural curiosity about the goings-on inside. Unfortunately, the confidence of the local working-class residents had never been won. There was still a pervading 'us and them' feeling about the place. Attempts had been made to integrate the good-will of the larger community in which Kingsley Hall stood, but to no avail. An opportunity to meet the residents of Kingsley Hall had been arranged, but only a handful of locals had bothered to turn up; their concerns for themselves and the children in the area were not thought to be adequately addressed. How would you explain to an ordinary working docker that this home, which was not a hospital, had no doctors in residence, and no 'patients' as such, and yet, for all intents and purposes was, as far as they had come to understand, full of potentially dangerous lunatics, posed no threat to the local community?

The battle over the cause of schizophrenia, indeed its very nature, seemed to avoid perpetually any 'showdown'. Those who claimed it was nothing whatsoever to do with the environment, including familial relationships or immediate environmental context, could provide evidence of sorts that the schizophrenic was merely suffering from some sort of chemical maladjustment. 'Radical' psychiatrists such as Ronnie were equally able to provide their own sources pointing towards a pathology that lay in the realms of inter-personal relationships. These two extremes were never going to meet. You believed in one or the other. But Ronnie was heading out of the detailed debate into another dimension. It was time, once and for all, for Ronnie to put his metaphorical cards on the table and state his allegiance, unequivocally, to a philosophical approach to madness (as opposed to the clinical term schizophrenia) with an emphasis on its contextual and relative nature, the challenge to the sanity of society as a whole, the questioning of the justice of the medical system, the reliance on personal experience over objective analysis – in short a total, all-out confrontation with accepted medical practice and those psychiatrists who practised within the mainstream establishment. To that end, *The Politics of Experience and The Bird of Paradise* was published in early 1967. The timing of this book could not be criticized. The R.D. Laing audience was perfectly prepared to receive a book that did not seem to address the nitty-gritty issues from a staid, academic perspective. What was delivered here was of a different order, written in the language of a philosopher-prophet, an application to the world for guruship, a statement of eternal truth.

The Politics of Experience and The Bird of Paradise was never written as a book. Very little of it was new, the vast majority having been delivered as lectures as far back as 1962. In a sense, it is an 'R.D. Reader' – a collection of what Ronnie considered his best (i.e., most controversial) utterances in the preceding five years. None the less, the combined chapters provided a unified philosophical perspective on the nature of madness, which owed more to Nietzsche and Marx than any clinical work on psychiatry. Extracts from the introduction to this slim volume were soon being reproduced in Ph.D. dissertations around the world:

We are all murderers and prostitutes – no matter to what culture, society, class, nation one belongs, no matter how normal, moral or mature one takes oneself to be.

We are bemused and crazed creatures, strangers to our true selves, to one another, and to the spiritual and material world – mad, even, from an ideal standpoint we can glimpse but not adopt.

We are born into a world where alienation awaits us. We are potentially men, but are in an alienated state, and this state is not simply a natural system. Alienation as our present destiny is achieved only by outrageous violence perpetrated by human beings on human beings.

Even the *British Journal of Psychiatry* – a publication that would avoid R.D. Laing if it could – took the opportunity to publish an article in the early part of 1969: 'Laing's Models of Madness', by three authors, Miriam Siegler, Humphrey Osmond and Harriet Mann, sought to undermine the credibility of R.D. Laing in general and *The Politics of Experience* in particular. The paper, financed by the National Institute of Mental Health, concluded:

Surely the young people who turn to Laing for help deserve to know what he is wearing, what role he offers them, what model he uses, what authority he speaks from. In this book, he offers three models which can be disentangled only with the greatest difficulty. None of them is the medical model, from which we believe he derived his authority. If Laing wishes to be a guru or a philosopher, there is no doubt a place for him, but young people who are suffering from schizophrenia may prefer to entrust themselves to a doctor who will treat their illness as best he can.

The latter part of this book, *The Bird of Paradise*, was given two working titles, neither of which survived: 'Entrances and Exits' and 'The Swordfish and the Moon'. *The Bird of Paradise* went through

many drafts. Among its more celebrated utterances was the passage:
'If I could turn you on, if I could drive you out of your wretched
mind, if I could tell you I would let you know.' The penultimate
draft of this much quoted promise was preceded by the words 'I am
trying to fuck you, dear reader, I am trying to get through', which
indicate a degree of desperateness, a desire to shock, a willingness to
go beyond the very concept of boundaries into a mode perhaps closer
to contempt than wisdom. The material that was subject to self-cen-
sorship at a late stage one can only presume was considered too over
the top, even for Ronnie. Here is another extreme example, contained
in a typewritten manuscript, which was dropped and then reinstated at
a later stage:

> How do you plug a void plugging a void? How to inject nothing
> into fuck-all? How to come into a gone world? No piss, shit,
> smegma, come, mucoid, viscoid, soft or hard, or even tears of
> eyes, ears, arse, cunt, prick, nostrils, done to any T, of man or
> alligator, tortoise, or daughter, will plug up the Hole. It's gone
> past all that, that, all that last desperate clutch. Come into gone. I
> do assure you. The dreadful has already happened.

What was Ronnie trying to say with this sort of material? Can one
say that such utterances were merely the effluence of Scotch whisky,
Californian grass and Czechoslovakian acid or was R.D. really crazy?
There is little doubt that much of *The Bird of Paradise* was written
when Ronnie was under the influence of a variety of mind-altering
substances, and at a time of day when most people were safely tucked
up in bed awaiting the late dawn of another day. This was Ronnie
living on the dark side of the moon; *The Bird Of Paradise*, presented
in such an unorthodox style, was designed to shock the middle-class
mentality, the established order, the fool living in ignorance of his
own ignorance. His mother was deeply shocked. It was probably the
first time she had ever seen the word 'fuck' in print. Amelia was deeply
ashamed, and remained so, for whether she read all of Ronnie's books or
not, she was perfectly aware, through local reviews and gossip, of what
her son was saying about families and society throughout the sixties.

Ronnie was still, even at this late stage in the formulation of his
new way-way-out-on-a-limb-self, putting in solid performances at main-

stream psychiatric events. In March 1967, after the publication of *The Politics of Experience and The Bird of Paradise*, Ronnie attended the First Rochester International Conference situated outside New York City on 'The Origin of Schizophrenia', where he delivered a paper entitled 'The Study of Family and Social Contexts in Relation to the Origin of Schizophrenia'. Here Ronnie was again among his peers, this time American establishment psychiatrists. A photograph of the speakers shows Ronnie in his best suit among equally well turned out colleagues, all of whom appear considerably older than the still under-forty, youngish looking Scottish psychiatrist.

But despite the formal nature of these proceedings Ronnie was hell-bent on giving the alternative view which, by now, was running along a well-trodden path. He could just about accept the use of the term schizophrenia but only in the sense that 'schizophrenia is the name for a condition that most psychiatrists ascribe to patients they call schizophrenic'. He was still trying to squeeze lessons out of David Cooper's anti-hospital experiment in Shenley Hospital, still arguing that an individual's apparent irrationality finds its rationality in the irrationality of the family. All behaviour has a context and the immediate context for most, is the family.

However, his ideas were progressing towards the concept of a 'Total World System'. However 'way-out' these views may have seemed to a psychiatrist who thought solely in terms of drug therapy to be administered by 'white-coat' authority, this line of attack against the establishment was gaining ground, particularly among the younger members of the medical establishment and on the campuses of the American university scene, and among wide-reading students in general.

'R.D. Laing' was becoming a byword for a whole system of ideas, the central theme of which was a challenge to the recognized order. Who had the right to call another person mad? Was not society clearly mad? If not, then was the violence in Cambodia the action of a sane and just society? The continuing battle raging in Vietnam did much to alienate the state from its younger citizens, not only in America but also in the UK. To liberal thinkers, R.D. Laing was a voice in the wilderness, a psychiatrist who had defected to 'true reality', 'true consciousness', in search of his 'true self'. It was as if Ronnie had embarked on his own spiritual journey in a very open and public manner, at a stage when political sentiment was polarizing. The 'anti-establishment' had good cause to believe that they could win the day — that peace and love would conquer violence and ignorance. Ronnie seemed to be finely tuned in to these sentiments. Indeed one could say that his writings, books, lectures, papers, television appearances and free-spirit reputation were having a serious influence on the possible outcome. Alas, it would not be long before the establishment would put its foot down, declare its supremacy and let everyone know that it was in charge, had always been in charge and would continue to remain in charge. That is not to say the battle was completely lost. In the hearts and minds of a generation lived the idea that their betters and elders had got it all wrong. But what was new about that?

There was much activity and excitement when Ronnie returned from the States in early April 1967. From his small flat in Belsize Park Gardens the main event of the year was being finalized by The Institute of Phenomenological Studies — a sort of trading name for Ronnie, David Cooper, Joe Berke and Leon Redler, who were gearing themselves up for a congress under the title 'The Dialectics of Liberation'. A star-studded Left-Wing line-up was promised including Gregory Bateson, David Cooper, John Gerassi, Allen Ginsberg, Erving Goffman, Lucien Goldmann, Paul Goodman, Jules Henry, Ronald Laing, Herbert Marcuse and Paul Sweezy. The most striking aspect to the Congress was the complete absence of publicized woman speakers, especially since it was supposed to be all about social injustice. The participants managed to secure the facilities of an enormous building in Camden Town, north London, aptly called The Round House. The publicity brochure was printed and distributed in hundreds, loudly proclaiming, like an eighteenth-century revolutionary pamphlet, that 'all men are in chains'.

The wording of the publicity material, a strange blend of radicalism through the ages from Nietzsche to Fanon, and its unequivocal revolutionary spirit, is more accurately attributed to David Cooper than Ronnie. It is no coincidence that this particular period marks the height of the guru wars between Ronnie and David. Onlookers were constantly awed by the sharp competition between Ronnie and David. One particular battle in the guru war can be detected by a careful reading between the lines of a series of articles in the New Left press in the weeks preceding the conference. In the *New Statesman* of Friday 16 June 1967 — less than a month before the congress — both

Ronnie and David were jostling for pole-guru-status. Ronnie was ahead – just. In this edition they reviewed five books between them, three of which are now regarded by many as landmarks in their fields. Ronnie managed to get his glowing review of Michel Foucault's classic, *Madness and Civilization*, ahead of Cooper's article, which reviewed *four* books – *Ecrits* by Jacques Lacan, *Being Mentally Ill* by Thomas Scheff, *Mental Health and Contemporary Thought* edited by K. Soddy and R.H. Ahrenfeld, and *The Mentally Retarded Child*, by Abraham Levinson. However, Ronnie could not resist establishing his perceived dominance over David by criticizing David's 'too short' introduction to Foucault's work which, in Ronnie's opinion, would necessitate the re-writing of the psychiatric textbooks. Never mind – David would soon get his own back. One must remember that Ronnie and David had a deep affection and admiration for each other which, by its exclusive nature, made others feel left out.

The congress, like all well-laid plans, did not go entirely smoothly. Erving Goffman indicated at a late stage that he was pulling out. Ross Speck was asked to stand in for him and had to make a hasty retreat to the Isle of Man to think of something suitable to say at very short notice.

Ronnie and Stokely Carmichael did not hit it off. For some reason Ronnie felt the need to establish his dominance over Stokely in a way that Joe Berke still recalls with displeasure. During one of the many *ad hoc* debates that occurred after the day's play, Ronnie blasted Stokely Carmichael with a 'number'. Ronnie had got it into his mind that it was a reasonable supposition that by virtue of Stokely's surname – Carmichael – he must have been a slave to Ronnie's Scottish ancestors 'the Viking-Laings'. In addition, Ronnie was keen on winding Stokely up because 'Stokely smelt real bad'. Apparently, by some human or divine intervention, a cat had defecated on Stokely's hotel bed. As a result, the rather offensive smell of cat shit seemed to follow Stokely around. Ronnie could not resist the temptation to let these two matters dominate their encounter. Although he obviously had a great time teasing Stokely in this fashion, others were not so impressed and felt Ronnie's behaviour to be rather childish. That no one thought of telling him indicates the level of Ronnie's charisma, but actually had more to do with raw dominance.

Ronnie delivered his paper 'The Obvious' on the morning of Saturday 15 July, the first day of this event. One witness to this talk,

Iain Sinclair, wrote up the opening day of the congress in a book called *The Kodak Mantra Diaries*. Ronnie's new-style delivery was not missed: 'Words are stranded, phrases knot together. The excitement of his idea ignites like brandy-breath. He swings dangerously between pub toughness and visionary withdrawal. Is committed to his argument. It is alive, with all the feathers on as he releases it.'

And so it went on for two weeks. Following Ronnie's talk there was Gregory Bateson on 'Conscious Purpose Versus Nature', Jules Henry on 'Social and Psychological Preparation for War', John Gerassi on 'Imperialism and Revolution in America', Paul Sweezy on 'The Future of Capitalism', Paul Goodman on 'Objective Values', Lucien Goldman on 'Criticism and Dogmatism in Literature', Stokely Carmichael on 'Black Power', Herbert Marcuse on 'Liberation from the Affluent Society'. David Cooper had the last word with a talk appropriately entitled 'Beyond Words'. It had been a very long two weeks, a great buzz for all concerned.

Not surprisingly, the congress received wide-spread attention. A film was made for the American education market, there was a Norwegian film crew, and a series of LPs were produced capturing all the major speeches. Perhaps the most poignant write-up of this gathering was a long article by Roger Barnard for the 3 August 1967 edition of *New Society*, in which summary judgement was given:

I submit the following two propositions: that for this kind of social engineering to come into its own, (1) the inequities of the present system must first be unmasked, and (2) a new politics will have to be developed which is able to create the possibilities for its use. The international congress on 'The Dialetics of Liberation' measured up admirably to the first proposition. With regard to the second proposition it was a nonstarter. That is the true measure of its failure.

Despite the failure described by the *New Society*, the congress, in its own way, rumbled on. David Cooper's book on the conference, published in America under the title *To Free a Generation – The Dialectics of Liberation*, included all the major speeches of the participants. The impact and effect of this book is impossible to quantify. It was certainly well read both in America and Europe. It was also a bone of contention between David and Ronnie for many years. David

Cooper's introduction included the following passage: 'The organising group consisted of four psychiatrists who were very much concerned with radical innovation in their own field – to the extent of their own counter-labelling their discipline as anti-psychiatry. The four were Dr R.D. Laing and myself, also Dr Joseph Berke and Dr Leon Redler.'

Ronnie made two mistakes with David's introduction. First, he did not insist on reading it prior to publication. Ronnie did not consider himself an 'anti-psychiatrist' and was not an advocate of the theory that the family scapegoated one of its members into the role of a schizophrenic, as stated. That was David's perspective and particular way of articulating 'the struggle'. The damage, however, had been done. David managed to label Ronnie an anti-psychiatrist. Ronnie was furious at this move, but made a more serious mistake in not taking immediate and effective action to rectify his position. It was as if he was content to be thought of as an anti-psychiatrist as long as he had the option of saying 'but I did not say that I was, nor did I perceive myself as being an anti-psychiatrist'. In short, Ronnie wanted to have his cake and eat it, the end result being that as far as the committed left-wingers were concerned he was the leading exponent of anti-psychiatry and the theories associated with that concept. By the time the book was insinuating itself into the minds of its readers during the 'revolutionary' period of 1968 and 1969, Ronnie was coming under increasing pressure to carry the flag of a movement with which he did not feel associated. His followers expected a definitive treatise on the political aspects of psychiatry and felt, no doubt, that Ronnie was abandoning the cause just when he was needed most. The R.D. entourage expected a political stance. Ronnie felt compelled to start an autobiography.

It is tempting to draw some sort of line after the events surrounding The Round House, not least because it marked the end of another phase in Ronnie's life. The urgency of the time had less to do with psychiatry than with a wider political movement, of which radical psychiatry was a relatively small but significant component. On a personal level, with Jutta expecting in September and another family about to begin, Ronnie was under greater personal pressure to 'cool off' than to head, or purport to be a major player in, a radical and outwardly political movement. Ronnie was now seriously considering his position, what he was trying to achieve, what he had achieved – a period of deep introspection which would culminate in a decision to live somewhere 'far away from it all' for at least one whole year. Yet there was constant pressure to provide financial security for both his new and his first family which now amounted to two 'wives' and five children, with another on the way. Besides, having laid the groundwork for his fame throughout the previous decade, he was much in demand.

Fundamentally Ronnie had a Christian-Marxist-Liberal philosophy to life as evidenced by the enormous amount of time he freely gave to the working ethos of the Philadelphia Association. He was consequently inhibited, on one level, from living a life which embraced all the trappings of a fully developed capitalist social system. Yet at the same time he enjoyed the best food, the best wine, first-class travel, constant supplies of Perrier water, the feeling of financial security, eating at good restaurants, holidays abroad and all the other comforts of middle-class life that he publicly condemned, implicitly or otherwise. He was tied in a knot, sometimes described as hypocrisy.

A few days before Ronnie and Jutta's first child, Adam, was born on 9 September 1967, Ronnie appeared on prime-time television, his first television appearance since March when he was on the less popular BBC 2 programme, 'Late Night Line Up'. Now it was 'Your Witness' on BBC 1. Ronnie was entering a new, uncharted league of fame. People wanted to know his opinion on everything – drugs, madness, religion, politics, childbirth, Vietnam, love and violence – the categories were seemingly endless. On 19 October 1967, for example, he gave a 'heavy' lecture entitled 'Psychotherapy in Schizophrenia' at the St Crispin Hospital for the Oxford University Committee for Postgraduate Medical Studies, followed the same evening by an Oxford Union debate on marijuana. The next month he was back on prime-time television for a brief appearance in the Omnibus programme, 'Tyger, Tyger'. His popularity seemed limitless, fuelled as it was by his active work in his field, his powerful charisma, intellectual reputation, and uncanny rapport with the rebellious anger of the sixties. But he was growing increasingly restless. Although he was associated with some vague political movement, Ronnie was too laid back to take politics seriously. He at no stage joined any political party; he boasted of never having voted, refused to create any sort of diplomatic relation with any Member of Parliament, and was quick to express scorn and ridicule, in private at least, over any person who was in a position of 'real' power.

The last entry in Ronnie's diary that is in any way remotely concerned with 'politics' was made on 23 March 1970 under the heading 'My Relation to Politics'. Here he admitted, to himself at least, that the political movement 'is far more vast than I can comprehend and apart from its existence there is very little I can say about it'.

On 7 October 1967 Ronnie celebrated his fortieth birthday and wrote a rough entry in his diary marking 'the transition from Icarus to Daedalus from Oedipus to Laius from *enfant terrible* to grand old man or everyman's favourite uncle from disciple to Guru from Isaac to Abraham. From simply son to father to one of the elders who has failed.... From Jesus to Joseph. From one of yesterdays [*sic*] young men of tomorrow to one of tomorrow's old men of yesterday'.

A surprising number of people who were close to Ronnie at this time recall this phrase 'from one of yesterdays [*sic*] young men of tomorrow to one of tomorrow's old men of yesterday'. It was as if Ronnie knew, from as early as 1967, that the consequence of reaching a pinnacle, of climbing to the highest height, embraced the glorious feeling of achievement and, simultaneously, the sadness that comes with the realization that the only way forward is downhill. There seemed to be little new to say. He was sick to the back teeth of the theoretical perspective on both 'normal' and 'crazy' families. The possibility of completing the second volume of *Sanity, Madness and the Family* was becoming more and more remote, and so, consequently, was his involvement with both the Tavistock Institute of Human Relations and the Tavistock Clinic. The real issue with Volume II was that Ronnie was deeply bored by 'normal' families. Indeed, on one of the rare occasions he could bring himself to write about 'normal' families, the pervading feeling is one of deep ambivalence:

> Normal families – perhaps best call them 'silent' families in the sense of making no noise to the world outside to signal any distress; indeed no noise to signal special joy or sorrow. In doing the IPM [Interpersonal Method] they frequently say we never think about these things yet their answers show almost total stereotyping to the second metalevels so they discipline our

lot in straight flushes of a sort of imploded consensus – how is this possible – perhaps just because they don't think about these things; they are not problematical they found the IPM (those who had never thought about it) surprisingly easy, surprising both for them and us; more easy than those couples who did think about those things. If you start thinking about it that particular game appears to be up.

Whether the abandonment of the book was the cause or the effect of his abandonment of his first family is a chicken and egg conundrum. He was clearly keen not to study families any more. *The Politics of the Family*, published in 1969, was derived from a series of radio talks, the 'Massey Lectures' for the Canadian Broadcasting Corporation, delivered reluctantly during 1968. No new material was added; the contents reflected the years of research between 1958 and 1963–4. One only has to look at a list of potential projects that Ronnie had in mind during late 1967 to see how far removed he was from 'all that family stuff':

1. The alphabets of the world, 2. Inner maps of the world, 3. A pictorial biography/autobiography, 4. Fundamental patterns emanations and their formula, 5. Apollo's Lyre, 6. Fundamental symbols of the world, 7. Fire of Life – A book of Mystic trees, 8. The Sun and the Moon.

Meanwhile Kingsley Hall continued, but in fact the Kingsley Hall story was turning into the Mary Barnes story. By now, on occasions when Ronnie spoke publicly about Kingsley Hall, the central idea of the place was personified by Mary and her regression. The extent to which Mary's role was dominating Kingsley Hall is evidenced by an influential talk Ronnie delivered at the Sorbonne on the 21st and 22nd of October 1967, 'Metanoia: some experiences at Kingsley Hall'. During that talk, Ronnie used Mary Barnes's experience to illustrate the principles upon which Kingsley Hall operated, and the talk proved to be an extremely lucid account of the methodology at Kingsley Hall. The lessons learned with Mary Barnes were very real. The talk was no longer of 'existential death' but of real death. The irony was that although much had been learned from the experience Mary went through it was clear that the horror of the experience was not going to be an everyday event. Who had the heart for it? The amount of time and energy required (without pay) to facilitate that extreme degree of regression was, in itself, a prohibition on any serious repetition. Besides, next time they might not be so lucky. Everyone was older if not wiser. Joe Berke was thinking of going his own way, as was Morton Schatzman, now writing his first book, *Soul Murder*. The lease on Kingsley Hall was not going to be renewed. The premises themselves, as early as 1968, were in a dilapidated condition, reflecting a lack of the attention required to keep such premises up to scratch.

The long hot summer of 1967 had come and gone with no indication that the hoped-for glorious revolution was going to take place. Never mind – there was still 1968 to come. On the political agenda was the growing student unrest in Europe and in the States. Marcuse was the voice of the young Parisians, Stokely Carmichael of the young black Americans. Would R.D. Laing take up the flag of freedom and revolt on behalf of the radical youth in the UK? Those who thought that Ronnie would wear the mantle of revolutionary leader made a serious miscalculation. Ronnie was keeping his head down, planning how to spend a year's sabbatical somewhere where he could think, meditate, clear his mind, find some tranquillity. He did not want a war; he was in search of peace – inner peace. But first he had to untangle a few knots.

CHAPTER FOURTEEN

End of the Revolution

In the midst of the world turmoil of 1968, Ronnie was interviewed by Rod Stokes in an article entitled 'Our Present Madness', in which he gave some views on the 'world scene'. He was not out to advocate unrest, or taking to the streets. In fact, he was clearly seeking to avoid taking a clear stance. When he was asked, 'Do you think that these pressure groups are helping at all? Do you think that the group pressures that have happened over the last six months have anything to do with LBJ's [Lyndon Johnson's] decisions?', Ronnie replied, 'That's the sort of question we should all resist attempting to answer. . . .'

This type of equivocation, expounded in both public and private, was confusing to many who had read *The Politics of Experience*. Where was the revolutionary spirit, the intellectual avant-garde? It is surprising how Ronnie managed to keep out of the main events of 1968. In addition to a profile published in the *Sunday Times* magazine in May 1968, a short interview of Ronnie appeared in the widely read *Student Magazine* (reprinted in the underground publication *IT*) which was neither for, nor against, the use of LSD, neither unequivocally on one side or the other on world politics. However, Ronnie did take the opportunity to give further guidance on certain passages from *The Politics of Experience*, which was gaining cult status:

When I said in *The Politics of Experience* that we are all prostitutes and murderers, I was trying to say that one cannot confine acts of destruction and the other anomalies that go on in the world within the lines that we call national barriers. Already these barriers are being broken down although before they completely disappear we can assume that a lot of people are going to die. But we cannot reject responsibility for this merely because one can see no immediate way of doing anything about it. We ought to be turning our attention towards achieving fuller control of the social system in which we live.

Ronnie, unlike 'Brother David' who was having a great time stirring up all sorts of trouble at the 'Anti-University' (situated about four miles away from Kingsley Hall in Shoreditch), was never in his heart a revolutionary. His mind was gearing itself towards peace, not violence, and beneath it all he was still a psychologist and philosopher, not a street-fighter. The interesting new dimension in the interview in the *Student Magazine* had nothing to do with world politics but concerned 'the politics of birth', which would occupy much of his intellectual attention throughout the seventies and early eighties, and was precipitated by Jutta's experience of giving birth to Adam in a hospital.

Nor were Ronnie's talks during 1968 overtly political. The type of issues that were of concern to him was evidenced by the meetings he attended and the contents of the talks he was giving. One of the last public symposiums he attended in 1967 was on 'Buddhism and Mental Health', at Hampstead Old Town Hall. During the early part of 1968 there were talks on 'Grandparents and Great-Grandparents' to the Association of Psychotherapists, 'A Re-valuation of the Theory of Regression' at a scientific meeting at The Tavistock Institute of Human Relations, and a lecture that 'ran and ran' called 'Intervention in Social Situations', first delivered at the Association of Family Caseworkers at the National Institute for Social Work Training in May 1968. This lecture was published in various forms right through to September 1969 when an abbreviated version appeared in *New Society* on 11 September. Indeed, even when Ronnie took a prolonged holiday on the Greek Island of Patmos during the summer of 1968, he was deeply preoccupied with matters of a spiritual, introspective nature. Inspired by the fact that St John had written the book of 'Revelations' while living on Patmos, Ronnie was moved to do the same. In addition, he wrote a long essay entitled 'Elements of an Autobiography' during the same month of July. This essay, some fifty-six typed A5 pages, covered his life from birth to the age of seventeen, and formed the basis of the second chapter of Ronnie's autobiographical work, *Wisdom, Madness and Folly*, completed almost fifteen years later.

The reality to which Ronnie returned in August of 1968 had narrowed down to the ongoing concerns of the PA, his family life at 65a Belsize Park Gardens, his private practice at 21 Wimpole Street, and the communities at Kingsley Hall and 23 Granville Road – the Tavistock and The Open Way having all but drifted out of his life. His mind was beginning to focus on a series of lectures due to be delivered over Canadian radio during November and December 1968, the 'Massey Lectures'.

The 'Massey Lectures' was an annual series of lectures delivered by the Canadian Broadcasting Corporation (much like BBC Radio 4 in the UK) in honour of the Right Honourable Vincent Massey, a former Governor-General of Canada. Since 1961, distinguished authorities had been requested to communicate the results of original study or research on a wide variety of subjects of general study. Ronnie was asked to give their eighth annual series, and so delivered five lectures over the radio during November and December of 1968: 'The Family, Invalidation, and the Clinical Conspiracy'; 'Family Scenarios: Paradigms and Projection'; 'The Family and the Sense of Reality'; 'Beyond Repression: Rules and Metarules'; 'Refractive Images: A World at Large'.

When the lectures were published in *The Politics of the Family*, the chapter headings were slightly modified for the wider market: The Family and Invalidation; Family Scenarios; Operations; Rules and Metarules; Mapping. These were packaged up as Part I, and three further previously delivered lectures added as Part II – The Family and the 'Family', Intervention in Social Situations and The Study of Family and Social Contexts in Relation to Schizophrenia. The introduction to the lectures was written in January 1969, although the final preface and the quotes from Plato's *Laws* were not actually added until March 1971 – one of Ronnie's last formal tasks before heading off for India and Sri Lanka.

Ronnie's involvement with his relatives in Glasgow, from the summer of 1966 until 1969, was almost non-existent. Susie, Ronnie's second daughter, made constant efforts to keep Ronnie informed as to how everyone was getting on, but the only time contact was made was when it was initiated from Glasgow – never the other way round.

Ronnie's father, David, had gone completely senile by the end of 1968, and was put into the psychogeriatric ward of Leverndale Hospital following an attempted outing for which he was fully dressed except for his trousers. Amelia, Anne and the children (now aged 10 to 16) regularly visited David in hospital as part of a ritualized Sunday visit.

When Ronnie decided that he should pay a visit to Glasgow, he was not prepared for the emotional onslaught ahead of him. Having kept out of touch he was distanced from all. His mother now hated him with a vengeance – on one level at least – because he had used the word 'fuck' quite liberally in *The Politics of Experience*. What would the neighbours say? And there was the shame of a separation (Ronnie and Anne were not legally divorced until 1970), in addition to a child born out of wedlock, five children 'without a father'. To make matters worse, Ronnie had not come to see his poor dad! No wonder Amelia was sticking needles into his effigy. . . .

Ronnie spent the 3rd and 4th of January 1969 in Glasgow. His meeting with his father was particularly upsetting for Amelia: David, by now, could not remember who Ronnie was. Those few moments that he spent with his dad haunted Ronnie for a long, long time. The idea of transcending familial ties, of releasing oneself from guilt, of seeking to rationalize neglect as liberalism, was no comfort when he came face to face with his father, now a pale shadow of his former, digni-fied self, being fed and cared for like a brain-damaged baby. The 'encounter' with his dad formed the basis of the opening passage of the book, *Do You Love Me?*, published many years later. The passage, intended to be read as a fictional meeting between a father and son, was called 'Return of the Prodigal'. One merely needs to substitute 'Ronald' for 'Peter' and 'doctor' for 'musician', and the end result is about as accurate an account of this meeting as one could hope for, set as it is in the psychogeriatric ward of Leverndale Hospital, Glas-gow. What pierced Ronnie to the core was seeing his dad in such a helpless position. David could not even remember having a son; Ronnie was remembered by his father as 'the chap who lived with my wife'.

By April 1969 Ronnie was completing a book that was not going to be a development of anything overtly concerned with politics, psy-chiatry, families, schizophrenia, mysticism, or birth, but a book of *Knots*. He was also far more money-conscious by this stage. In a banal twist he found himself having to earn more and more money in order to receive what felt like less and less. The Labour government was imposing punitive tax rates on the 'wealthy', which by now, with all the royalties flooding in, included Ronnie. He had to earn a lot of money to keep his head above water.

Knots was a commercial popularization of *Interpersonal Perception*, conceived and written at a time when four main influences were in effect. Ronnie had had enough of schizophrenia and families; he was seriously disengaged from any form of politics; he needed to make a lot of money; and such a book had the potential to form a bridge out of psychiatry into a more creative world. The best way of achieving his immediate aims was to write entertainingly about the communication between people, about men and women typified by 'Jack' and 'Jill', who found themselves stuck in an emotional rift.

Knots was a long time in the writing for such a short book. Ronnie worked very, very hard on it – harder than on many of his books. At least eight drafts were handwritten, carefully analysed and modified. To Ronnie it was also a great gamble. It was like nothing he had ever written before and, inevitably, would be in for a rough ride no matter what. A few passages were open to clear association with his previous works. Others seemed to come from absolutely nowhere. Although effectively written over many years as jottings, loose thoughts, scribbles, notes and truisms, *Knots* did not come together until spring 1969, and was not published until the early part of 1970, first in hardback by Ronnie's old safeguard Tavistock Publications (where he was the editor), and a few months later in paperback.

It was enormously successful. Ronnie had, in his own mind, proved to himself that there was life after radical psychiatry, life after the sixties. By now there was a lot to juggle. There was also the ongoing saga of Kingsley Hall.

Throughout 1969 the Kingsley Hall story was drawing to an end, the trustees having confirmed that the lease was to be handed back by May 1970. An argument had already begun over the compensation the PA should pay the trustees for the appalling condition of Kingsley Hall. Knowing that its days were numbered, Ronnie decided it was time that Kingsley Hall was written up and made a tentative, rambling start in a diary on 19 March 1969 at 9.10 p.m., during a quiet moment at Belsize Park Gardens, and later during the same month at Kingsley Hall:

Aaron Esterson and I had been talking about doing 'it' for years. It was not at all clear what 'it' was or rather it was sometimes one thing then another thing. None of the things was it. But it could only be done by doing one thing or another. We had to do something. Take off to a remote island, where the fall-out would be less than most places, set up a place in the country, go to a Greek island, buy a village in Wales or Scotland or in the Dordogne. We were sometimes six and sometimes more like sixty.

But the story of Kingsley Hall was never to be written, at least not as envisaged by Ronnie, Sid Briskin, Leon Redler and Paul Zeal in 1969. Who had the heart to go through all that again? Besides, Joe Berke, the key to any serious book about Kingsley Hall, was doing his 'number' with Mary Barnes, not R.D. Laing or the Philadelphia Association.

Mary Barnes had received public attention as early as June 1968, as a result of the publication of an article entitled 'How Mary Barnes grew up again at 42' published in the *Sunday Observer*. By April of the following year Mary was becoming something of a celebrity in her own right by virtue of the first major public exhibition of her paintings on Friday, 11 April at the Camden Arts Centre. The book she was writing with Joe Berke, *Mary Barnes – Two Accounts of a Journey Through Madness*, would be published in early 1971 after a long and tiring editorial process.

There came a time during October and November 1969 when Ronnie, Leon Redler, Sid Briskin and, to a lesser extent, Paul Zeal, sat down together and went over the history of Kingsley Hall. They planned for the tape-recorded and transcribed discussions to form the basis of a book about Kingsley Hall and the PA. These discussions, hours and hours of them, mostly covered material which is, unfortunately, too libellous and professionally confidential to be repeated in writing or otherwise. Reading this material over twenty years later, one gains the impression that the purpose of the exercise was more to do with a re-evaluation of the respective roles of the key players than the recording of a dedicated history of the previous five years of Kingsley Hall. Any material selected from these discussions is, necessarily, taken out of context and edited with pronounced subjectivity. None the less, as the hours and weeks pass the conversation becomes perceptibly more honest, self-critical and self-effacing. Eventually, during the last of these recorded conversations on 17 November 1969, Ronnie states: 'I wouldn't live in that fucking place as it is just now, at all. And if I lived in it it would only be on the condition of changing it. Because it's a miserable dump.' He also felt that his hope of Kingsley Hall providing a safe environment where acute schizophrenic episodes could occur without electric shocks, tranquillizers and sedation 'never happened as far as I know throughout the whole of the $4\frac{1}{2} - 5$ years of Kingsley Hall'.

Sid Briskin threw a few names at Ronnie to see if he was being merely provocative. Ronnie stood by what he said and was quite adamant that the experience of Kingsley Hall had not proven his original theories. One of the problems, and a frequent one, was that the intended social therapist was just as likely to go through his or her own 'dishonest flip-out' as to provide support for others.

Moreover, the historical coincidence of the closure of Kingsley Hall coming at the end of the 1960s attracted the argument that the experiment of Kingsley Hall was merely part of a psychiatric and social history. Even Ross Speck, Ronnie's American friend of many years, wrote an article for publication in America under the title 'Kingsley Hall: A Metaphor', which told the story, in great detail, about one of the last nights at Kingsley Hall conducted in 'the spirit of The Last Supper' and in a 'Breughel-like atmosphere'. This pertinent and hilarious story was written not with malice or envy, but a subdued weariness and well-earned wisdom derived not only from Ross's experience with extremely disturbed family networks over many years, but also with a familiarity with state mental hospitals' routines prior to the widespread use of drugs or electric shocks. Ross was not impressed with the theatrical dimensions of people's behaviour (Ronnie had dressed up in drag saying 'if Sartre can do it so can I'). Even Ian Spurling, one of the more entertaining characters, was ready to admit that the crazy behaviour 'was all an act, put on to impress the visitors'.

On 31 May 1970, Kingsley Hall finally closed its doors to the PA. An extraordinary era in the life of R.D. Laing and many others had came to an end and with it, another chapter in the history of the Philadelphia Association. In the meantime the revolution had come and gone. If there were winners and losers, Kingsley Hall was not on the winning side. Ronnie was older, and older still for being none the wiser.

CHAPTER FIFTEEN

Mystical Journey

The same weekend that Kingsley Hall closed, the diehards moved into two adjoining properties in Archway Road in north-west London, not far from where Ronnie was living with Jutta and their children: Adam, now aged two, and Natasha who had been born in April. The Archway Community, as it became known, picked up more or less where Kingsley Hall had left off. Ronnie was little concerned on a day-to-day basis with Archway Road, the baton having been effectively handed over to the American doctor and medical school friend of Joe Berke, Leon Redler. Redler not only obtained the premises but assumed *de facto* control.

The new PA community was less idealistic than Kingsley Hall and better for it. No longer was there a need to go crazy, to emulate Mary Barnes, no longer the informal pressure to 'let it all hang out'. This was idealism tempered with experience. In an interview with L.J. Comba in February of 1970, Ronnie explained the new ethos:

> One thing I would like to see happen, is a set-up, however
> limited, (it does not matter how limited as long as it is feasible),
> as a practical alternative to what has come to be the prevailing
> mental hospital procedures. An alternative in practice would be to
> take on in a place maximally disturbing people, not just people
> who, if too disturbed, will be passed to mental hospitals
> eventually. An 'end of the line' place: the end in a mental
> hospital is when you are naked, incontinent, huddled in the
> corner of a padded cell: it is the last place you are going to go;
> you know that once you are there, there is no further.

Although there was no gap between the closing of Kingsley Hall and the opening of the Archway Community, the reputation of Kingsley Hall was such that its closure was seen as evidence of its failure, especially by the American psychiatric world. And the fact that Joe Berke was actively getting his own organization, Arbours, off the ground was also seen as an indication that Ronnie's powers were fading. Morty Schatzman, despite holding Kingsley Hall together for most of 1968, was also viewed by the R.D. Laing camp (and Ronnie in particular) as a defector to this threatening new splinter group. Ronnie viewed dissent as betrayal, and Joe and Morty were therefore viewed as traitors, much to their own bewilderment. The lines were now clearly drawn between the PA, and Arbours as represented by Joe and Morty. You were in one camp or the other.

The Philadelphia Association had now received a transfusion of new blood – Mike Yocum, a community therapist, Paul Zeal (who had a degree in Law from Bristol University) John Heaton (an eye surgeon who had turned his attention to phenomenology, he had known Ronnie since The Open Way days back in 1964), Chris Oakley (a Cambridge-educated admirer of R.D. Laing) and his wife Haya (who was educated at the Hebrew University of Jerusalem). There were also a rugged and forthright Scottish doctor – Hugh Crawford, Francis Huxley (a well-respected anthropologist, writer and member of the Huxley clan) and the loyal Sid Briskin. The PA was, in at least one sense, alive and well.

However, it was clear to Ronnie and Sid Briskin that some effort had to be made to counteract the inevitable negative reaction to the closing of Kingsley Hall. To that end, the 'Philadelphia Association Report' was prepared and published shortly before Kingsley Hall closed. Not surprisingly, the report cut no ice with the medical establishment and gained only scant attention in the press. After five long, controversial and heavily publicized years, a great deal more was expected than 1,500 words of text and four quasi-medical tables. A short review of the report which appeared in *New Society* in the first week of July, highlighted the practical problems the PA faced: 'the association has a certain amount of difficulty in explaining itself to outsiders or indeed in being itself comprehended'.

If there was one single issue that caused more dissent than any other it was money. Ronnie, as such a professional individualist, detested the idea of comprising fundamental principles, to the extent that he was completely useless at raising much-needed funds unless all he was required to do was give a lecture. He preferred others to go out there and do the dirty work for him. Sid Briskin explains Ronnie's attitude to money as

> not only his achilles' heel but he showed enormous destructiveness in making null and void the many ideas I had to get money which he was forever saying we must get. I was very clear in my own mind that Ronnie, who was in many ways so generous, became envious of any plan that did not originate with him.

High ideals, pseudo-scruples, personal objections - they all seemed to prohibit the taking of the cheque, rightly or wrongly, on one ground or another. It was one of Ronnie's true weak spots, and one that would play a major factor in his eventual defeat and downfall at the hands of the new PA order in the early 1980s. In any event, he was now thinking in detail of how to get away from it all for a year or so. Away from madness, away from his patients, away from the PA. He really had had enough of the whole scene.

1970 was a year of preparation for Ronnie and his family. *Knots*, written some time previously, was due for publication in September 1970. *The Politics of the Family* was to be republished in the UK and needed only the addition of a quote from Plato's *Laws*. Ronnie was winding down his practice in Wimpole Street and was living once again with a young family.

By December 1970, the PA had crystallized its identity as a charitable organization providing alternative treatment and accommodation for those who would otherwise be in a mental institution. It was also coming to terms with the need to provide a training programme, with registered, fee-paying students, regular seminars and lectures all functioning within a recognized organizational hierarchy. This was no easy task. At first there was talk of an 'A' Group and a 'B' Group. Some people did not seem to be aware of such a distinction, others who were did not know to which group they belonged or the basis of the distinction between the two. If there was a *de facto* 'A' group, it was Ronnie, Leon Redler, Sid Briskin, John Heaton, Hugh Crawford and Paul Zeal. In addition, on the fringe at this stage were Chris and Haya Oakley, Jerome Liss (a charismatic friend of Joe Berke and Leon Redler) and numerous other people who seemed to float in and out of the PA without any definable purpose or course. At this stage Mike Yocum, a community therapist, performed an increasingly important role within the PA *vis-à-vis* the Archway Community. And in the immediate aftermath of Kingsley Hall there was a growing interest in early morning Hatha Yoga groups and Zen-style meditation.

This new concentration within the PA on the personal and the physical, created a deeper polarization of the ideals and aspirations of the PA as opposed to those of Joe Berke, Aaron Esterson and David Cooper, who was still busy attacking the family as an institution. By 1970 the 'Guru Wars' were settling down. Joe Berke and David Cooper both had their own followings and, partly by virtue of *The Leaves of Spring*, so too did Aaron.

Ronnie always managed somehow to keep one step ahead of this group. In January 1971, for example, a mammoth article accompanied by a front-page portrait of Ronnie surrounded by a symbolic intertwining rope appeared in *The Atlantic*, a popular American magazine with a wide circulation. This adoring piece, 'Who Is Mad? Who Is Sane? – R.D. Laing: In Search of a New Psychiatry', written by Dr James Gordon, ran to nearly 15,000 words over fifteen pages. Gordon, a 1967 graduate of the Harvard Medical School, and at that time Chief Resident in Psychiatry at the Albert Einstein College of Medicine, made a thorough examination and critical appraisal of Ronnie's theories and practice, from *The Divided Self* to Kingsley Hall. His glowing article, although published in January 1971, was researched and written almost one year previously, at the time Kingsley Hall was winding down. Although there is no reference to Ronnie's religious beliefs throughout the whole of the article, only a few weeks after meeting with Gordon, on Wednesday 18th March 1970, Ronnie recorded a BBC radio programme produced by the Rev. H.H. Hoskins: 'Is There a Future for Religious Belief?'. During this twenty-minute talk (broadcast on Friday 27 March), Ronnie described his background as 'lower-middle-class Lowland Presbyterian corroded by 19th century materialism, scientific rationalism and humanism'. He mentioned some of the intellectuals who had influenced to his beliefs – Darwin, Haeckel, Voltaire, J.S. Mill and Thomas Huxley. One telling passage during this broadcast provided a link between his theological beliefs and his own reality as represented by Kingsley Hall – the concept of metanoia:

If one hasn't been brought up to take religious propositions seriously, it's almost impossible to do so short of a radical transformation of one's whole mind, what in the New Testament was referred to as metanoia, a fundamental change of mind. Otherwise one's only relationship to religious propositions can be that of a naturalist comparing and classifying them as one would compare and classify plants, butterflies, ants and other species of animals.

Despite his tendency to avoid religious commitment, there came a moment when Ronnie put his cards on the table: 'God is spirit, and those who worship Him must worship Him in spirit and in time. I believe that is the case.'

Perhaps it was because Ronnie's friends and colleagues (with the notable exception of Leon Redler and John Heaton) found it hard to accept that he had any firm religious beliefs, other than a passing intellectual interest in Eastern thought, that he felt it necessary to spend time away from them. To Joe Berke, for example, the idea that Ronnie was in any sense a 'believer' was a bad joke. But Ronnie was deadly serious in his pursuit of the 'higher order'. He had enjoyed theological debate throughout his days at school and, till he left home, with his father. His mind was too complex and informed to dismiss without reservation any possibility of a God. His profound scepticism, as he admits in *Wisdom, Madness and Folly*, was mainly due to the doubt he had as to whether his own thoughts were merely the product of infant indoctrination by his father and years of Sunday school.

But behind Ronnie's theology lay a curiosity in the unknown which always came back to the same theme and one that recurs throughout his life – the answer to the question: What is the chief end of Man? Even in *Wisdom, Madness and Folly*, the issue is raised at an unlikely, early stage:

> I was four. I was sent to Sunday School a year earlier than to primary school. At Sunday School we sang hymns, read the Bible, learned by heart passages from it and the Short Catechism of the Westminster Divines, said prayers.
>
> Question: What is the chief end of Man?
> Answer: Man's chief end is to glorify God, and to enjoy Him for ever.

This question, first raised in Ronnie's mind, if we are to believe him, at age four, was ever present throughout his life. He took it to Sri Lanka and India with him, hoping for an answer. If we do not believe him it was, none the less, as he honestly remembered it.

Ronnie was keen to get his affairs in order prior to leaving for India and Sri Lanka, and this required a great deal of work. He decided to bring his practice at 21 Wimpole Street to an end many months in advance of leaving; no new patients were taken on, and legal affairs were put into place on advice from his lawyers. Belsize Park Gardens needed sorting out, immunizations and notifications were required. Eventually, by the middle of February 1971, it was settled that the rough plan would be to leave for Sri Lanka sometime in the second half of March.

At 11.30 on the morning of Tuesday 30 March 1971, Ronnie, Jutta, Brenda (the au pair), Adam and Natasha left 65a Belsize Park Gardens for Heathrow Airport to catch the 15.45 flight to Colombo, Sri Lanka (then Ceylon). Ronnie had made some rules for himself: he would take no books, no writing matter, leave behind his much-beloved clavichord, take no extra clothes and no drugs. He had waited all his life for a spiritual journey of this magnitude, and had no intention of compromising his high ideals.

Although it was clearly Ronnie's intention to rid himself of as much of the material world as he could, including such mundane items as books and writing material, barely a week after his arrival he could not resist opening up his diary and making an entry or two for the sake of posterity. Ronnie did not seem to have much of a plan for his sojourn. The family arrived at the Mount Lavinia Hotel south of Colombo, and a few days later drove by jeep for nearly six hours to a guest house in Kandy and then to the Bandarapola Tourist Lodge – situated about forty minutes from Kandy.

Sri Lanka was in the midst of a civil war. There was fighting in Kandy and by 9 April, within a fortnight of their arrival, a twenty-four-hour curfew was imposed on all residents in the vicinity of Bandarapola. But despite the fear at the time, this was recalled on subsequent occasions as an exciting start to a great holiday.

Although the Bandarapola Tourist Lodge was little more than an isolated piece of civilization in the midst of a coconut plantation (the nearest village, Matale, was twenty minutes away), Ronnie soon decided he wanted to spend time in even more remote surroundings. He left the family for a Buddhist meditation retreat in Kanduboda, central Sri Lanka, where he stayed for six weeks.

Jutta was extremely relieved to receive a short letter from Ronnie dated 26 June informing her that he was returning to Bandarapola. There were times when she wondered whether he would, in all seriousness, abandon his worldly responsibilities and 'take the robe and bowl'. However, he did return, and quickly settled into a daily routine based around abstinence and meditation. Despite the interruptions by former patients and unwelcome friends who made the pilgrimage to see him (it would not have mattered where he was in the world, he would eventually have been found) Ronnie began to loosen up, meditate, eat sparingly, study Sanskrit and relax. He recorded the following as a 'typical day':

03.00–05.00	wake Meditation (M)
06.30	Rice
06.45–c. 08.00	M
c.08.00–09.00	breakfast
09.00–11.00	reading Majjhinne Nikaya swimming pool
c.11.00–12.00	M
12.00–13.15	lunch
c.13.15–15.00	reading
15.00–17.00	M
17.00–18.00	afternoon tea
18.00–20.00	M
20.00–21.00	sit with others after their supper
21.00–22.00	M
22.00–c. 03.00	sleep

Ronnie and the family stayed at the Bandarapola Tourist Lodge for most of their time in Sri Lanka, although intermittently they went on sight-seeing adventures around the island and for a short while they occupied the summer residence of a friend who owned a bungalow in Trincomalee, a small village overlooking Kottiyar Bay on the northeast coast of Sri Lanka.

By the beginning of September Ronnie felt that it was time to move. Although he had decided to travel from Sri Lanka to India, the precise destination was uncertain. As recorded in his diary, Ronnie was thinking of Madras, Calcutta, Delhi, Goa or Bombay. On 23 September the family flew to Madras and from there on to New Delhi, eventually settling at the Snow View Hotel – one hour's walk from the village of Almora situated in the foothills of the Himalayas and about 200 kilometres from Delhi – where they were based for the remainder of their time in India until returning to London in April 1972. During this second part of the holiday Ronnie decided once again to retreat into wilder territory and eventually left for a place called Naini Tai, 50 kilometres south-west of Almora, where he stayed with an old wise man by the name of Gangotri Baba in the foothills of the Himalayas.

A few days after Ronnie's forty-fourth birthday on 7 October 1971, he recorded in a diary a visit to a wise man by the name of Mufti Jal al-Ud-din. The note Ronnie made of that encounter indicated what they discussed. Ronnie numbered the topics: '1. What is man's chief end in life?; 2. What is the correct way to live?; 3. What is the method to rid oneself of the corruptions that defile the heart and weaken wisdom?' In answer to these questions, the wise man replied: 'if you wish to help your fellow man there is no better way to do so than to give up the world, renounce everything and take up the robe and bowl'. This did not seem to provide Ronnie with a satisfactory answer. He wrote in his diary: 'It would be a blessing were I to find the right man for me. Maybe there is not such a man, maybe I cannot recognize him.'

In London and elsewhere, there were many rumours circulating regarding Ronnie's activities in the East. Peter Sedgwick, a psychologist and libertarian Marxist based at York University, was writing a critical analysis of Ronnie's work under the title 'R.D. Laing: self, symptom and society' for the forthcoming book, *Laing and Anti-Psychiatry*. His dismissal of Ronnie's mystical involvement as transitory and marginal was premature. Before the book went to print Sedgwick had time to add a postscript, dated December 1971:

The most recent turn in Laing's development has invalidated my conclusion that his mystical involvement was transitory and somewhat marginal. For Laing has now withdrawn from Western and psychiatric scenes, departing to Ceylon in order to devote himself full-time to a prolonged task of mystical meditation.

Dr Ageha Bharati, the Chairman of the Anthropology Department of Syracuse University, New York, met Laing for long discussions during a field trip to Ceylon and (in a letter to me in November 1971 for which I am deeply indebted) writes that Laing:

'has virtually broken his bridges with things British and psychiatrical. He is not only doing Theravada Buddhist meditation there – he does it seventeen hours a day, for the past five months. He spent six weeks in a training monastery in Kanduboda, in Central Ceylon, and the senior monk there told me that Laing has been doing better, much better, than long-time meditation experts, Sinhalese Buddhist and foreign.'

Ronnie came back with many wondrous tales of Sri Lanka and India. Perhaps the one that had the most impact was the story of the four weeks he spent with an old wise man in a cave while in India. This was how he told the story to Israel Shenker of *The New York Times* a few months after his return:

I spent a month up a mountain with an Indian holy man who lived under a rock cranny up a ravine. He had let his hair grow and spent much of the time naked wrapped in his hair to keep warm. I sat with him all day, tuned in to the rhythm of daytime and nighttime, watching the sun go down and the moon go up. The largest lessons I learned are ineffable and I don't even begin to put words to them.

I was doing nothing all day except watching one's own bodily sensations. One's stomach got empty, one's colon got filled up, one's hunger rose up and abated. Food was one of my heaviest addictions, and it took a week to get out on the other side.

On another occasion he told much the same story to the *Boston Globe*:

I went to India to take up the adage that you can't buy a camel in a donkey market. I spent two months in a monastery in Ceylon going through the intensive mind training of a Buddhist monk. I sat with an Indian Baba under a crag in the Himalayan foothills for another month. I was doing less and less until I was doing nothing at all, including not doing the guilt number because I wasn't doing anything. . . .

I stopped doing anything except standing, sitting crosslegged, walking, eating, breathing. About desire, I learned that nothing comes which does not go. I let the wheels slow down. I gradually got to that inner silent place and bathed in it. Very refreshing. That's what I was doing, gradually doing nothing at all, not even meditating.

Ronnie often talked about Sri Lanka and India in private and in public. It is curious that he usually talked as if he had spent the whole of that time in some monastery or other, or living in the forest/jungle with some wise old man who looked like an old bird, the two of them 'wallowing in silence'. There were clearly two distinct phases to this period of meditation: the first was a period of six weeks in Kanduboda, Sri Lanka, when he stayed at the Buddhist training monastery learning his trade; the second was the 'hanging out' with the old wise man in the foothills of the Himalayas where he practised what he thought he had learned.

Nearly six months in India followed the same amount of time in Sri Lanka. Back to humdrum England from the magical world of Hindus, Sufis, Sikhs, Muslims, Tamils, elephants, tigers, forests, exquisite sunsets, sunrises, moonrises. Back from the weird and wonderful to his real world of a cramped flat in Hampstead, the Philadelphia Association, socks and shoes, the West and the rest. Ronnie's year in Sri Lanka and India had been a once-in-a-lifetime experience; but there was a price to be paid.

CHAPTER SIXTEEN

The Guru Returns to the Facts of Life

When Ronnie and his second family returned from India on 20 April 1972, much had taken place since their departure for Sri Lanka in March of the previous year. Ronnie had deliberately kept out of touch with events not just in London but the West as a whole. He had been reading a great deal but his interests were confined solely to books on Eastern theology and philosophy. He had a lot of catching up to do. Moreover, shortly after his return to London he experienced a serious collapse in his own self-confidence, prompting the following entry in his diary in May 1972:

> I've got to keep my nerve – or lose it – everything is completely uncertain. I've lost my motivations and beliefs – there is nothing I want to do and I don't want to do nothing. It's really like starting a new life and I would be just as glad not to. I'm already demode, depasse [*sic*]. I have depassed myself into a void.

During the sabbatical in Sri Lanka and India between March 1971 and April 1972, some important events had occurred in what Ronnie (and many others) would have considered to be his domain. David Cooper's book, *Death of the Family*, had been published in the UK in June 1971. The book written by Mary Barnes and Joe Berke, *Mary Barnes – Two Accounts of a Journey Through Madness* had appeared on the bookshelves in October 1971, as had Ronnie's own book, *The Politics of the Family*. Aaron Esterson's off-shoot from *Sanity, Madness and the Family*, *The Leaves of Spring*, originally published in 1970, had provided Aaron thereafter with his own platform. A compilation of articles, *Laing and Anti-Psychiatry* published as a special Salmagundi issue in 1971 was now, in 1972, to be published as a Penguin paperback.

Ken Loach's film *Family Life** was a dramatic cinematic portrayal of a young girl victimized into schizophrenia, and was released throughout cinemas in the United Kingdom during December 1971 and January 1972. The effect was confusing. Depending on which review one read, Loach was variously influenced by David Mercer (*In Two Minds*), R.D. Laing (*Sanity, Madness and the Family*) and David Cooper (*Death of the Family*). In fact, David Mercer had written the screenplay for *Family Life* as an adaptation of the play, *In Two Minds*, which was written in 1967. Mercer had been influenced not only by Ronnie but also by David Cooper, whom he had met and knew before Ronnie. Very quickly however, Ronnie was associated with the film *Family Life*, with which he had nothing to do in any practical sense, and *Family Life* was associated quite clearly with the idea that the very cause of schizophrenia was the family itself. In a front-page article from a December 1971 issue of *Time Out* – London's leading entertainment guide – the connection was perfectly clear: 'the film is rooted in the relatively recent development of psychiatric/political investigations and hypothesis, which are certainly most popularly understood through the work of psychiatrists Ronald Laing and David Cooper'.

In America, Ronnie's guru image had been given an incredible boost by the popular and prestigious *Life* magazine. In October 1971, *Life* took a 'striking look at R.D. Laing, controversial psychiatrist and author' under the banner 'Philosopher of Madness'. Here Ronnie was put in the same gallery as two of the best-known American 'messiahs' of the time: 'Like Marshall McLuhan and Timothy Leary, R.D. Laing is a professional scholar transformed into an oracle and prophet', whose book *The Politics of Experience* had sold 400,000 paperback copies and was now 'a campus classic'. The most striking aspect of the *Life* feature was a series of photographs by John Haynes. The wide readership of *Life* saw Ronnie in his underpants, on his elbows, upside down in what can only be described as an advanced Yoga position. They saw him sitting in bare feet on a rug, staring guru-like into space; they also saw the young and extremely handsome philosopher-poet

---

* Released in the United States under the title *Wednesday's Child*.

squatting like a forest-elf in the branches of a tree on Hampstead Heath. Ronnie had truly 'arrived' in the States.

Also in Ronnie's absence, another very lengthy article, by Peter Mezan, a musical acquaintance of Ronnie's, was published in *Esquire* magazine. This dissertation of over 16,000 words had an enormous influence on the public perception of R.D. Laing, particularly in the States, as Ronnie was to find out during the latter part of 1972. Under the large-captioned title, spread out over six pages, Ronnie found himself 'multi-labelled' in the following manner: 'AFTER FREUD AND JUNG, NOW COMES R.D. LAING POP-SHRINK, REBEL, YOGI, PHILOS-OPHER-KING, LATEST REINCARNATION OF AESCU-LAPIUS, MAYBE?'. With perfect timing, Peter Mezan had put Ronnie forward as a guru of the modern age. All Ronnie had to do was to live up to the image.

Not only had the public perception of R.D. Laing been crystallized, distorted or reinforced depending on one's initial premise, but the PA had gone through its own process of evolution in Ronnie's absence. Premises in north London – commonly referred to as 'The Grove' – had been purchased and were operational as a PA household. Sid Briskin had assisted in organizing a star-studded charity-do at the London Hilton Hotel on the evening of 5 September 1971. At this gala event were celebrities by the score: Michael Caine, Suzy Kendall, Alan Bennett, Peter Cook, Dudley Moore, John Cleese and many others. Enough money – £3,000 – had been raised from one night's activities to purchase the one and only household ever owned by the PA. Sid thought Ronnie might be delighted but realized the possibility of a puritanical backlash. Ronnie, having spent a year eating nuts, berries, rice and fruit, could not bear to hear of the gluttonous activities, despite the beneficial consequences. Sid thought he had done the PA a good turn; instead he had unwittingly engineered his own downfall, and by the spring of the following year he was isolated and marginalized – particularly by Hugh Crawford – until he felt the need to resign from the PA in March 1973. The PA were also lucky not to lose John Heaton, who at this juncture threatened to resign over Sid's treatment.

But the real blow to Ronnie was the growing recognition of the Arbours Association, originally brought into being by Joe and Roberta Berke, Morty Schatzman and Vivien Millet. Crawford and Heaton had used their influence to keep Joe and Morty out of the PA, and the Arbours began its life in the home of Morty and Vivien in the spring of 1970, to Ronnie's intense irritation. Like one of the possessive mothers he so frequently went on about, Ronnie had great difficulty in accepting the assertion of another's individuality and independence, and he was obviously concerned that Arbours would eclipse the PA.

Ronnie would have also noticed on his return from India the growing dominance of explanations of schizophrenia which had no basis in existentialism, phenomenology, therapy or analysis. There was always a battle with what Ronnie and others around him viewed as the 'drug-pushing element' of the psychiatric world. Those who advocated the use of pharmaceuticals for the treatment of schizophrenia had put up with what they viewed as mumbo-jumbo psycho-babble throughout the whole of the sixties, and were now seeking to regain the upper hand they had had in the fifties. In an article in *The Sunday Times* published in October 1971, Dr Norman Imlah of the All Saints Hospital in Birmingham quoted a 90% decrease in readmission to his psychiatric wing through the use of fluphenazine (an injected tranquillizer developed from the phenothiazine drug). One could now read the occasional article about madness or schizophrenia without any reference to R.D. Laing, the Philadelphia Association or David Cooper. Villa 21 was history, Kingsley Hall was history, R.D. Laing as a psychiatrist was history. Even in an article in *The Times*, 'Busman's Holiday', published to herald R.D. Laing's arrival back in the UK, Ronnie gave advice that seemed to have no connection with modern-day psychiatric practice: 'He recalls the dictum of the 16th century French surgeon, Ambroise Paré, who said: "I dressed him and God healed him." This philosophy should be applied to psychiatry, says Laing.'

R.D. Laing was now in the guru business. There was growing interest not so much in what Ronnie was saying but what he had said, what he meant, what he *really* meant, *ad nauseam*. In May 1972 Peter Sedgwick, for example, delivered a talk on Radio 3 concerned with R.D. Laing's sympathy or otherwise for new left politics. A new industry was developing, which concerned itself with R.D. Laing almost as if he no longer existed. Even as early as 1972, the publishers Fontana had engaged Professor Edgar Friedenberg of Dalhousie University in Canada to write a short, though engaging, book about R.D. Laing for their Modern Masters series, thus putting Ronnie in the same rogues' gallery as Samuel Beckett, D.H. Lawrence, Georg Lukacs, Karl Popper and Bertrand Russell. The R.D. industry was in full flight.

After Ronnie's return from India he became, for a while at least, a committed vegetarian, and he soon became a connoisseur of the various types of brown rice, lentils, cold soups, pastas – anything considered consistent with the Buddhist way of life. Red meat was out in those days. Arthur Balaskas, a South African who had become friendly with Ronnie and Jutta during 1970 through Mina, his wife at the time, was in 1972 running a very successful vegetarian restaurant in St John's Wood in north London. As the restaurant was not far from Belsize Park Gardens, Ronnie regularly attended for vegetarian sustenance, and he and Arthur established a close and productive friendship, which lasted nearly twenty years.*

Ronnie used to needle Arthur about his relationship with money. Arthur, as a successful restaurateur in the natural-food boom days of the early seventies, spent a good deal of his time counting money. He also had a very bad back due to the demanding physical work in his busy restaurant. Ronnie had the answer. He told Arthur to lie flat out on his back in order to relax and straighten out his body. He told him to breathe in a conscious and deliberate manner, through one nostril and then the other. He told him to take up and practice yoga, pranayama (breathing) and hatha (physical) yoga. He told Arthur that his life would be more fulfilling and, consequently he would achieve even greater success and personal happiness, if he followed these instructions. Was counting money, in itself, an enjoyable experience? Arthur heeded Ronnie's advice and became part of a mischievous trio consisting of himself, Ronnie, and Francis Huxley, rather like the Indians from the writings of Carlos Castaneda, with Ronnie playing Don Juan, Francis playing Don Genaro and Arthur playing the novice. They had a lot of fun over many years.

The hardest blow Ronnie was delivered upon returning from India came during the course of a phone call to his American publisher Andre Shiffrin in the second week of May 1972. Ronnie thought he had planned his finances in such a way as to enable himself and the family to take a year off without generating any income. He believed that the royalties from the worldwide sales of his books would be more than sufficient to provide a capital base deep enough for money

---

* In addition to presenting a television series on yoga techniques during the 1970s, Balaskas wrote several books on various forms of yoga, including *Bodylife* (1977) which contains a foreword by Ronnie.

not to be an issue. He was wrong – terribly wrong. Following his call to Andre he wrote: 'I discovered that apart from the trust money and royalties due in June and July as from Sept. 71 he is holding no money of mine at all. So I was all this last year at least $100,000.00 out in my calculations! I thought we had enough to live off now we have nothing.' Ronnie was in deep financial trouble and decided he had to do something that would generate a lot of money in a relatively short space of time. He therefore took immediate steps to arrange a coast-to-coast tour of the United States, to be completed before the year was out.

But first there were other events to be sorted out – the first public showing in New York and London of a film made by Peter Robinson and based on the day-to-day experiences of those living at the Archway Community. Called *Asylum*, it was 'a feature-documentary in colour – an experiment in communal living that arose from the theory and practice of R.D. Laing'. *Asylum* was shown at the Paris Theatre in New York followed by the Collegiate Theatre, 15 Gordon Street, Euston Road, on Sunday 7 October 1972, which coincided with Ronnie's 45th birthday. The film featured little of Ronnie, the principal dramatic thread being Leon Redler's relationship with David Bell – one of the die-hards from Kingsley Hall whom Ross Speck had so vividly portrayed in his paper some two years previously. The film had already attracted considerable praise in the States and Canada for its warmth and humanity. The *Toronto Globe and Mail* wrote, for example, 'almost terrifyingly involving.... Barely has a movie screening ever seemed such an important and intellectual event'. This was also a major financial boost for the PA – the proceeds from the screening of *Asylum* in New York raised £5,700.

On the day of the screening of *Asylum* in London, Ronnie met, for the first time, the author of an incredibly popular book, *The Primal Scream* by the west-coast American Arthur Janov. Ronnie recorded Janov as 'the most modest and unassuming of men' but thought of him as a 'jig man' – someone who knows a lot about a little. Janov advocated therapy through literally screaming and screaming until one got to that primal scream, which had the cathartic effect of releasing tension, pent-up emotion, frustration, anger, hatred – all manner of feelings that would otherwise fester inside one's emotional being. Ronnie sympathized a great deal with Janov and might well have gone down that route himself. On a cynical level Ronnie could see that this was an ongoing lucrative business, which required no more than obtaining a suitable space and letting people 'hang it all out' – money for old rope. But it was Janov's number and that was that.

Three days after the *Asylum* showing in London Ronnie lectured in front of a British public for the first time since leaving for Sri Lanka. The venue was the Friends' Meeting House in Euston Road, and the lecture was reviewed by Victoria Brittain in *The Times* on 9 October, under the heading 'An end to fashionable madness'. A few days later on 28 October, Ronnie delivered a powerful speech on the subject of birth at the Inaugural Meeting of the British Section of the International Society of Psychosomatic Obstetrics and Gynaecology at the Royal Society of Medicine. He advocated an analysis of the practice of birth, and claimed that the baby, before and during birth, is a human being more alive, alert and capable of feeling pain than most adults. His recent experiences of witnessing childbirth in Sri Lanka and India, his purported ability to remember his own birth and the many, many stories told him by people in analysis prompted him to recount his own birth, and the cutting of his umbilical cord:

> I can remember it happening to me as a body blow, a searing pain, a complete total organismic reflex, unguarded by any segmentalisation, which took my breath away before I got my breath, and produced a triple red light, emotional, physical, and mental state of emergency and danger. Quite suddenly the only status quo I knew was, within seconds – the time it took for scissors and clamp to sever that connection – abruptly ended. It happened just after being born, which could be regarded as out of the frying pan into the fire. Being born was an experience I certainly wouldn't like to repeat.'*

Although Ronnie's views were considered 'way-out' at the time, others present, including Professor Norman Morris, a consultant gynaecologist at the Charing Cross City Hospital and President of the International Society of Psychosomatic Obstetrics and Gynaecology, agreed that the new-born baby was capable of feeling pain. Morris went so far as to mention his daughter's recollection of her own birth in support of the proposition. These lectures served as a sort of 'cold shower'

* Quoted in Danae Brook, *Nature Birth*, 1976.

for the main event of Ronnie's year – thirty-two major talks across the States over thirty-five days. Ronnie knew that this would be a killer.

The lecture tour that Ronnie made across the States from 5 November to 8 December 1972 was the most gruelling he had ever undertaken. Ronnie used his connections well. He had established contact with Chris Stamp, the manager of the pop-group The Who. Also part of The Who's management team was Kit Lambert, who in turn knew a rough American diamond by the name of Danny Halpern. It was agreed that Chris would make the necessary arrangements using his unique experience in the pop world. Danny was thrown in as Ronnie's guide, confidant, fixer, roadie, companion, front-man and bodyguard. It was a wise decision. Danny Halpern, by all accounts, was a good man to be on the road with.

On 4 November, Ronnie and Danny met up at Heathrow Airport. Just before they checked in Danny thought a confession was in order. 'Ronnie, before we get into this there is something you should know.' Ronnie said nothing, waiting for the worst. Danny continued, 'You should know that I'm a heroin addict, but I'm giving it up today.' Ronnie shrugged his shoulders. It could have been a lot worse.

Ronnie hung out in New York for a few days, settling down before his first gig at Hunter College on 11 November. He quickly acclimatized to being the centre of intense interest. He appeared on New York's Channel 13 on Wednesday 8 November, with Norman Mailer, and the following evening was live on Dick Cavett. Meanwhile, Peter Robinson and the film crew followed Ronnie almost everywhere throughout New York before parting and then joining up with Ronnie and Danny later during the tour.

The talk at Hunter College, Ronnie's first, did not go down so well. Glenda Adams of *The Village Voice* showed no mercy:

The house was sold out, and so had R.D. Laing. This revolutionary psychiatrist, friend of the so-called schizophrenic, who has opened the eyes of so many of us, entertained a house full of fans in what turned out to be a Dick Cavett Faith Healing Exercise. And R.D. was laughing at them as he pocketed their money.

Adams was not at all impressed with the performance. She rounded off her sustained attack in the following manner:

> The dogma handed out that evening was: sitting cross-legged
> and barefoot on the floor for an hour was good; wearing glasses
> was bad; a stiff upper lip was bad; organic materials were good;
> living in New York was bad; shit, in its place, was good.
> R.D. Laing played dirty with that audience. It is significant that
> he chose to wear brown, but that kind of brown is dangerous,
> because you can't detect the smell.

New York, although not a complete disaster, would have to be
improved upon rapidly. Even Danny thought Ronnie was below par
that first night. But Ronnie quickly sharpened up his act as they moved
on to Stony Brook, Boston, Buffalo, Philadelphia, Baltimore, Virginia, Tampa, New Orleans, Salt Lake City, Los Angeles, Berkeley,
Chicago, San Diego and back to New York.

The gigs soon turned into a routine. The 'stage' would be set up
with either a single chair or no props at all. Danny would peer through
the curtain to sus out the audience and make sure everything was in
order. Ronnie would take the stage and talk for about an hour, take
a break of about ten minutes, and then reappear to field questions
for a further period of thirty to forty-five minutes. Danny noticed a
peculiar pattern developing. As a result of the intense guru persona
of R.D. Laing, propagated by *Esquire*, *The Atlantic*, *Life*, untold
articles, interviews and television appearances, the young American
campus-based audience viewed Ronnie as something of a minor God
to be listened to in awe, touched with reverence, viewe d in wonder.
The true dream was to sit at the wise man's bare feet and share a
joint. It became part of the norm for a stack of joints to be ritually
placed on the chair or on the floor during the interval. Ronnie impressed Danny with his deft touch in placing the booty into his pocket
before commencing the second session in a way that was hardly noticed. The prize was invariably all 'good gear' to be savoured in the
relative peace of the hotel by Ronnie and Danny after the show was
over.

By the time Ronnie and Danny hit Baltimore Ronnie's presence
was causing more and more of a stir. The review section of the Baltimore *Spectator* painted the scene:

The hand-lettered signs began as far out as Dulaney Valley road – 'R.D. Laing Lecture Sold Out!' They were dotted along the road leading onto the Goucher College campus, and appeared yet again in the parking lot, as if to convince those so determined to get in that one sign would be insufficient to deter them.

Outside the Kraushaar Auditorium, a crowd milled about and pressed against the metal doors. Security guards occasionally opened one a few inches, and a camera was thrust out, filming the crowd. Scalpers hawked tickets, people yelled, and although the young and the hip predominated, there were many older people trapped in the crush. One white-haired woman looked around helplessly, pinned by her neighbours. 'My God,' said a young man, 'it's like trying to get in to see the Rolling Stones!'

Tampa, Florida was a turning point. Ronnie was feeling more and more deprived of real food and pure water. Everywhere he went the food seemed to be artificial, the water contaminated with chemicals and additives. Ronnie was losing his patience and persuaded a cab driver to engage in a quest for something wholesome to eat or drink. After several hours they eventually found a shop on the outskirts of Tampa, which sold Perrier water. Ronnie consumed the best part of six bottles in a single session while exclaiming: 'I'm fucking dehydrated.'

It was then on to New Orleans where they were met by Peter Robinson and the film crew. The next stop – Salt Lake City – scared the hell out of Danny. Jutta had warned Danny about Ronnie's drinking, as she had seen Ronnie go truly bananas while on holiday in Morocco during 1969. The Americans had just landed on the moon, and Ronnie was furious at this invasion of the outer wilderness. He howled like an animal in the general direction of the moon, telling Armstrong and the others to 'Get the fuck off!'. Danny was warned but not prepared for what was in store.

On their way to Salt Lake City, in the otherwise uninhabited first class compartment of the plane, an air hostess had words with Ronnie about not wearing any socks or shoes. This was against regulations and, for some reason, was Ronnie's cue to order a double vodka. The debate continued. The plane stopped at St Louis and Ronnie was told the plane would not take off unless and until he covered his feet.

Annoyed even further, Ronnie requested another double vodka. Ronnie and Danny were then joined by a lady with a young child on the pretext that the lady had read and wished to talk about *Self and Others*. Ronnie was now on his third large vodka and Danny was feeling increasingly uncomfortable. As the plane approached Salt Lake City Ronnie starting making noises to the effect that he had no intention of getting off the plane. 'I can feel vibes and they're horrible, horrible, Danny,' he said. Danny reminded Ronnie that they had a gig. Ronnie was adamant that the atmosphere was 'poisoned'. The plane landed; Ronnie refused to move. In an effort to humour the now heavily inebriated guru, Danny told Ronnie that if the kid could get off so could he. All other passengers got off except for Danny, Ronnie, the lady and her four-year-old son. Only after the woman departed, taking her son with her, was Ronnie open to persuasion that the air, although not perfect, was not going to have the effect of killing him off; he eventually departed, eager for more alcohol and now completely inebriated.

Peter Robinson met them at the terminal, and they all made their way to the hotel. Danny had secured a room opposite Ronnie's suite. Ronnie was due to be interviewed by the press and television, including CBS and NBC, first thing in the morning. Ronnie phoned for a large vodka, changed his mind during the phone call and asked for two large vodkas. He downed them rapidly and then for no conceivable reason physically attacked Danny, landing a couple of sloppy blows while ranting and screaming.

The violence escalated. Ronnie tried to pull one of the venetian blinds from its mooring shouting, 'I'm going to get you, you bastard.' It was now about three in the morning. Ronnie seemed out of control. All Danny felt he could do was try to placate and reason with him. In desperation, Danny called the film crew. A young lady appeared, and helped persuade Ronnie to go to sleep in a bundle, on the floor. Danny left him snoring happily, but he knew that he would have to try and revive him in about four hours.

At about 7.30 a.m., Danny tried to wake Ronnie. To his amazement, Ronnie woke up, got up, showered, and within a few minutes was absolutely all right. Ronnie then sat on the couch for an hour and a half, being grilled by nearly twenty journalists, handling the whole scene beautifully. Danny was stunned. And that was Salt Lake City.

They moved on to Los Angeles and stayed in the Beverly Hills

Hotel's most exquisite rooms, where the massive roaring fireplace prompted Ronnie to order buckets of champagne, ask a few people round, and run up a bill of stupendous proportions.

Ronnie's talks were getting better. He was learning what to expect, listening to the questions in a more alert fashion, becoming more and more interesting. The next stop was the Chicago Medical Center. Ronnie, perhaps feeling more himself through having had an old-fashioned Glasgow-style blow-out, was now hitting back, no longer portraying himself as the gentle, wouldn't-t-harm-a-blade-of-grass-Buddhist. It was time to let rip. He took the opportunity during question-time to vent his feelings about 'the land of the free'; details were captured by the newsletter of the Chicago Medical Center, *Illini*:

Since in America I've been living in hotels, and airports, in planes and taxis, a month of this environment is enough for me. It's been over a week since I've actually tasted any water, real water, actual water, you know, water. I mean I wouldn't touch the milk, I mean it's dead, homogenised, pasteurized: it's not milk any more. I've found it difficult to get any real fruit, the fruit here is pretty tasteless and completely chemicalized. The bread that one finds most places I don't know what to compare it to; I would compare it to the soles of my shoes, the swabs of meat one is given to eat. The stuff that a large sector of the population has to eat is not at all appetising. The air is dull and static.

A brave medical student gave the rebellious Ronnie the perfect opportunity to let everyone see the Glaswegian in him, behind all the airy-fairy bullshit. The student accused Ronnie of rambling, of being totally unprepared, and generally handing out 'his dirty luggage'. Ronnie suggested that those who did not like his spontaneous exchange of ideas should listen repeatedly to the various tapes that had been made of the talk in order to get the meaning. 'And before doing so how dare you have the fucking cheek to ask me that,' Ronnie blasted out to a stunned audience.

Before leaving Chicago for San Diego, Ronnie was invited to examine a young girl diagnosed as schizophrenic. The girl was naked and engaged in no activity other than rocking to and fro. The doctors wanted to know what Ronnie thought. Without warning he stripped off naked and entered her room. There he sat with her, rocking in time to her rhythm. After about twenty minutes she started talking to Ronnie – something she had not done since being admitted several months previously. The doctors were stunned. 'Did it never occur to you to do that?' Ronnie enquired afterwards, with mischievous innocence.

From San Diego, it was back to New York for one final lecture to his peers at the famous Algonquin Hotel. Out of the blue an 'emergency' arose. Ronnie went into Danny's room and said he was not well and wanted to see a doctor. They got a cab to a doctor in Madison Avenue. They proceeded up Park Avenue, and as they turned left the cabbie said they would have to get out because of the traffic jam. By chance, the two men noticed a lady, and Ronnie remarked that they would see her again. They walked the rest of the way to the doctor's surgery and there in the waiting room was the same lady. Danny was perplexed, but Ronnie just brushed it off. By now his left arm was hanging uselessly by his side. Danny waited for him to come out of the surgery. When Ronnie reappeared he was brandishing a prescription. He cried, 'I have gout!', and burst out laughing in the middle of Madison Avenue. Ronnie went to a drug store, obtained the medicine, and promptly threw it in the gutter. The two got a cab back to the Algonquin. Ronnie told Danny he did not know what 'it' was. He said he had had 'it' before and he still didn't know what 'it' was.

Later that day they returned to business. Ronnie addressed the 'shrinks of America'. He stood and lectured them about the necessity for losing the ego, about materialism, about Sri Lanka, Zen, mysticism and Noble Truths. The next day, Ronnie and Danny boarded the plane for Heathrow, leaving behind the confused and unhappy audiences. The tour was over.

A few days after returning to London, Ronnie was invited to participate in a studio discussion with Professor Morris Carstairs, on Thames Television's programme, 'Something to Say'. Although broadcast only within the greater London region, Ronnie's performance had quite an effect on those whose had never seen 'R.D.' before. The growing crowd of 'Laingians' were expecting Ronnie to slaughter Carstairs, to debate him into the ground, to ridicule him. It didn't happen. Ronnie did not pick or win a fight with Carstairs. They talked as equals on the perplexing subject of schizophrenia, each apparently open to the other's arguments. Ronnie gave the impression of a mellowed rebel, a radical whose experience had tempered his anger. Even when the host, John Morgan, confronted Ronnie with his disapproval of the use of drugs or electric shocks, Ronnie casually replied:

I don't say I disapprove of these things quite in the way that a lot of people think I do. What I would like to see is that people should have the option of having electric shocks if that is what they have come to feel is what they need to relieve the suffering they're undergoing.

This was mild stuff indeed coming from Ronnie. It might seem simplistic to suggest that he was still exhausted from the American tour. But it was not vintage Laing.

Ronnie invited Danny to attend a lecture at Westminster Hall a few weeks later, in January 1973. The PA records demonstrate that all proceeds of this talk, as with the money from the Friend's Meeting House lecture back in October, went to the PA. Although the posters indicated that Ronnie was going to talk about meditation, he was past the point of giving a damn about what he was supposed to do or not do. When he discovered that the piano on the platform could not be moved, he took the opportunity to sit down and go through a rendition of some of his favourite George Gershwin numbers. Once he had tired of that he stood up and delivered an uninspired lecture, which prompted one lady from the back of the hall to shout 'But Dr Laing, what is the purpose of meditation?'. Now Danny could understand Ronnie when he bounded to the front of the stage and exclaimed: *It has no purpose!*', paused for a few moments, said, 'Thank you ladies and gentlemen', and walked off.

Danny learned a lot about Ronnie during this lecture tour: he witnessed at first-hand how Ronnie could oscillate between brilliance and mediocrity; he experienced Ronnie's incredible powers of self-recovery; he came to believe, in all sincerity, that 'Ronnie was hungry for the truth'. Ronnie, too, learned a great deal from this tour. One of the many cranky and 'far-out' scenes he experienced during this visit was a rebirthing ritual enacted together with a rebirth-midwife, Elizabeth Fehr. It was unusual for Ronnie to adopt someone else's 'number'. But with rebirthing he was going to make an exception, and in doing so he precipitated the split that was now widening within the Philadelphia Association.

CHAPTER SEVENTEEN

The Politics of Love

All in all, 1973 was not a good year for Ronnie. He was experiencing extreme difficulty writing in the fluent and flowing manner which he had taken for granted since his early school-days. His interests were becoming more and more remote from his professional roots, and he was in a quandary as to what his next move should be. *The Politics of the Family*, the last book published before he left for Sri Lanka, provided him with no lead into the future; his intellectual interest in families had almost completely waned. The effect of having taken a whole year off was becoming apparent: while he was still incredibly healthy physically, mentally he seemed static and distinctly lacking in what had been one of his hallmarks – originality. He was also under financial pressure of a severity and constancy that he had not previously experienced.

There was, however, one promising new dimension to his work. Although *Knots* had been published back in September 1970 without making much of a splash in the UK, interest in the book was now reawakened due to its adaptation for BBC Radio 3. This was sufficient cause for further publicity in *The Radio Times*, which advertised the broadcast of *Knots* on Tuesday 27 March. Here was an opportunity to tag Ronnie with yet another slogan, which had the effect of reducing his work to a single headline. This time, he was 'the man who said the mad weren't mad'. When *Knots* was first reviewed, Ronnie had been 'the man who says we're all mad'.* Whether these two isolated examples reflect the opinions of a wider public is dubious. They

* Roy Perrott in *The Observer*, 20 September 1970.

174

do, however, go some way to pinpointing a generality that Ronnie learned to live with. He was the man who said the mad are sane and the sane are mad, the man who said families cause madness, the man who said there is no such thing as madness, the man who said society was mad, the psychiatrist who was mad. . . .

By the beginning of April 1973, the PA bore little resemblance to the original group. In the beginning (e.g., late 1964), there was Ronnie, Sid Briskin, David Cooper, Aaron Esterson, Clancy Sigal, Joan Cunnold and Raymond Blake. On 21 March 1973, Sid Briskin formally resigned, having served his time for nearly a decade. Raymond Blake felt totally disillusioned by the whole experience, which he described as having nearly driven him crazy and he formally resigned in 1973. Aaron Esterson had long since left, because of what he considered to be Ronnie's mental instability; he had dramatically resigned during the course of a PA meeting on 4 September 1968, asking that the minutes record his dissatisfaction with the way Kingsley Hall had been managed since its beginning. Joan Cunnold, too, had drifted away to start a new life. Clancy Sigal had left feeling angry and betrayed but lucid enough to fictionalize his story. David Cooper was turning into a guru with a drink problem, creating havoc and emotional anarchy wherever he could; he formally resigned from the PA in 1971. Ben Churchill, one of the 'guardians' of Granville Road, had resigned from the PA during 1969.

The new PA consisted of Drs Hugh Crawford, John Heaton, Leon Redler and R.D. Laing as the four corners of a professional hierarchy now called 'the convenors', with the self-described status of Members of the Council of Management of the Philadelphia Association Limited. In addition there were members and associates. But this quasi-legal tagging was the reflection of the *de facto* hierarchy. There were really three layers: the top, the middle and the bottom. Everyone knew who was at the top – they were all doctors. Then there were the trainees, followed by the students and patients.

For the PA, the very concept of a 'trainee' was a painful issue; some accepted it as the reason why David Cooper decided to go his own way. There were many trainees; Haya Oakley, Paul Zeal, Mike Yocum and Mike Thompson, who was the PA secretary from 1973 to 1980. Many others followed. Between 1970 and 1973 the PA became very active as a training centre providing accommodation for people in distress, supervision of patients, a whole selection of therapies, regular seminars, study groups concerned with community therapy, lectures on phenomenology, Zen, hermeneutics, dialectic philosophy, hatha yoga, the *Bhagavadgita*, *The Platform Sutra*, Winnicott, Freud, Jung and Laing, by members of the PA and specially invited guests (e.g., Mary Barnes on Mary Barnes). This formal background bore little relation to the original purpose of the PA, which was to provide constant practical advice to those having difficulty living in the world on a day-to-day basis.

The PA functioned along these lines for the next ten years. It gradually metamorphosed into a network of people, most of whom lived in and around north-west London, from Hampstead to Kilburn, from Camden Town to Maida Vale, from Highgate to Archway. Ronnie remained at the head of these multifarious activities, and by 1974, he was wearing the hat of 'Chairman'.

During the late spring of 1973, Ronnie went through a deep emotional crisis from which he was lucky to survive. He had discovered that Jutta was having an affair with a television producer, and his heart was broken. During most of the summer, he sank into an alcoholic depression. He retreated to the delightful Cornwall country home of one of his former secretaries, to weep his heart out and write endless passages reflecting on himself and his relationship with Jutta which, at this stage, was hanging together by a very thin thread. In a photograph of Ronnie in the August 1973 edition of *Rolling Stone* magazine, one sees not the slim, handsome, sagacious man recently returned from a year's meditation, but a bloated, double-chinned, glazy-eyed boozer.

In the midst of this mammoth binge Ronnie went to see his first family in Glasgow. Although he had reconciled with Jutta by September, he was still in an extremely emotional state on 26 October, when he went round to Ruskin Place. His daughters, Karen and Fiona, had gone down to London in Ronnie's absence a few weeks previously, and had behaved rather badly; the police had called round to Belsize Park Gardens and accused Jutta (wrongly) of having supplied illegal substances. Ronnie was still furious. No sooner had he got through the door of Ruskin Place than he attacked Karen, then aged seventeen, and started to beat her unmercifully, until Paul and I intervened and restrained him. It was very frightening for all concerned. Years later when this story was put to him as an explanation as to why his relationship with Karen was so distant, he swore blind that he had absolutely no recollection of the incident.

Ronnie managed to redeem 1973 in part by virtue of a two week mini-tour of Canada during February 1974. This time his companion was Barrie Reynolds, the thirty-year-old president of a Toronto PR firm, Software Productions Limited. It was during this visit that Ronnie participated in a widely screened film, *Approaches*, with the American psychoanalyst Dr Harold Searles. In the film, a young girl referred to as 'Jane' is seen alternately by Dr Searles and Dr Laing. During both sessions, the girl complains of a pain in her neck. Searles ventures a psychoanalytical interpretation, but when 'Jane' does the same with Ronnie, he stands up and rubs the back of her neck. Different folks, different strokes.

In other respects, Canada was a rerun of the previous year in the States – intense media attention and lectures. He was interviewed on CityTV, CTV's Canada AM and CBC–TV's 'Weekday' and 'Take Thirty'; he lectured to packed auditoriums and lecture halls, he shared the peace-pipe with young journalists of the campus newspapers of York and the University of Toronto, and he hung out in the best hotels while lecturing his devotees about living under a crag in the foothills of the Himalayas with a spiritual master. But the magic was wearing off. A newspaper covering his sell-out lecture at the University of Toronto's Convocation Hall reported:

When we left him in his tower suite, he was sipping Vichy water, taking a drag of his cigarette, and evidently meditating. I asked one of the girl reporters, a 19-year-old named Cathy, what she thought of her interview with Laing. 'Disappointed', she said. 'It was as though he were talking to an empty room.' 'Yeah,' agreed her fellow journalist, a 22-year-old named Shelley. 'But I guess that's what he means when he says he's found his private sanctuary.'

By 1974, two years after Ronnie's trip to India, there was still no sign of any book. However, there was enough money coming in on a regular basis for him to think about purchasing property. He felt he knew Devon and Cornwall well enough to take the plunge, and bought a delightful three-acred property called Batworthy Mill, near Exeter. The site was also close enough to friends of Ronnie's second family, David and Sarah Salmon and their children, for Batworthy Mill to be used as a base for long weekends. This was merely intended to be a country retreat from the London 'scene', for he also had his eye on an old vicarage in Eton Road, round the corner from where he had been living since moving out of Kingsley Hall in 1966, into Belsize Park Gardens. His second family was growing rapidly (Adam was now six and Natasha three) and, having reached the grand old age of forty-six, Ronnie felt it was time to think about moving out of his rented flat into more spacious surroundings in neighbouring Chalk Farm. Altogether, 1974 marked Ronnie's intention to turn over a new leaf, reinforced by his marriage to Jutta on Valentine's Day.

Some months later, Ronnie invited my brother Paul and me to attend our first 'R.D. conference'. The elderly but alert Dr Winniford Rushforth, a pioneer of therapeutic workshops in Scotland, had invited Ronnie to spend a weekend talking to students and staff of Fatima House, a Christian residential community south of Kilmarnock. This was an opportunity for us to experience our dad at close range in a professional context, albeit much to our mother's protestations.

The weekend did not start well. Possibly because of his gnawing sense of guilt at having left his two elder sons 'out of it' for so long, Ronnie decided to turn the event into an episode of vintage dimensions. He was supposed to be at Fatima House for dinner on Friday night. Not until nightfall in the West End of Glasgow did he persuade a reluctant cab driver to brave the long journey into the back of beyond, in the quest to find 'Fatima House – somewhere south of Kilmarnock'. Too many public houses were popped into for a quickie en route for the journey to be recalled in any detail.

We arrived sometime after midnight. Everyone was in bed, having all but given up any hope of seeing the great Laing. But there he was, sons in tow, completely inebriated and still singing 'Four and Twenty Virgins'. It was a close shave with the cab driver, who not only had to put up with three drunkards in the back of his cab all the way there, but also with the truly unforgettable, pungent smell of Ronnie's vomit all the way home.

Ronnie rapped the door loudly, until it was eventually answered by people roused from their beds, wondering what the racket was all about. As we fell inside, Ronnie noticed a life-size sculpture of Jesus on the cross at the end of the hall. 'Just the man I want to talk to', he exclaimed, staggering over to the silent, dignified icon. He began embracing the sculpture in what can only be described as a familiar manner. By now, quite a crowd had assembled from out of the numerous guest-rooms. There was absolutely no doubt what was going on – R.D. Laing had arrived and he was steaming drunk. As if making the ultimate 'fuck you' gesture to the world in general, and the good Christian residents of Fatima House in particular, Ronnie began slobbering over the statue's arse. Paul and I could no longer restrain ourselves, and convulsed in hysterical laughter on the floor. What a guy!

The next morning Ronnie delivered a sober and thoughtful lecture on sin and redemption and, after dinner, played 'Four and Twenty Virgins' on the piano. His party mood was extremely infectious and the singing, dancing and drinking continued until the early hours of Sunday morning. We left thirty-six hours after our dramatic arrival, Ronnie having made his peace with all concerned, in particular with Winnie Rushforth, who was very forgiving and in a Christian way quite grateful.

This was a serious turning point in the relationship between Ronnie and me. Having been initiated into what Ronnie was truly like, on one level, both Paul and I were trusted enough to spend some time with Ronnie and his second family at Batworthy Mill during the summer. Ronnie had set a high standard on how to disgrace oneself. It was the first of many such events over many years.

Not wishing to be outdone, Susie, Ronnie's second daughter, decided to spend a few days with her dad in London during November of the same year. Susie always seemed to be the most forgiving towards Ronnie, the most honest and the most attached. While she was down in London she stayed with Ronnie's secretary, John Reilly, who recalled Susie coming back from Belsize Park Gardens sobbing uncontrollably. Try as she might she could not get through to Ronnie and felt completely rejected. She was yet to learn that the only way to get through to Ronnie was to share at least one bottle of whisky with him – something he rarely did with a woman. However, there was a small consolation in store for her. The *Sunday Times* did a feature on children of famous people – 'Heirs to a Name' (24 November 1974). Richard Whitehouse was interviewed about his mother Mary; Tracy Tynan on her father Kenneth, Mark Collins about his father Canon Collins, Connie Eysenck talked of her father Professor

H.J., Maxwell Aitken of his father Sir Max, Mark Thatcher had a few words to say about his mother Margaret, Dominic Freud talked of his MP father Clement, John Duane talked about his father Michael and Martin Amis about Kingsley. Susie had quite a lot to put forward about her dad and finished off by stating: 'The worst thing for him is the five of us. He can't get used to us all being so grown up. We've got too many problems for him. He can solve everybody else's but not ours.'

By 1975 Ronnie's preoccupations were specific and focused: he was Chairman of the PA, which occupied some, but not all of his time; he was seeing fee-paying patients (this confused some people); trying to write too many books to be completed within their tentative deadlines; and he was 'rebirthing'. In an autumn 1974 interview with Claude Steiner and Spence Meigham which was published as 'Issues in Radical Therapy' a year later, Ronnie explained his rebirthing trip:

Last winter I had a weekly session in the evenings to which about 40 to 50 came in which we cultivated a rather simple ritual which started off as what we called 're-birthing'. We found it increasingly easy as a number of people stand around one person at a center spot to just give the word 'go'. People would start to go into, God knows what, all sorts of mini-freak-outs and birth-like experiences, yelling, groaning, screaming, writhing, contorting, biting, contending. A lot of physical handling might ensue and a lot of energy would be released and redistributed. I should mention massage, bodily sculpture, improvised games, etc., are all part of our ordinary ongoing culture: wearing masks, dancing. . . . I met Janov here a couple of years ago. Lowen has also been over here, and a number of people I work with had sessions with him. Some people are drawn to this or that way of releasing energy and we have a fair array of competence within and around our network. We are not identified with any special developed technique but we are into it, as the saying goes, for me particularly, music rhythm and dancing. When I go to one of our households for an evening usually music, drumming, singing, dancing starts up. This often continues after I leave.

He added reassuringly, 'There is also pottery.'

In April 1975 Karen, Ronnie's third daughter, who was then living in Glasgow, gave birth to her first child Mark. Ronnie and Jutta's third child, Max, was born on 24 June 1975. Ronnie's family was becoming very extended, but he took many years to adapt to his new identity of 'Grandad'.

As a counterpoint to rebirthing activities, Ronnie and Jutta were now part of a group that promoted natural birth – although the film that was made of Max's birth showed that natural could be long, painful and life-threatening. Ronnie's life was centred to a large extent around his second family in London and for most of the time he lived and wrote at home which, with the addition of Max, was becoming too crowded for comfort – once again, it was time to move.

A few minutes' walk from Belsize Park Gardens is the quiet and exclusive Eton Road. In 1974, the vicarage of All Saints Church in Eton Road was up for sale. Number 2 Eton Road was in a very run-down state, but had a great deal of potential principally by virtue of its size – eight rooms situated over three floors and a basement; relatively large front and back gardens; a massive kitchen and two bathrooms. Eton Road was the sort of house Ronnie's parents could never have imagined; there were stairs galore, open spaces, wooden-panelled window shutters, enormous fireplaces – all within a short walk from two London Underground stations and right in the heart of one of the most sought after areas in north-west London: a dream home. There was only one small catch. The house, the former vicarage of a church run by a well-known practising exorcist (the Revd Neil Smith, reputed to have over five hundred exorcisms to his credit), had an eerie feel to it. After they had purchased the house in the summer of 1974, both Ronnie and Jutta made endless visits to check up on the extensive refurbishments. Ronnie became convinced that Eton Road was haunted. On one occasion, as if to confirm his belief, a ceiling collapsed just after he walked out of a room. He decided to let 'them' have it. One night he went round to Eton Road and told 'them' to 'fuck off and never return', as a result of which the atmosphere, as he remembered, changed dramatically, and that was the end of that.

In early 1975, Ronnie's second daughter from his first marriage, Susie, was twenty-one years old and engaged to be married. Late in the year she fell very ill and was eventually diagnosed with monoblastic leukaemia. The doctors in Glasgow decided that drugs and radiation treatment were the only course of action available. It was obvious that she had very little time left. To pile on the misery and heartbreak, a major row developed between Anne and Ronnie. They were always at each other, but this was war. Anne did not think anything was to be gained by telling Susie of her condition. Ronnie had a different view. He felt it was imperative that she should be told. Ronnie wrote a letter in early 1976 informing me of his intentions: 'There's no doubt in my mind that she will have to be put in the picture, and if it doesn't come from elsewhere, it will have to come from me.'

Ronnie went up to Glasgow and, in the face of fierce opposition from the doctors, Anne, and Susie's fiancé, Roddy, told Susie that she had a form of leukaemia for which there was no known cure and that in all likelihood, barring a miracle, she would not live very long – perhaps six months. There was at the time a tremendous amount of anger directed at Ronnie, who had no difficulty in adopting the authoritarian role of father, only to leave everyone else, particularly Roddy and Anne, to deal with the emotional fall-out. He left for London almost immediately after putting Susie in the picture. Nevertheless, a sense of relief prevailed after it had been done. Very shortly afterwards Susie was taken out of hospital as the doctors agreed that there was nothing further they could do. Susie returned to her fiancé's house to die with dignity in the midst of an overwhelming family love which, for the first time in over ten years, reunited Ronnie's first family, albeit momentarily.

Following Susie's burial a reception was held at the Grosvenor Hotel in Glasgow. After the sit-down meal, the serious drinking continued. At the tail-end of the evening, I was crying uncontrollably on my mother's shoulder. After a while I felt a strong, indeed painful, grab on my left arm, and was forcibly pulled away by a social worker who had been assigned to Susie's 'case', a large, fat, ugly female. As she pulled me away from my mother, she said, 'Now pull yourself together Adrian, you've cried enough!'. Before I could 'pull myself together', Ronnie lunged at her with all of his might. He dragged her by the lapels of her jacket and began violently pounding her against a wall. He shouted at her at the top of his voice 'Don't you fucking understand (thump), that what I am fucking going on about (thump), is that fucking social workers (thump), have no fucking right (thump), to fucking interfere (thump), with *families*!' She was then unceremoniously thrown out. I reread *The Politics of the Family* in a different light. Ronnie and I returned on the same flight to London and hired a cab back to Belsize Park Gardens, still ranting and raving about the whole episode until the early hours of the following morning.

CHAPTER EIGHTEEN

Birth and Rebirth

Soon after Ronnie moved into Eton Road, the house was burgled and the matter duly reported to the local police. To Ronnie's utter amazement the police reappeared shortly after, not to inform him of the results of their investigations but to arrest and charge him with possession of LSD. During their 'routine' check of missing items, they had inexplicably forced open a locked cabinet and found ninety-four ampoules of LSD–25. Unknown to Ronnie, the Misuse of Drugs Acts 1973 restricted the possession of the drug to specific prescribers and he, at that stage, was not one. He was therefore charged with unlawful possession of a Class A drug. It was not until July of the following year that the case came before the local magistrates for committal to the Crown Court for trial. Ronnie was smart enough to secure the best lawyers he could, the solicitor David Offenbach who instructed the barrister Geoffrey Robertson. The defence advanced the argument that the prosecution could not prove that the offending drug had been obtained after the passing of the 1973 Act, and therefore the presumption was that the LSD had been obtained at a time when it was lawful for a doctor to do so. The chairman of the magistrates, Mrs Manna Sedgwick, agreed. Despite the ruling, the prosecution persisted in arguing that the costs of the case should be borne by R.D. Laing. On 28 July, *The Daily Telegraph* reported the conclusion of this mini-saga, stating that costs of £500 were awarded to R.D. Laing, following the withdrawal of the case by the Director of Public Prosecutions.

As one might imagine, Ronnie felt unseen forces at work behind this strange episode. At the time of the burglary in April another court case was hotting up. John Stonehouse, MP – the former Postmaster

General of the Labour government who had feigned his death in England only to reappear in Australia, was now on fraud charges to be heard at the Old Bailey in London. Stonehouse had visited Ronnie in Belsize Park Gardens and persuaded Ronnie to give evidence on his behalf. As *The Guardian* reported on 20 July 1976, Ronnie duly did his bit:

> Earlier, Mr Stonehouse called a fifth psychiatrist, Dr Ronald Laing, the author of The Divided Self.
>
> Dr Laing said that he had examined the MP in October last year, and March this year. He had also read his book, Death of an Idealist, and read interviews taken by other psychiatrists. He had seen a great many cases in which patients had tried to pull the wool over the eyes of psychiatrists. Mr Stonehouse's account of his breakdown was plausible.
>
> Dr Laing said that Mr Stonehouse's story was unusual in that his two personalities were joined by an umbilical cord, when most dual personalities were not really aware of each other. 'If that story is to be believed it is what would fall into a psychiatric category of partial psychotic breakdown.'

Not surprisingly, Ronnie's evidence made little impression on the jury, who found the idea of a man defending himself while pleading insanity difficult to swallow. Ronnie himself regretted giving evidence on behalf of Stonehouse and was constantly bugged by the possibility that his own case and that of Stonehouse's were, in some way, connected. Besides, he did not have any sympathy with Stonehouse's account and recorded in his diary after coming back from a gruelling and humiliating cross-examination:

'– Stonehouse: Either a sick man behaving like a criminal
or a criminal behaving like a sick man
If, a criminal behaving like a sick man he is sick;
and conversely why not say he is both, a sick criminal,
a criminal lunatic.'

The Facts of Life, Ronnie's ninth book, was published in the States shortly after Ronnie and his second family moved into Eton Road.

At the same time, *R.D. Laing: The Man and his Ideas* by Richard Evans (Professor of Psychology at the University of Houston, Texas) was also put into print. Almost coincidentally Professor Anthony Clare's critique of modern psychiatry, *Psychiatry in Dissent* was published in the UK. *The Facts of Life* appeared during the latter part of November 1976, and was reviewed in *The New Review* by Anthony Clare along with Thomas Szasz's book, *Anti-Psychiatry – The Paradigm of the Plundered Mind*. The simultaneous publication of these four books created another wave of publicity about R.D. Laing and 'anti-psychiatry', which continued unabated throughout the latter part of 1976 and eventually culminated in the publication of a lengthy off-print from *The New Review* under the title *Anti-Psychiatry – A Debate* in 1977.

Ronnie had found the whole 'anti-psychiatry' debate rather tedious ever since David Cooper had set the hare running in 1967 in his introduction to *The Dialectics of Liberation*. By 1976 Ronnie was not in the mood to go over old ground, and preferred Leon Redler to enter the affray with a detailed response to all the chattering about Laing, Szasz, Cooper, Esterson and now Anthony Clare, which seemed to go on *ad nauseam*.* Others found the complex rivalries between Szasz, Ronnie, Esterson, Redler and Berke, totally absorbing. *The Observer* stated on 10 April 1977:

> For months now, an astonishing debate about the uses and abuses of psychiatry has dominated the pages of the literary magazine, The New Review. In its way the acrimonious attack on the unorthodox views of R.D. Laing by his fellow psychiatrist, the American Dr Thomas S. Szasz, is as important to psychiatry as the famous Leavis-Snow debate of the 1960s was to literature.

But Ronnie felt ambivalent towards the whole affair. Besides, Anthony Clare had committed the ultimate sacrilege against Ronnie's ego when, in the course of his review of *The Facts of Life*, he described it as 'boring, very boring indeed, I regret to say'. This was the first time the word 'boring' had been used to describe Ronnie's writing. *The Facts of Life* contained three distinct elements. As Ronnie's first foray into a quasi-autobiographical work, the book contained deeply personal anecdotes from his family life. It also attempted to pull together

* Redler maintains that he wrote on his own initiative.

two strands of Ronnie's working life. On an intellectual level he was trying to present a theory which was not an entirely new idea in the field of psychoanalysis, but was derived from his own experience of dealing with extremely disturbed patients over many years, and concerned the effect of pre-natal life on adults. Finally, he was attempting to explain – also from his own practical experience – the potential beneficial therapeutic effects of his rebirthing workshops. But nobody seemed to want to take any of it seriously. Ronnie had to face up to the facts of life himself: the book was badly written, poorly researched, unpopular and almost without exception viewed as a great disappointment, coming from the man who had written *The Politics of the Family* over five years previously.

Perhaps one of the reasons for the hostility towards *The Facts Of Life* was that it did not concern itself in any shape or form with what was expected and hoped for from R.D. Laing at that juncture – a comprehensive and detailed analysis of present-day psychiatry and anti-psychiatry, addressing such questions as the clinical basis for ECT, drugs and physical restraint, the efficacy of existential-phenomenological analysis, the economics of community care and the relevance of avant-garde therapies including rebirthing. But such a book was of no interest at all to Ronnie. Besides, the point was lost during the course of the debate that there had been and was only one 'anti-psychiatrist' – David Cooper. Even the radical Italian psychiatrist, Franco Basaglia, described himself as far back as 1968 as being a proponent not of anti-psychiatry but of 'non-psychiatry'. Thomas Szasz was not an anti-psychiatrist, nor was Aaron Esterson. Ronnie had himself denounced the concept many years previously as had Joe Berke in his letter to *The New Review*. The idea of Michel Foucault being an anti-psychiatrist was ludicrous. His book *Madness and Civilization* was intended as one in a series of books in the history of ideas. Even by 1980, when both David Cooper and Michel Foucault were living in Paris they rarely met, despite rumours to the contrary, nor even wished to meet. Ronnie and Foucault did not meet until November 1975, and only once thereafter in 1983, after I had made a bridge with Foucault, having studied with him throughout 1980 and 1981 while simultaneously cultivating a close friendship with David Cooper, whom Foucault found both intellectually and physically rather coarse.*

* Details of the meetings between Michel Foucault and the 'anti-psychiatrists' have recently been published in Didier Eribon's 1991 biography of Foucault.

No one seemed to want to accept that the whole idea of anti-psychiatry had been abandoned by those with whom the term had originated. Even David Cooper had moved on. In his last, 'brotherly' letter to Ronnie, written from Argentina in October of 1972, David described his life as 'intense beyond words, beautiful, exciting and above all dangerous – that's what I've always wanted – a sort of 'unknotted' existence like stone floors in finally unromantic prison cells and the nudging of one's false rib by the end of an automatic rifle'.

During August of 1976 Ronnie once again visited the USA. He had been invited by Dr Bruce Larson, the resident pastor, to spend a week at a theological seminar at Princeton University, New Jersey. For the first time in a professional context Ronnie was accompanied abroad by one of his children, his eldest son Paul, then eighteen.

After a week of impressing the theologians of Princeton, Ronnie and Paul flew to New York and, as if to counterbalance the previous week's good behaviour, Ronnie started drinking heavily. Paul received an 'education into politics' with a guided visit to 'no-go' areas for whites in Manhattan, including Harlem, the Bronx and Spanish Harlem. Ronnie was due to appear live on the television show, 'Good Morning America' the next morning.

When Paul returned with his black minder to the opulent suite on the sixth floor of the St Moritz in Central Park South, he found Ronnie in a heavy drinking session with an American psychiatrist, Gene Nameche, who was based in Philadelphia. Gene wanted to talk about a possible biography of Jung; Ronnie had other issues on his mind. Ronnie, outraged that Gene had interviewed his mother in Glasgow on the pretext of the Jung project, was letting Gene have it: 'You're a total fucking schmuck, Gene – a real, total, fucking schmuck! How dare you fucking treat my mother like that, you bastard.' Gene had visited Amelia in order to extract as much information as he could on Ronnie. The *quid pro quo* for Amelia was a box of mouldy chocolates. Ronnie was absolutely furious at Gene's 'fucking cheek'. Gene, in an advanced state of contrition (tears), pleaded for mercy. But Ronnie was only warming up. He decided that words were insufficient to get the message across and delivered an uninhibited right hook to Gene's face, followed by numerous other blows in quick succession. The completion of Gene's physical education was having an Italian marble coffee table hurled at his head. Launching into a complete *non sequitur* which can only be understood within the logic of alcohol, Ronnie then proceeded to say 'the final act which results in somebody being taken to a mental hospital is the smashing of the television set', whereupon he launched a large fragment of the remains of the coffee table at the television. It bounced off, leaving the television unharmed. But the destruction of the set became a point of principle, and resulted in all of those present 'having a go'. The television set finally got the message and it blew up with an extremely loud noise – loud enough to attract the attention of the armed hotel security guards who burst into the suite, guns drawn. Ronnie, instantly sober, said, 'I'm seeing a psychiatric patient', (indicating Gene) 'and I'm responsible for the bills.' Ronnie explained to the guards that his patient had caused the damage to the television. Poor Gene did not have Ronnie's talent for instant sobriety in adverse circumstances. 'This man' (again pointing to Gene) 'has a severe history of psychiatric disorder.' The guards then examined Gene's identification, which showed that he was a psychiatrist. Ronnie went on, 'See what I mean, his delusion is complete – he's even managed to obtain false identification.' Gene Nameche found himself being handcuffed and escorted off the premises by the guards. It was not long before Gene talked himself out of it, by which time Ronnie and Paul were on the plane home. Ever forgiving, Gene eventually saw the funny side, although the Jung project was never completed.

Paul did not have to wait long before the next R.D. beano – a week's filming in Glasgow under the directorship of the Canadian producer John McGreavy. The award-winning cameraman, Charles Stewart, was part of the crew. McGreavy was making a series of films for the television market about European cities from the viewpoint of a 'famous son'. The amount of money Ronnie was paid – $8,000 for one week – not only helped his cash-flow but was sufficient incentive for him to work flat out. The small crew (including Paul who was co-opted as a 'fixer') commenced work usually before 6 a.m., and shooting continued sometimes past midnight. Considering the scope and depth of the film, which included interviews with the Scottish poet Hugh McDiarmid, the trade union leader Jimmy Reid, the mayor of Glasgow and the evangelist Jack Glass, 'R.D. Laing on Glasgow' surprisingly failed to make an impression on British television executives and was only transmitted in the London region, safely out of peak time, about two years later.

Shortly after the McGreavy film, Ronnie was invited to front another documentary called *Birth*, which was to take 'a critical look at childbirth practices in Western society'. The New Zealander Helen Brew persuaded Ronnie to take a leading role in the film. In 1950, Brew had founded in New Zealand the Parents' Centre movement, which was concerned with parent education in the field of mental health. Brew was also deeply involved in the way women were treated during childbirth in state hospitals and through the combined experience of mother, actress and film producer decided to make a no-holds-barred film portraying the insensitivity of childbirth practices in the Western world. Although the film would, in all likelihood, have had the desired effect of shocking the British television viewers into some kind of action, there really was not much hope of it ever being broadcast in the UK. Perhaps because of the aura of censorship surrounding the film, it was a great success in its own right and caused a minor sensation wherever it was shown. Following an early presentation at the New Zealand High Commission in London, with Yehudi and Hepzibah Menuhin as the honoured quests, the public reaction, as gauged by the press reviews, was extremely favourable. Ronnie's commentary was suitably controversial and the following passage was guaranteed to produce sighs of incredulity wherever it was shown:

There couldn't be any event, I think, that is more centrally located within the fabric of any human society and any civilisation than the procedures around birth. If we judge our civilisation by what we do to assist this process, then it certainly looks to me one of the disaster areas of our culture.

Birth was an uncompromising film, showing how the process of birth is conducted on the false premise that a new-born baby could not be fully sentient. Ronnie said that the film, which showed a new-born baby in extreme physical distress being circumcised without an anesthetic, left him in tears every time he saw it. Many shared that sentiment when they saw the film at film festivals in Edinburgh, Sydney and Melbourne, Cannes, MIFED, Milan and The International Forum of Young Cinema. The film picked up awards for the Best TV film: Melbourne Festival 1978, and the Best Documentary of the Year: Feltex

Award New Zealand the same year. Despite the international acclaim, *Birth* could not break into the mass market in the United Kingdom. Ronnie thought the powers that be (i.e., The Royal College of Obstetricians) were 'too frightened' for the film to be broadcast on national television in the UK, and had 'put the blocks on it'. Helen Brew campaigned tirelessly for *Birth* to be shown to more and more people; she found herself trying to persuade the BBC to air the film as late as 1983. Deborah Fosbrook, then in the acquisition department of the BBC and, at that time, my girlfriend, remembers Helen's efforts very well. Ronnie had little understanding of the detailed rules and regulations governing the broadcasting of material in this country and never understood what *Birth* was up against in the commercial and public UK broadcasting world even before the up-and-running days of Channel 4. It was a tremendously moving and powerful film. But as a balanced portrayal of medical practice it was a non-starter. What the film did was to give further ammunition to the natural birth movement, already well in its stride.

Frederick Leboyer, who came to see *Birth* in London, had taken the high ground on the issue. The popularity of his book, *Birth Without Violence*, was gaining great momentum as were the writings of Arthur's second wife, Janet Balaskas. Ronnie was caught up in a movement that had its own dynamics, rooted in the experiences of mothers themselves. Perhaps this was one of the reasons why another intended project of Ronnie's, 'The Politics of Birth', was neither published nor fully completed. In this particular struggle he was way down the pecking order behind Leboyer, Odent, Sheila Kitzinger, Janet Balaskas, Sarah Salmon and many other active and dedicated midwives, and the growing and vociferous army of angry mothers who had had their vulvas shaved, were pressurized into accepting epidurals, had their legs held high in stirrups, and whose normal bodily functions during labour were treated as secondary to their doctors' plans to play a round of golf.

Ronnie took the opportunity to use the film as part of a strategy to advance the cause of the PA. A series of lectures was organized at the Logan Hall Institute of Education at Bedford Way in central London during the end of June and the first week of July in 1977. The PA was now fronted by Ronnie, Francis Huxley, Leon Redler, Hugh Crawford and John Heaton, and the five of them took to the stage to deliver their pieces under the banner 'Our Approach to Psychiatry' on

28 June. *Birth* was screened the following week. *New Society's* banal review of Ronnie's first talk left him raging:

> Laing sat to one side, looking like his picture on the front of NEW SOCIETY a fortnight ago. He was dressed up with an almost excessive conservatism (to forestall medical criticism?): well-dressed suit, cuff-links, shiny black shoes, quiet tie, and socks that seemed held up by suspenders. His fellow associates were on a different wavelength: open shirts, fancy shoes, light-weight suits, beards. If clothes do make the person – or at least announce the person – there was a range here that Marks and Spencers could be proud of.
>
> Dress and let dress, is part of the message, too, perhaps.

Birth provided Ronnie with a *locus standi* in the ferocious natural-birth debate; its reverberations lasted throughout the late seventies and into the early eighties, at a time when his preoccupation was not only the process of medical birth but the therapeutic process of rebirthing, now gaining its own momentum under the reluctant auspices of the PA.

By late 1976 Ronnie had completed his second book since his return from Sri Lanka and India. *Do You Love Me?* was originally entitled, 'Why did the Peacock Scream?', and was published in 1977 amid the anti-psychiatry debate. Following hot on the heels of *The Facts of Life*, it gave even more ammunition to Ronnie's critics. The book was intended as a further development into 'entertainment' and passages were often read aloud by Ronnie in the company of his friends and family to hilarious effect. But Ronnie's public reputation was still firmly placed in the context of madness and the family. He now wished to be regarded more as a poet than a radical psychiatrist, but it was never going to be easy persuading the intelligentsia on both sides of the Atlantic that a complete chapter, which consisted of 'Was that a kiss?/or a hiss/from the abyss?', was anything other than complete rubbish. Although the reviews ranged from the sympathetic to the savage, the general reaction to the book was summed up in the *Sunday Times* by the poet Dannie Abse: 'We do not expect an eminent psychiatrist however unorthodox, to tap-dance (like an amateur) and let his trousers fall. No weak philosophising can compensate.'

Others were not so kind. Professor H.J. Eysenck, an old foe of psychoanalysis in general and of R.D. Laing in particular, could not resist putting the boot in: 'As for me I would much rather read the report on drains of the Melbourne Department of Sanitation. At least it does not pretend to be other than it is.'

The reviews continued in the same vein throughout 1977. Perhaps the nadir was the review in the *New Society* which rose to the challenge of *Do You Love Me?* by avoiding a review in any accepted sense of the word, and letting forth a stream of abuse ending with:

> *and misery. knots? no.*
> *more like spots clots rots.*
> *all men are pigs man. and woman seem*
> *so well, so well well well, well then. um*
> *ah shit. no as I call myself a*
> *turd. life? no well. well then.*
> *what I am really no really what I am trying*
> *no*
> *saying is*
> *can you love me anyway*
> *this old nit-wit?*

Ronnie was at least consoled by finding a review that was worse than the book. Perhaps in former days he might have taken it all to heart but to a seasoned writer these utterances were confirmation that because of their own perception of what R.D. Laing was, or should be, about, others would neither permit nor tolerate Ronnie's change in direction. Besides, the harsh words of the critics did not succeed in killing off *Do You Love Me?*. Edward Petherbridge, a well-known National Theatre actor and moving spirit behind the Actors' Company, which had previously performed *Knots* for the radio, was sufficiently moved by the book to make arrangements for its adaptation to the stage. During the summer of 1977, Ronnie and I regularly attended the rehearsals of *Do You Love Me?* at the Old Vic at the back of Waterloo station. Ronnie was not particularly impressed with the way things were going, although surprisingly, he kept his criticisms to himself and did not seek to interfere with Edward Petherbridge's direction. Privately he expressed some dismay at the way some potential great numbers were being thrown away. In particular, the delivery of the song 'St James's Infirmary', to Ronnie, was lacking in the passion he felt it deserved. The performances were hanging together, but Ronnie knew the adaptation was never going to be a blockbuster, much to his disappointment.

The year 1977 was dominated, on an emotional level, by Fiona, Ronnie's eldest child from his first marriage to Anne. The messy and protracted split between Anne and Ronnie was a hard blow for all of the children, but even more so for Fiona who, being the eldest, took the brunt of it. Susie's death in March 1976 was so traumatic and painful that emotionally the Glasgow family were hanging on by a thread.

In her personal life, Fiona had gone though a tough patch with her boyfriend, Gordon, who had rejected her. Fiona 'cracked up', and when she was found weeping outside a church off Bryes Road in Glasgow, she was taken into Gartnavel Mental Hospital for examination. Once again, a bitter battle broke out between Ronnie and his first family, over the reasons for Fiona's breakdown. I phoned up Ronnie and asked him in despair and anger what he was going to do about Fiona. He reassured me that he would visit Fiona and do everything in his power to ensure that she was not given any ECT. But when it came to the crunch, all he could say was 'Well, Ruskin Place or Gartnavel – what's the difference?' At this stage, spring of 1977, feelings within the family were running very high. Once again it felt as if all the old wounds were wide open. Perhaps understandably the drinking on all sides became heavy.

A full front page photograph of Ronnie promoted an interview by David Cohen in *New Society* in May 1977. The purpose of the interview was to provide advance publicity for *Do You Love Me?* and David Cohen's book *Psychologists on Psychology*. During the interview it was put to Ronnie that *Sanity, Madness and the Family* might be understood as an attack on the family. Ronnie retorted:

You're interviewing me right now in the midst of my family. I enjoy living in a family. I think the family is still the best thing that exists biologically as a natural thing. My attack on the family is aimed at the way I felt many children are subjected to gross forms of violence of their rights, to humiliation at the hands of adults who don't know what they're doing.

David Cohen did mention that Ronnie 'left his first wife and family who still live in Glasgow, but then remarried' but, as one might expect, no mention was made of Fiona. Even at the time of Ronnie's death in 1989, Fiona's predicament was little known outside a small circle of people. Ronnie had good reason to keep the matter under wraps. He knew his critics would have a field day. He also knew that Fiona could not possibly benefit if her condition were made public. It would not be fair to say that Fiona was callously abandoned. Ronnie and I went with Fiona to one of the PA households in Ealing the following year, with a view to her moving in on a long-term basis. But it was obviously not going to work out. Fiona was firmly rooted in Glasgow and felt even more disorientated in semi-squalor in the outskirts of London. Eton Road, with Ronnie and Jutta's three young children about, was not considered a viable option.

In the meantime, in September 1977, I stayed with Ronnie at Eton Road while Jutta was in Germany visiting her parents with the children. Ronnie knew that I was still sore about 'all the family stuff' and was keen to 'make things up'. As a result, every day for a week and more the two of us painted the town red. On the first night Ronnie suggested going to see *Jesus Christ, Superstar* which was still pulling in large audiences at the Palace Theatre in the West End. True to form, Ronnie ordered several large drinks to be at the ready for the interval: large whisky, large Pernod, large Bloody Mary, to be washed down with at least one pint of lager in the space of about fifteen minutes. We staggered to our seats for the second half. 'Ah, next act must be the crucifixion – can't fail!' Ronnie muttered. While we waited with bated breath the curtain rose. To the tortuous sounds of blaring pop music the chorus launched into an appalling, wailing song of some description while Jesus appeared on a plastic cross, neon lights and all, rising from a trap door. Ronnie put his head in his hands and started wailing, 'What the fuck is this? I can't believe it, I can't believe it, no, no, no.' We sat it out to the end so that Ronnie could let them have it. Rising to the challenge he booed continually for what must have been a full ten minutes, interlaced with 'What a load of absolute fucking rubbish.' As the week progressed Ronnie's selection improved immensely. Both Dame Alicia Markova's production of the ballet *Les Sylphides* at the Royal Festival Hall and the Sir Henry Wood Promenade Concerts at the Royal Albert Hall moved Ronnie to light sobbing, which was his way of showing appreciation.

During these few days Ronnie came to the conclusion that I was deeply uneducated – 'a dim light shrouded in darkness'. Ronnie thought I was ignoring everything else apart from becoming a lawyer. I asked Ronnie to write out a short list of books in order to counteract this constant criticism. Never one to ignore such a challenge, Ronnie picked out some paper and quite spontaneously wrote the following:

Ancilla to the Pre-Socratic Philosophers (Oxford. Blackwell 1956, Kathleen Freeman. Sophocles. Oedipus Rex, Oedipus at Colonus, Antigone (The Theban Plays), Penguins. Euripides The Bacchae. Aeschylus The Agammemnon. Plato The Symposium, The Republic, The Phaedrus, The Parmenides, The Laws. Aristotle a la carte. Dionysus the Areopagite, The Mystical Theology. Macmillan Co. trans. C.E. Rolt (Society for Promoting Christian Knowledge). (perhaps the shortest text to have had such enormous influence on the whole tradition of 'negative theology'). Plotinus a la carte. Spinoza Ethics. Selections to take of Berkeley, Hume, Locke, Hobbes, Machiavelli The Prince. Kant, Critique of Pure Reason. Hegel The Phenomenology of Mind. Kierkegaard 1) The Concept of Dread 2) Either/or 3) The Sickness unto Death. Nietzsche Thus Spake Zarathustra, The Anti-Christ. Leo Chestov or Shestov In Jobs Balances. Pascal Pensees.

Before Jutta and the children returned, Detective Inspector Lee, who had investigated one of the largest conspiracies to manufacture and supply LSD in Great Britain (codename 'Operation Julie') paid Ronnie a 'social visit' at Eton Road. During the course of their investigation, the police had made several arrests, including a close associate of Ronnie's – David Solomon – who was eventually given a ten-year prison stretch.

Lee came round to Eton Road 'out of curiosity'. He wanted to inform Ronnie, in the presence of another absolved suspect, the psychologist Steve Abrahams, that for some time during the early part of the international enquiries, Ronnie and Steve had been major suspects, but that there had come a point during Lee's investigations when the manufacturing plant (a farm in Wales) and the international distribution of the drug in vast quantities could no longer be associated with either Ronnie or Steve.

The evening was completely bizarre. Ronnie, Steve and I had waited, in trepidation, for Lee and his sergeant to arrive at seven o'clock in the evening. They arrived about three hours late. Paranoia was the order of the day. The drink began to flow as the intricacies of Operation Julie laid out from Inspector Lee's side and the psycho-analytical theories behind the use of LSD from Ronnie's. At one point Lee asked Ronnie what he meant by the word 'ego'. Ronnie began a speech/soliloquy with the preamble 'Well', (long, long pause) 'there are twenty-seven definitions of "ego".' Steve and I relaxed, knowing that we would not be on the receiving end of a loaded question for at least half an hour. By six o'clock in the morning, the strain was beginning to be felt, particularly by Ronnie, who insisted in lying flat out on the floor doing breathing exercises after audibly throwing up in the upstairs toilet *circa* 4 a.m.

Lee and his sergeant got the hint that the three of us were dead beat, and they finally left to go their own ways. The whole experience of Operation Julie had somehow changed Lee's perspective on the world. He had 'banged up the villains', men he regarded as exceptionally intelligent, but after careful reflection, he decided to leave the police force for good. Inspector Lee said that he was going to write about it all, and he did; *Operation Julie* was later adapted for television.

Although *Do You Love Me?* was not a resounding success as a book or as a staged performance, it created sufficient momentum for Ronnie to make a foray into the world of entertainment. Two musicians and producers, Ken Howard and Alan Blaikely, came to Eton Road during the afternoon of Saturday 24 September 1977. The idea being bartered around was a serialized TV show or musical of some kind. Ronnie, being imbued with implantation and birth, suggested a sort of ballet involving a dance of the spermatozoa racing and fighting to fertilize the egg. He enthused about the possible chaos and competition, the fight and struggle and finally 'the bliss of implantation'. His idea was to have a whole musical about sex, conception, fertilization, prenatal environment, early childhood, puberty, adolescence, maturity, old age and death wrapped up into a musical. As the day wore on it became clear that Ken and Alan were not too impressed with Ronnie's idea – nor was Ronnie taken by the sample of music they had brought round. None the less the following weeks resulted in a growing friendship and mutual respect between Alan, Ken and Ronnie. The objective of their collaboration was to find some common ground which would combine their music with Ronnie's words, and the end product of these creative forces was an LP called *Life Before Death*. It was released in 1978, and featured Ronnie reading and singing his words to the background of Ken and Alan's music.

Ronnie had at one stage taken voice lessons from Georges Cunelli, the world-renowned singing teacher described as 'the pioneer of the logical approach to vocal problems'. Despite what many people thought of Ronnie's often sloppy public speaking, he could deliver a poem with all the trained professionalism of a seasoned actor. He maintained a habit throughout his adult life of reading aloud to his friends and acquaintances from his works and the writings of others. He enjoyed reading and engaging other people's attention in what he and others had to say; when he was on form, he was a delight to experience. During an intense poetry phase in 1978, there was one poem he performed again and again. At one stage it seemed as if he had little on his mind besides that poem: 'The Windhover: To Christ Our Lord' by Gerard Manley Hopkins. If Ronnie read that poem out once, he read it a hundred times – sober, drunk, tired, exhilarated. To him, 'The Windhover' was poetry of a higher order.

1978 was, therefore, essentially a continuation of Ronnie's multifarious activities during 1976 and 1977. *Conversations with Children* was due to be published in June, by which time the final recording of *Life Before Death* was made. The work in hand was 'The Politics of Birth', never to be published, a second volume of *Conversations with Children*, which was only published outside the UK, and the writing of a collection of thirty-nine sonnets and adages. But before Ronnie settled down to what was beginning to shape up into a relatively hassle-free year, fate dealt him another blow. At 5.15 p.m., the exact time of his birth, on Thursday 21 April, in Ward 7 of the Psychogeriatric Unit of Leverndale Hospital, Glasgow, Ronnie's father David died, aged 85. Ronnie wrote in his diary:

I feel that now I'm the children's grandad and dad, rolled, as it were into one. The dead live through us. I feel in a way, his representative, in a way I never did as far as I remember, while he was alive. I often wondered how I would react to his death. One of the surprises is that I hadn't realized the extent to which I have incorporated him. I don't mind. I'm glad. I have feared, loathed and despised him. But, especially in the last ten years I have come to love, respect, admire and honour him. I feel very sorry for the travail he has had to undergo, but he seldom entirely lost his sense of humour, and then he could be awful. But I can never remember him being spiteful (except once maybe), and not revengeful. He was not a perfect saint, I don't think, but he was basically a holy man, although he would have been very embarrassed had he thought I held such an opinion of him.

CHAPTER NINETEEN

The Warrior Trip

The year 1978 saw the beginning of the end of Ronnie's relationship with the Philadelphia Association. Despite the concerted front publicly presented by Ronnie, Hugh Crawford, John Heaton, Francis Huxley and Leon Redler, the seeds that would result in Ronnie losing control of the PA three years later were already being sown. There were several active households in operation at the time: the three houses collectively referred to as the Archway Community (135 Tollington Park, 95 Mayfield Road, 74 Portland Road — number 60 was used for administrative purposes), The Grove, Ascott Park and Crychell Cottage; none of these was under Ronnie's direct authority. Hugh Crawford was in charge of the houses in Portland Road, Ascott Park and Crychell Cottage, all of which he either owned or was the principal tenant. Leon Redler was effectively running the Archway Community. A 'sub' PA group, of which Robin Cooper,* Chris Oakley, Haya Oakley and Mike Thompson formed a part, was doing much of the work, often to Ronnie's scathing sarcasm. Weekly PA meetings were held at Eton Road, but Ronnie's involvement in the PA was becoming more and more supervisory in nature. After many years of dedicated work provided without formal or regular payment, Ronnie felt entitled to disengage himself from the day-to-day hassle of the PA households. He took frequent holidays and trips abroad: during 1978 he went skiing with his family in Davos over Easter, held rebirthing workshops with Jutta in Brazil in May, travelled to Greece in the summer and booked another skiing holiday before Christmas. It was against this background

* Robin Cooper is now one of the leading members of the Philadelphia Association.

that an event was organized which contributed to the irreversible division within the PA.

Apart from Ronnie's interest in poetry his main intellectual pre-occupation during 1978 was to do with birth and rebirth. In July 1978 he published a long article, 'Existential Topology', in which he gave 'Special Thanks to Winnicott', in a 'Birth and Rebirth' issue of the magazine, *Self and Society*. On 17 August a flysheet proclaimed that the 'Philadelphia Association presents An Encounter with Carl Rogers and R.D. Laing and others at an all-day workshop at the Grand Ball-room' of the London Hilton Hotel in Mayfair (admission £10). This was intended to be a major money-spinning, rebirthing extravaganza. Unfortunately, as many suspected, the venue was somewhat ambitious for its intended purpose. The grand ballroom of the Hilton Hotel was capable of accommodating 800 people but only 270 tickets were sold – barely enough to cover the administration and booking costs. Carl Rogers, a famous therapeutic figure in the States, had been persuaded to 'invest' $1,300 up-front. Afterwards he wrote a polite but demand-ing letter to Mike Thompson, the PA secretary, requesting the return of his advance. His request was refused with equal diplomacy. The idea of rebirthing by numbers in the grand ballroom of the Hilton Hotel proved too much for some of the PA, particularly Haya and Chris Oakley. From that point Ronnie's control over the PA became increasingly tenuous.

Ten days after the Hilton fiasco Ronnie gathered his rebirthing team in one of the large rooms at Eton Road to sharpen up their act. The team on this day consisted of Arthur Balaskas, two extremely amiable physical instructors, John Stirk and Peter Walker, Jutta and, for the first time, myself.

To start the meeting, a discussion took place in Ronnie's room for an hour or so, during which he expounded his theory behind the thera-peutic value of rebirthing: within each person's muscular system there are locked up countless experiences and feelings of fear, pain, de-spair, hatred, sorrow and pity. By undergoing a reconstructed birthing experience, with human beings as the simulated womb, closing up tight, a person could fight 'free' of the enclosure and by so doing, experi-ence 'not exclusively a rebirth scenario but more a physical realiza-tion of one's existential impasse'.

This rebirthing became an important part of Ronnie's life. Frequent workshops took place in the church hall across the road and Ronnie's team developed a cohesiveness only partly attributable to the rebirthing sessions. Eton Road became the centre for PA meetings, occasional rebirths in the consulting room, dinner parties, gloriously outrageous sing-songs round the piano, supervision sessions – all pervaded by a *joie de vivre*. Ronnie's work, his family life and social life became increasingly part of one scene. In the midst of all this, Ronnie continued with his main occupation: trying to square the notion of living the life of a king with the income of a poet.

By late 1978 Ronnie was concentrating on a wide variety of issues, none of which had any direct concern with psychiatry. The LP *Life Before Death* received scant attention. *The Observer, Music Week, National Student, Gay News* and Ronnie's local newspaper, *The Hampstead and Highgate Express*, were among the few periodicals that found space for Ronnie's latest venture. A brief interview on Michael Parkinson's television show on 27 September failed to contribute to the LP's success. *The Observer* made a gallant attempt to describe its contents:

Each poem has been treated very individually by Howard and Blaikely, employing a wide range of musical idioms, instruments and top musicians. There are rock tracks, heavy and sweet; classical guitar; harmonica; Creole-style jazz trumpet; softly swinging clarinet; and a Brecht/Weill pastiche evoking the image of Laing as Expressionist cabaret star.

With hindsight it is easy to realize that by the late seventies Ronnie was becoming more and more marginalized. Since returning from India each of his works had achieved a certain amount of success but the sales of his books were declining in tandem with the interest in R.D. Laing. Had *The Facts of Life, Do You Love Me?, Conversations with Children* and *Life Before Death* been the work of a young aspiring writer/poet/musician, the sales would have seemed very healthy. But for R.D. Laing, used to selling books by the hundreds of thousands, the public's reaction to his post-1972 creativity was slowly but surely undermining his confidence and financial solvency. Ronnie was now accustomed to spending relatively large amounts of money. He owned an enormous house, enjoyed travelling and eating out, had seven children, three of whom were still at school, and was living in chic middle-class comfort. Sooner or later the growing differential between income and outgoings would become too acute to avoid. Ronnie knew this, as did others. But he was not destined to zoom suddenly back on to centre stage. Despite the unremitting financial pressures, he was adamant that he would finish *Sonnets* before anything else, knowing that no matter how good others might consider his poetry to be, there was no hope of the book making serious inroads to his ever-present overdraft. The cumulative effect of these worries was very depressing. A small entry in his diary, dated Thursday 2 November 1978, indicates his state of mind: 'October 7th. was my 51st. birthday. I haven't felt so old since I was 21.'

'The Politics of Birth' was gathering more and more dust. Ronnie was aware of the female hostility surrounding his involvement in the natural birth scene. He did not really have much to add to Leboyer, Kitzinger, Odent or Janet Balaskas. Besides, there was little interest from publishers – a book by R.D. Laing was no longer a guarantee for the recovery of any advance. Ronnie started to turn his attention to two other books, a book of memoirs and a disciplined analysis of the relationship between experience and science. The former would make money, the latter would regain some of the credibility that had drifted away over the years. Ronnie realized another fight was on, and this time the stakes were very high. Without a major success of some kind in the near future he knew his life, his house, his marriage and his own health would gradually but inevitably fall apart.

During the late seventies, Ronnie's participation at a conference aroused less and less interest. He was no longer the star attraction delivering the 'key-note' speech, and the conferences were becoming more and more fringe in nature. But there was still fun to be had. In September 1978 he attended a conference in Sheffield. The subject was the 'catastrophe theory', which purported to provide a mathematical model of events in a wide-ranging sphere of human life. The practical function of the theory was to predict a sudden and violent change in personal and interpersonal behaviour. One speaker, who applied the theory to manic depressives, was a civil servant working with Home Office psychologists on the theory's potential application to prison riots such as those brought on by the experiences in Gartree Prison in 1972 and 1973. Professor Gordon Pask, an extraordinary character resplendent in a mauve and black silk-lined cape, explained to a stunned audience his theories of 'essential and non-essential bifurcations' by leaping up and down from a table while drawing circles in the air with his hands. Ronnie's own impromptu talk went down like a lead balloon. The audience expected a catastrophe model to be applied to schizophrenia. Ronnie explained, with some force, that they did not know what they were talking about.

Ronnie knew how to enjoy himself at such events: deliver a controversial speech, field a few questions, head straight to the bar and get loaded. That night Ronnie, Gordon Pask and I got totally inebriated while intermittently ranting and raving about the barefaced cheek of the Home Office coming to a medical/mathematical conference in order to find out what they could to assist them in the control of prison inmates. At least Ronnie had met a soul mate in Gordon Pask – his bifurcation talk stayed in Ronnie's mind for many years.

1979 was tedious and unsuccessful for Ronnie. As if to emphasize his waning success, Joe Berke and Mary Barnes had a great revival when David Edgar's adaptation of their book was performed at the Royal Court on 10 January. Ronnie, meanwhile, was attending a conference in honour of Dr E.F. Schumacher (author of *Small is Beautiful*, 1973) who had died the previous year. Also lecturing at this conference was Amory Lovins (on a publicity tour for his book *Soft Energy Paths*) and the celebrated Ivan Illich. Ronnie delivered an intense speech on the 'Ecology of Mind', whose central theme was that 'disordered minds produce disordered environments and disordered environments produce disordered minds'.

Ronnie continued to flirt with the growing 'green consciousness'. In April he participated in the 'World Symposium on Humanity', based simultaneously in Los Angeles, Toronto and the Wembley Conference Centre in London. The primary object of this world gathering was to 'save the world'. There were contributions from Allen Ginsberg, Carl Rogers, Marshall McLuhan, Fritjof Capra and many others. Ronnie realized that he was way down the pecking order. The publicity brochure did not even list him as a 'secondary speaker'. It was time to concentrate on 'getting back in there'.

Throughout the previous year, Ronnie had been immersed in poetry. Perhaps in accepting that *Do You Love Me?* fell short of the mark, he wanted to let the world know that he was capable of writing decent, structured, disciplined poetry. He had been encouraged by the publication in *The Times Literary Supplement*, July 1977, of three of his early poems.

Sonnets was published in 1979. Each of the thirty-nine poems has its own small history, and provides an insight into Ronnie's state of mind and concerns at the time he wrote it. Although the book's publication met with an almost deathly silence, and in some cases provided more ammunition to old foes, Ronnie was delighted with the critical acclaim it did receive. It created another series of talks, another circuit to join in on, something new.

Following its publication, Ronnie settled down to produce the book intended to re-establish some of the intellectual credibility he knew he had lost over the years. Originally entitled 'Testament of Experience,' and published in 1982 as *The Voice of Experience*, this book was written and rewritten for nearly three years. All hopes that *The Voice of Experience* would catapult Ronnie back to centre stage were misguided. By the late seventies, Ronnie had sunk into an obscurity from which *The Voice of Experience* was not going to rescue him. In the meantime his concern with rebirthing continued, as did his heavy drinking.

In July 1979 Ronnie considered the rebirthing team good enough to take on the road to Geneva. By now the team was kitted out in pastel coloured track-suits, members were fairly fit and healthy and presented quite a sharp image. Many practice sessions had taken place in the All Saints Church hall across the road from Eton Road (with various degrees of success). The team's repertoire had been extended to include various forms of encounter therapy including 'body sculpture' (a game whereby one person directed another into a posture designed at the other's whim, often to hilarious effect); 'the gauntlet' (in which an individual would walk between two lines of people to the spontaneous reactions of the others, ranging from boos and hisses to cheers and whooping); 'trust games' (a person closed her eyes and fell forwards and backwards, relying on those in front and behind to prevent her from falling; another game entailed being thrown in the air and caught by the others); 'bustling' (participants were told to walk amongst each other as if caught in a city rush-hour) – all of which was the warm-up prior to the rebirthing sessions themselves. It was a tough way to earn a few quid.

The visit to Geneva did not get off to a good start. A peculiar and sometimes annoying aspect of Ronnie's personality was his obvious need to be always the centre of attention. If someone else took centre stage, even in a relatively informal situation, Ronnie would, at some stage, 'let them have it'. The 'Geneva team', comprising Arthur Balaskas, Mel (Arthur's sister, who had married Francis Huxley), Steve Gans (a PA therapist and philosopher), Dodo Von Grieff (a German friend of Jutta's who had also stayed at Kingsley Hall during the early days), Jutta, Peter Walker, Johnny Stirk, Paul Zeal, Leon Redler, Ronnie and me, was held up at Gatwick Airport. 'Who the fuck suggested Gatwick, why aren't we at Heathrow?' Ronnie growled. There was a faint hint of danger in the air.

The team arrived in Geneva on a Saturday night. The organizers had laid on a meal, and members of the PA were invited to make speeches afterwards. Leon Redler, Paul Zeal and Steve Gans each took the microphone in turn and made impromptu pleas on behalf of the PA. Ronnie was neither pleased nor impressed. He thought the speeches were pretty awful and during an intense debriefing held in the basement of the hotel, he emotionally brutalized the speakers with uninhibited venom. One of his favoured means of humiliation was the imitation of another: body language, subtle intonation and all. He had the ability to mirror another person with the skill of a professional mimic. To be on the receiving end of a performance of this type was devastating, and Ronnie was ruthless that night. However throughout Sunday and Monday morning the workshops went down quite well and the team returned exhausted late on Monday evening to 'carve up the dosh'. Understandably, things were never quite the same after Geneva. A large workshop was conducted in a four-star hotel in Cambridge and a business associate of Ronnie's, Theo Knippenberg, funded the filming of these activities in the Shepperton studios outside London. But it was clear that the standard of what was being done was not sufficient to gain any commercial interest. One by one, the group drifted away or lost interest. It was fun while it lasted.

The dawn of the new decade, 1980, held no promises on the horizon. Ronnie had had no real success since *Knots* and he knew it. *Knots* had sold hundreds of thousands of copies all over the world, had been adapted for the radio, the stage and television. It was now relatively big news for me to report going to see *Est-ce Que Tu M'aimes?* at the Théâtre Marie Stuart in Paris. Throughout 1980 Ronnie worked on *The Voice of Experience* and read his poetry to relatively small audiences. R.D. Laing became more and more obscure. It is quite likely that for the first time in his life since 1962 Ronnie did not read a significant piece about himself in the press or see himself on the television for a whole year. A long-time friend and editor of *New Departures*, Michael Horovitz,* managed to inform the increasingly uninterested world of the activities of R.D. Laing in a letter to the *Sunday Times* in June 1980. Horovitz was responding to a suggestion that nothing like a French poetry festival could happen in this country:

> It may or may not interest your ill-informed commentator to know that last weekend in the 3 Horseshoes Pub, Hampstead, I presented American, Canadian and British poets to an enormously responsive crowd....
>
> On Sunday, July 20, Live New Departures continues the 'World's Best Jam' series at Ronnie Scott's club, Soho, with concerted articulations by R.D. Laing, Jeff Nuttall, woman poets, Lol Coxhill and myself, plus Stan Tracey's beautifully word-inflected jazz extensions.

One of most important events in Ronnie's life in 1979 was the permanent replacement of his secretary by a woman from New Zealand — Marguerite Romayne-Kendon — for it was with Marguerite that Ronnie would spend the last few years of his life. The following year Ronnie saw many friends and other people he felt attached to pass away. He wrote in his diary on 3 August, 'Sartre died two/three months ago, then Roland Barthes, yesterday Hugh Crawford. Peter Sellers and Ken Tynan.' The next month he added the name of Franco Basaglia. Before the year was out there were others to mention: David Mercer, Jesse Watkins (the sculptor who was the subject of 'A Ten-Day Voyage' in *The Politics of Experience and The Bird of Paradise*), Steve McQueen, John Lennon. Of 1980 Ronnie wrote, 'death has had a good harvest this year'.

Hugh Crawford's death was not only a great loss to Ronnie personally but also to the PA. With Crawford went three PA establishments, 74 Portland Place, 20 Portland Place and Ascot Farm, leaving only Mayfield Road and The Grove operational, the trio of households referred to as the Archway Community having been closed down by January 1980. The PA was falling apart, and so was Ronnie.

* See Michael Horovitz's obituary of R.D. Laing in the *Independent*, 2 September 1989, for further details of their relationship.

In September 1980 Ronnie attended a three-week conference at the Monasterio de Piedra, a converted twelfth-century monastery, near Saragossa in Spain. For this marathon event Ronnie made a concerted effort to pull himself together and impressed the distinguished guests including Stan Grof, Jean Houston, Rollo May and Fritjof Capra,* who was writing a book called *The Turning Point*. Also present was an American psychologist, Roberta Russell,+ who met Ronnie for the first time. Many of the PA crowd were there including Arthur Balaskas who was becoming more and more involved in Ronnie's personal life. Although Balaskas was at no stage a formal member of the Philadelphia Association he was, none the less, very much part of the PA scene.

Throughout the 1980s, Jutta and Ronnie's relationship became increasingly acrimonious, eventually culminating in their divorce in 1986. During the conference, Jutta had a short affair with a German lawyer. When Ronnie found out about this later in the year, all hell broke loose, releasing all the pain and humiliation of the spring of 1973. There were constant arguments and confrontations, compounded by Ronnie's drinking, which was reaching unbearable new heights.

On 19 April 1981 *The Observer* featured Ronnie in 'A Room of My Own', a series intended to give readers an insight into people through a look at the space in which they work. The article captured Ronnie in 'his' room at Eton Road almost to perfection: the glass coffee table, the art nouveau lamps, the 'character' chairs, the unused carved oak fireplace, the dark brown hessian wallpaper, the long oatmeal-coloured Conran sofa, the Steinway baby grand, the manuscripts, and the endless piles of books. Ronnie, however, was losing his touch both in private and in public. When asked about the Yoruba drum, a present from Leon Redler, he said: 'I have had it two years and haven't yet made its acquaintance. But I wouldn't want to offend it as I feel the spirit of someone's grandmother may be there.'

It was during this period immediately after the conference in Spain that some members of the PA remembered Ronnie as going 'over the

---

* See Fritjof Capra, *Uncommon Wisdom*, for further details of this meeting.
+ Roberta Russell and Ronnie agreed the following year to co-author a book provisionally entitled 'How to Take Your Own Advice'. Although this project was abandoned, Roberta Russell wrote about her subsequent relationship with Ronnie at great length in her book, *R.D. Laing and Me: Lessons in Love*, 1992.

top'. There were too many drunken occasions to list separately. Ronnie, feeling deeply betrayed, seemed to be constantly three sheets to the wind and worse still, increasingly aggressive. One crisis followed another until the PA decided enough was enough and on 26 May 1981 Haya Oakley sent a letter to Ronnie:

> On behalf of the members and associate members of the P.A. I would like formally to acknowledge your resignation from the day to day management of the organisation and all committees. We are very pleased you are not resigning your membership and would be honoured if you would accept the position of honorary consultant.

Ronnie's formal resignation was not tendered for another year. In the meantime the power struggle continued, which had the effect of creating two distinct factions within the PA. On the one hand there was Ronnie, Francis Huxley and Arthur Balaskas and on the other the rest of the PA headed by John Heaton, Haya and Chris Oakley. Leon Redler's was a difficult position, divided between his loyalty to the PA and his friendship with Ronnie, but he somehow managed to ride two horses. Ronnie was never going to win this battle. The gripes of the PA were not fanciful; Ronnie was fortunate to have survived for so long.

In September 1981 there was another major conference, 'The International Convention of Humanistic Psychology' in Leuven, Belgium. Once again Ronnie managed to pull himself together (at least for his speech), but once back at Eton Road the drinking intensified. Ronnie's drinking was now a source of concern to all who knew him, particularly those living or in close contact with him. He seemed to oscillate between abstinence and indulgence in equal measures. The completion of *The Voice of Experience* provided a much-needed respite from this self-destructiveness; the delivery of the manuscript an excuse to start another binge.

As if to compound the misery, the publication of *The Voice of Experience* was not an event heralded as the comeback of R.D. Laing. The book was carefully and painstakingly written and rewritten with the ultimate aim of setting out once and for all Ronnie's intellectual critique of scientific methodology, the psychological relevance of intrauterine experience and the application of phenomenological analysis to prenatal life. The subtitle, 'Experience, science and psychiatry', reveals the hopes Ronnie had for this book. But, in Ronnie's terminology, it 'bombed'. An unhelpful coincidence was the publication of Peter Sedgwick's book, *PsychoPolitics*, which contained two quasi-biographical chapters on Ronnie: 'The Radical Trip' and 'The Return to Psychiatry'. Ironically, *The Voice of Experience* was overshadowed by a book about its author.

The minutes of the 1982 Annual General Meeting of the Philadelphia Association quietly record the acceptance of Ronnie's resignation, although it was not until some time later – the end of 1983 – that Ronnie finally accepted defeat and disengaged himself from the activities of the PA.

In the meantime life went on in a constant blur. In November 1982 Ronnie accepted an invitation to spend a weekend in Dublin. The idea was to deliver a couple of talks at Sutton School and Trinity College. He also made a celebrated appearance on Gay Byrne's programme, 'The Late Late Show'. Ronnie came back from Ireland boasting about this performance. He had, it seemed, upset his television host (and quite a number of viewers) by virtue of his inebriated condition. Ronnie thought the whole thing was a bit of a giggle. The idea that some sections of the Irish were up in arms because he was drunk on a chat show brought tears of laughter to his eyes. When boarding the aeroplane on the way back to London he was greeted with a loud cheer, and a large whisky was anonymously sent over to his seat. He even took a certain amount of solace from the fact that for some days afterwards he received a new wave of fan mail; some of the letters ironically expressed the view that he had been treated rather harshly by his host. This was fodder for a new state of mind – the 'warrior trip'. For some time he had argued against those who expressed the view that his drinking was doing him no good whatsoever on the grounds that he was 'a Viking spirit'. To some extent he was led on by Arthur Balaskas and Francis Huxley, who were also caught up in Ronnie's new found identity. To those who merely passed through the doors of Eton Road during the early eighties the scene was depressing and verged on violent collapse. It was almost routine for dinner parties to end in drunken uproar. Ronnie had entered a wild, dangerous period.

During 1982 Ronnie continued to travel, see patients, attend conferences, join in the occasional jam session with his jazz mates, and make attempts at starting and finishing various books. On Sunday 30 October he was at the International Conference on Active Birth at the Wembley Conference Centre in London, where speakers included Peter Dunn, Faith Haddad, Caroline Flint, Melody Weng, Juliet Buckley, Beatrice Smulders, Penny Simkin, Michel Odent, Janet Balaskas, Yehudi Gordon and Sheila Kitzinger. He was still showing the *Birth* film and talking of 'The Politics of Birth', but was cutting less and less ice. It was time for new blood to fight the fight. R.D. Laing was considered a spent force in his own field of psychiatry, and in the contentious world of obstetrics and radical midwifery of the early 1980s he had no chance of establishing any real credibility unless he published a well-received book on the subject. And there was no chance of that happening.

It would be wrong to believe that at this point Ronnie was completely 'past it', despite his heavy drinking. Even at this late stage in his life he could engage in enjoyable and sophisticated conversation, derived a great deal of pleasure from playing the piano, and could still be great fun to be with. The only prerequisite was his sobriety. His charm and warmth were still capable of shining through to others as and when required. Laurie Taylor, Professor of Sociology at the University of York and a well-known sociologist, came to Eton Road to interview Ronnie for a full-page spread to be published in *The Times* on Monday 31 January 1983. Taylor had obviously heard all the stories:

> I was mildly surprised to see him looking so well. When I had mentioned my intended visit to some colleagues, they had made remarks along the lines of him being 'past it'. One had even said in a casual voice that he rather thought Laing was dead.... But a little of my surprise was also occasioned by the nature of Laing's good health. His build suggests pugilism rather than asceticism and he still retains the sort of Scots accent which you feel would ensure healthy respect in a crowded bar.

At the same time, during the latter part of 1983, Ronnie was constantly touring the world delivering lectures, doing workshops, giving interviews, reading and writing, although the novelty of travelling had long since passed. 'Travel narrows the mind,' he wrote his Aunt Ethel. He was tired, bored and depressed. From 21 to 30 January 1983, Ronnie did a 'world mini-tour', taking in the United States (Los Angeles and

Seattle), Norway, Finland (Helsinki and Ivalo), Sweden (Stockholm) and Denmark (Copenhagen). The nature of the talks Ronnie was giving at this time is probably best described by a long and wide-ranging interview in the May/June 1983 edition of *The Family Therapy Networker*, an American publication. It devoted its entire front page to an article by Richard Simon entitled 'Still R.D. Laing After All These Years':

> It is late January and R.D. Laing is sitting in a large New York City hotel ballroom in front of 60 attendees at this year's Eastern Regional Conference of the Association for Humanistic Psychology. At 55, Laing seems to have less the intense manner of an angry Jeremiah than that of an amiable English gentleman who, at the moment, is trying to cater for the needs of the unwieldy social organism before him. He is nothing if not painfully solicitous of his audience. Would they like the chairs to be rearranged in a circle? What would they like to talk about? Would they mind if he smoked?
>
> The first 20 minutes or so of the workshops are taken up with these matters, culminating in an elaborate discussion on the subject of breaks. How long should they last? When should they be taken? Is 90 minutes long enough for lunch?
>
> Eventually the audience manages to make it clear that there is nothing in particular they wish to hear – they just want to listen to R.D. Laing say whatever he wants to say. So R.D. Laing begins to do what he claims he typically does 'at these types of things' – he begins 'to voice my thoughts as they occur to me'.

Throughout the Richard Simon interview Ronnie was very guarded, an indication of a high degree of sobriety, but also an acceptance – to some extent – of how he was being perceived by others at the time: 'At the moment, people don't know what to make of me. They think I'm in some sort of semi-retirement or that I've bombed out. But that's not the case. I continue to write books. It's just that people in America no longer read them.'

In May Ronnie was again in the States, this time at the Ojai Foundation near Los Angeles, as a prelude to an extraordinary conference to follow the next year. The introduction to a long piece by Lewis MacAdams in *LA Weekly* (13–19 May 1983) gives an indication of how people in LA felt about Ronnie:

> I have never been in a room packed with as much pain as greeted R.D. Laing when the 55-year-old Scots-born psychiatrist walked into the Ojai Foundation seminar earlier this month. Usually, we think of saints as people who, like Mother Teresa in Calcutta or the Catholic Workers' Dorothy Day, house for the homeless, tend the sick, feed the hungry and comfort the dying. But in our time there may be another kind of saint – people like R.D.

Ronnie decided a visit to the Scottish island of Iona would do him some good, and while he was there he laid the ground for a further visit the following year. Iona had been close to his heart since his days at university and a visit to this small, barren island was always an emotional and spiritual event. His personal life was in tatters and by the end of 1983 he had, for all intents and purposes, split with Jutta and had formed a new relationship with a woman called Sue Sunkel, a German-born therapist who gave birth to Ronnie's ninth child and fifth son, Benjamin, on Saturday 15 September 1984. To complicate matters, Ronnie became involved with his secretary, Marguerite, who by the spring of 1985 was accompanying Ronnie abroad. Ronnie was well and truly into the 'warrior trip'.

Between 4 and 6 May 1984 Ronnie attended the fourth annual Conference in the Humanities at the Fawcett Centre in Columbus, Ohio. The conference, 'Vision and Reality', organised by The Ohio State University, was intended to be international in scope, and focused on Orwell's vision of 1984 and its implications for life in the present day and age.

Another conference had begun at the Ojai Foundation, in California, but Ronnie was not due to deliver his speech until the evening of 23 May. Ronnie's participation at the Ojai Foundation's 'four week interdisciplinary program for professionals and students in the humanities and sciences and those concerned with the investigation of mind and spirituality' reverberated not only throughout California but found its way into the gossip columns of the London *Evening Standard* and the satirical magazine *Private Eye*. Entitled 'Awakening the Dream: The Way of the Warrior', the conference was organized by a remarkable woman, Joan Halifax, the author of *Shamanic Voices, Shaman, the Wounder Healer*, and co-author of *The Human Encounter with Death*. The other co-leader, besides Joan Halifax and Ronnie, was Harley Swiftdeer, described in the publicity brochure as 'a Metis medicine chief' with 'extraordinary knowledge of Native American medicine wheels and keys'. Swiftdeer's contribution promised to 'provide a basis for our understanding of the relationship between all sacred systems'. Also giving lectures and workshops were Bob Aubrey (an instructor in Aikido who had, by chance, been my teacher in Paris), Lama Chakdud Tulku Rinpoche (recognized at the age of five as 'the incarnate lama of the Nyingmapa Monastery and College of Tibet') and Francis Huxley. Contributors included Don Jose Matsuwa, 'a 105 year old traditional Huichol shaman of Mexico' and Seung Sahn Soen Sa Nim, a Zen Master 'renowned for his presence during dharma combat' and more usually known as 'The Ten Thousand Cart Monk'. An article by Gregg Kilday in a local paper described the setting as 'a sleepy agricultural community 80 miles north of Los Angeles where Frank Capra's 1937 adaptation of James Hilton's novel Lost Horizon was filmed'.

Ronnie's reputation had, of course, preceded him. The local shop, 'The Wild Store', was selling tapes of talks he had delivered there the previous year, 'The Politics of Knots and Thorns'. In addition, partly by virtue of the publicity he had received the previous year and partly because he was the author of *The Politics of Experience*, Ronnie managed to secure centre stage. Readers of a review of this conference were reminded that in 1970, car stickers declaring 'I'M MAD ABOUT R.D. LAING' were being sold in France.

It became clear from an early stage of the conference that Ronnie was playing games. Joan Halifax and Swiftdeer began to refer to Ronnie as their 'Heyeohkah' (trickster). Francis Huxley remembered the 'main event' of the conference well. There came a time when the talking had to come to an end and for 'the real stuff' to commence. Participants were instructed that there was a 'free-for-all', during which any one person could attack another without warning. Ronnie was bored with the whole scene and retired to a local bar to have a few drinks. Having forgotten what was afoot he became increasingly inebriated and thought fit to start howling – loudly – at the moon from inside this bar. An attendee, sober as a judge, was on the hunt for Ronnie, to attack him as instructed. To that end he was carrying a pickaxe of the type carried by serious mountaineers. In due course he found Ronnie in the bar, howling. Without warning, he pounced and began delivering fairly serious blows to Ronnie's head and body with the flat side of the spade-like end of his pickaxe. He then insisted that Ronnie should 'do him over' and the two went outside. Unfortunately Ronnie was not up to the job and the blows that he delivered failed to make an impression on his opponent, who was feeling extremely disappointed at the sloppy treatment he was receiving. The assailant launched into a fresh attack which resulted in Ronnie lying on the ground facing an extremely angry young man who threatened to stick the pickaxe through his testicles unless he immediately 'renounced the devil forever'. According to Francis, Ronnie had no hesitation in acceding to this demand before making his escape and recovering his composure. The next morning, much to everyone's admiration, he delivered an impassioned speech on the subject of contrition.

Ronnie returned to London and recorded in his diary: 'enjoyable week at the Ojai foundation'.

Ronnie's warrior fantasies were now being played out more and more in public. Encouraged by the possibility of writing another never-to-be-completed book, 'The Way of the Warrior', with Bob Aubrey, he was living life with the brakes off. It was no great surprise to me (at this stage I was practising as a criminal barrister) when I was contacted in the early hours of 18 September 1984 by the Police Inspector at the Hampstead police station, who informed me that Dr Laing had been arrested and that I had been requested 'as R.D. Laing's lawyer' to attend the police station at once.

I was told the story by the duty Inspector upon my arrival: Ronnie had been passing a Bhagwan Shree Rajneesh Centre in England's Lane, Hampstead, round the corner from Eton Road at about 11.30 p.m. Upon passing the Rajneesh place he had, for no apparent reason, thrown a full bottle of wine through the window and sat down on the pavement outside muttering obscenities about 'the orange wankers'. He was duly arrested and taken to Hampstead Police Station, very drunk. At the station he was asked to empty his pockets and a brown substance – 'presumed to be cannabis' was discovered. When asked why he had thrown the bottle through the window he had said 'for spiritual reasons'.

While Ronnie was sleeping in the cells, a debate was going on as to whether he should be charged, and if so, with what. I spoke with a Rajneesh lawyer over the telephone and it was agreed that if an undertaking was given that the damage to the window would be paid for, the Rajneesh lawyer would withdraw any charges. The lawyer also wanted an undertaking that Ronnie would pay them a 'social visit' with a view to their sorting out his obvious 'spiritual disturbances', an invitation that was politely declined on Ronnie's behalf. Further charges were to be considered by the police upon analysis of the brown substance.

A behind-the-scenes debate went on for some weeks before the police, having taken advice from the Director of Public Prosecutions, decided to charge Ronnie with possession of cannabis. An appointment was made for 8 o'clock in the evening and I agreed to accompany him as his lawyer. When I turned up at Eton Road at about 7.30 my heart sank. Ronnie was steaming drunk and looked awful. A ferocious row ensued between us as my immediate plan was to phone the police station, make some excuse, and cancel the appointment. Ronnie would have none of it. Despite my protestations Ronnie had a shower, put on a suit and tie, fumbled endlessly with his cuff-links, and we got a cab up Haverstock Hill to the police station.

Following the now routine argument with the cab driver as to whether he was to be paid cash or 'on account', we entered the police station. 'Once more into the breach,' I muttered, with a premonition that my career was about to come to an abrupt end. Ronnie paused and held my arm: 'Once more into the breach, *dear friends, once more*!' he said. The Inspector quickly picked up Ronnie's condition and stated that he felt deeply insulted that a doctor should turn up the worse for drink. By this time Ronnie was slouched up against a wall and giving about ten astounded police officers 'the evil eye'. Matters came to a head when the Inspector flatly refused to charge him, saying that there were too many legal complications in charging someone who was obviously drunk. Ronnie then shouted at the assembled crowd of police officers: 'Good! All I have to do is fucking stay drunk then!' A further argument followed during which the Inspector explained his powers of detention. I managed to make a diplomatic intervention and Ronnie was allowed to leave on the understanding that an appointment was to be made by telephone the next day, and if Dr Laing again turned up drunk he would be detained in the cells until he had sobered up.

I was furious with the stupidity of it all and told Ronnie to find another sucker for the next visit. As we walked down the road, Ronnie, well aware by now that I was none too pleased with his performance, gave me one of the few hugs I ever had out of my dad and said, 'Aw, come on.' My anger subsided and, like two eighteenth-century cavaliers, we laughed all the way to the nearest pub.

Shortly thereafter Ronnie paid another visit to Iona, the purpose of which was to establish a new organization, the 'Oran's Trust', later renamed 'Sanctuary'. Ronnie had assembled a new 'crew' consisting of a retired monk by the name of Kevin O'Sullivan, of whom Ronnie was very fond, Marguerite (later Ronnie's female companion), Bernard Spalding, a former patient and one of the few people who remained friends with Ronnie until the end, Steve Ticktin, a Canadian child psychiatrist, Elaine Zanger, Elke Gieiss, Kevin Rose, Rob Brown and Mina Balaskas. He was also accompanied by a small film crew.

Ronnie had high hopes of finding a base somewhere in Scotland – preferably on the west coast. He became aware of the island of Oronsay south of Iona and a boat was hired for the day so Ronnie and his entourage could view the island. As luck would have it, the sight that greeted the hung-over and freezing cold team was an estate agent's board declaring the island 'SOLD'. Unknown to Ronnie, two Americans had already purchased the island in May. Although the trip was a complete farce, a great deal of time and effort were afforded to the Oran's Trust/Sanctuary project, particularly by Kevin O'Sullivan, Bernard Spalding and Steve Ticktin.

The trip video was, in the main, excruciating. There were some beautiful shots of Iona and the Abbey and a few engaging moments of Ronnie in conversation with the Reverend Donald MacDonald. But the sight of Ronnie sitting in front of an audience that was cringing with embarrassment at his self-indulgent crying was too much to bear.

Ronnie's case was due to come up before the Hampstead magistrates on 27 November, the charge being that he was, on 17 September 1984, in possession of 6.98 grams of cannabis resin. Ronnie was boasting that he would beat the rap and intended to plead not guilty. I was horrified, admittedly for personal and professional reasons, at the idea of a full-blown trial, and persuaded a friend of mine – a senior and distinguished barrister, Peter Morrish, to attend a social meeting at my flat a few days before the hearing. Ronnie turned up in a foul mood. He was faced with three seasoned lawyers (myself, Peter and my girlfriend, Deborah Fosbrook) who were willing to spend several hours with him going over his defence to determine its credibility. After an entire evening of ferocious cross-examination Ronnie's 'defence' was torn to shreds, and he reluctantly agreed to 'go guilty', much to everyone's relief. On the condition that Ronnie would adhere to the legal formalities, Peter agreed to represent him at the hearing and persuaded the lay justices to impose a nominal sentence – a twelve-month conditional discharge. Even after the case Ronnie bemoaned the injustice of it all, telling anyone who would lend him an ear that he had received a suspended prison sentence instead of the conditional discharge which had, in fact, been imposed. He had been lucky. But his luck was running out.

By the end of the year Ronnie's behaviour was alienating almost everyone around him. On the rare occasions when he visited Eton Road he created mayhem, and by New Year's Eve of 1984, he wrote in his diary 'I have left Eton Road'. Ronnie's final chapter was about to begin.

CHAPTER TWENTY

Closing the Circle

Moving from Eton Road was no easy task. Although Ronnie had recorded in his diary that he had left Eton Road by the end of 1984, the truth was somewhat more complicated. He needed somewhere to stay, to see patients, to play the piano, to receive mail and, above all, an emotional base. For some time Marguerite's flat in Clifton Villas, Maida Vale provided a solution to the immediate problem of where to crash out. But trying to maintain some sort of professional stability in his life was not proving so easy. His latest book, *Wisdom, Madness and Folly*, an autobiographical work covering the first thirty years of his life, was about to be published by Macmillan. Ronnie had a lot riding on its success and was even contracted by the same publisher to deliver a second volume on the tenuous basis that the first would be a great success.

On 25 February 1985, the National Portrait Gallery of Scotland unveiled a portrait of Ronnie by the celebrated artist Vicky Crowe. Despite Ronnie's waywardness he was, and still is, part of the Scottish folklore. As though to confound his critics he was capable of impeccable social behaviour as and when he saw fit and, on this particular occasion, was well behaved, charming, courteous, engaging and went so far as to make sure that his daughter Fiona attended the ceremony as well as his old pal Johnny Duffy. Ronnie's wild temperament was controllable as long as he was sober, and this time he was.

A full-page interview by the Scottish journalist Kay Carmichael appeared in the *Glasgow Herald* and made only passing reference to the events in Iona the previous autumn, which Carmichael had witnessed firsthand. It concentrated instead on the human, Glaswegian side of R.D. Laing:

Listening to him talk about his childhood is painful. He acts out in front of you the terrible dilemma of the human being whose heart has never been satisfied, who has never felt totally loved, totally accepted, who knows that the time for experiencing that has passed, who understands why it hasn't happened, who would like to forgive his parents because in his head he knows that they were acting out their own dramas, but at the same time is still screaming for the unconditional love they couldn't give him. His anger is still raw.

This was the intention of *Wisdom, Madness and Folly* – to persuade others that Ronnie had been brought up in an emotional wilderness without love or affection from his parents, had spent a childhood subjected to physical violence and deprived of the company of other children. He told a story in *Wisdom, Madness and Folly* intended to support this view:

> When I was three I heard my father say to my mother: 'I'm going to beat him to an inch of his life this time.'
> I knew I was in for it.
> He beat me. As he did he began to 'literally' smash me to pieces.
> I knew there was nothing more to be done.
> I contracted to a point.
> There no one could get me.
> On the other side of that point was where I came from?
> After a while the coast was clear. The damage was not irreparable.'

Ronnie might have put the beating into context; if he was capable of remembering such detail at three years of age he might have informed his readers what he did to produce such violence (exaggerated or otherwise) from his otherwise placid and doting dad. Any punishment seems unjust without knowledge of the circumstances behind it. In any event the 'beatings' to which Ronnie was subjected probably occurred on no more than two isolated occasions during the whole of his childhood, as evidenced by a small passage in *Wisdom, Madness and Folly*: 'For most of the time (*except for one or two incidents*) . . . I was as free as a bird.' The private sentiments he felt towards his dad, quoted from his diary earlier, also indicate that ritualized beatings were extremely rare. Those who knew Ronnie's mother and father and the social context of Glasgow in the late 1920s and early 1930s would find this sort of chiding hard to swallow. Ronnie was an only child who received endless attention from both his parents, grandparents, aunts and uncles. Despite his parents' lower-middle-class standing they made sure – at great personal sacrifice – that 'wee Ronald' received the best education from the best schools, and privately financed his musical education from the age of seven. By the time he was nine he was regularly seen with his father on the Royal and Ancient Golf Club at Prestwick, Ayrshire. He also enjoyed a close musical relationship with David until the time he left home at the age of twenty-two. He bemoaned being told that his parents were Santa Claus at a time when most children of Govanhill would have been overjoyed at receiving a special treat, whether on Christmas or any other day. He attended Sunday school and won prizes for regular attendance and good behaviour. It was no wonder that more than one review criticized the book on the basis that Ronnie had little to complain about.

During the early part of 1985 there was talk of divorce, money and the children. A divorce, as any lawyer knows, is an extremely costly exercise. If you try to cut a cake in two invariably you are left with less than two halves. The emotional fall-out is usually so great that the earning capacity of one or both of the bread-winners is seriously undermined. And the whole messy affair, usually conducted in a deeply acrimonious and recriminating atmosphere, is invariably compounded by the involvement of numerous lawyers trained to behave in an adversarial manner.

Ronnie had high hopes that *Wisdom, Madness and Folly* would see him through. But that was not to be. Initially the book sold only a few hundred copies and even at the time of his death had only sold three thousand hardback copies in the UK. By Ronnie's standards it was a catastrophic financial disaster and forced him to devise some entrepreneurial activity that would save the day. He tried to venture into the publishing world with the launch of two 'newspapers' – the *Journal of Original Ideas* and the *Fleet Street Journal* although he had little to do with these papers other than writing an article about the topical miners' strike for the Italian daily newspaper *L'Unità*. The other enterprise he was trying to get off the ground was an Institute for Dream Research; it fizzled out when the General Medical Council took umbrage at an advertisement in a local newspaper which breached their rules concerning the promotion of medical activities by qualified doctors. Ronnie was turning into a running joke, now subjected to the same ridicule he was pouring on to the revised American text-book of psychiatric disorders (DSM III – *The Diagnostic and Statistical Manual of Mental Disorder*). A short piece in the *Observer* of 17 March by Peter Hillmore set the tone to which Ronnie was now becoming accustomed:

> 'Life, you see, is a sexually transmitted disease and there's a 100 per cent mortality rate'. If R.D. Laing had said that to me in the late Sixties/early Seventies, I would have immediately done two things: (1) I would have rushed away and told all my friends that the great guru had actually spoken to me, and (2) I would have pondered the meaning for ages and found deep significance in it.
>
> Tempus fugit. When R.D. Laing said it to me last week, two completely different reactions were provoked: (1) I recalled having seen it as a piece of graffiti on a lavatory wall some months previously, and (2) I got to thinking what exactly did it mean? I relegated it to the meaningless and ponderous statements such as 'Who digs deepest deepest digs' and 'Never look for apple blossom on a Cherry tree.' I also wondered which one of us had changed.

In March 1985 Professor Anthony Clare invited Ronnie to participate in his Radio 4 series, 'In the Psychiatrist's Chair'. Much to Clare's surprise Ronnie agreed to do so. The interview was recorded over many hours during late March and a heavily edited version was broadcast on Radio 4 on 14 July 1985. Clare had adopted a softer, more understanding approach to Ronnie since the days of *The Facts of Life* and even went so far as to describe *Wisdom, Madness and Folly* in *The Listener* as a 'remarkable' book. However, Ronnie made a serious mistake by 'confessing' to his state of mind at that time. When asked by Anthony Clare about his sanity Ronnie responded in the following terms:

The thing that I think has beset me most, in my own personal life, has really been depression.... I've been thinking that it might do me a lot of good just to write about so called 'heavy drinking' or alcoholism, and 'depression'.... I'm quite a typical type of crypto-psychomotor retardation depressive....

Both Ronnie and Anthony Clare felt that the interview had gone rather well and neither thought much more about it. Others, including the General Medical Council, had different views, as Ronnie was to find out over a year later. Ronnie had other matters on his mind, mainly of a financial nature.

Ronnie's financial safety net for many years was the international lecture circuit, particularly in the States and Canada. During 1985 he once again embarked on a world mini-tour lecturing in Scandinavia (Horsholm and Alborg), Dublin, Seattle, Vancouver, Vienna, Baden, Budapest and Athens, in between spending some time with David and Sarah Salmon in Devon. During his visit to Vancouver he stayed with a psychologist friend, Andrew Feldmar, and he revisited Andrew and his family each successive year until June 1989. During those visits a film crew recorded some of the workshops and lectures and a heavily edited programme, 'Did You Used To Be R.D. Laing?'), was eventually broadcast late at night on Channel 4 in the UK shortly after his death.

This living-out-of-a-suitcase was extremely tiring for Ronnie. The excitement of the 'big conference' had long since gone and was now replaced by the tedium of booking in and out of hotels, listening to 'numbers' he had heard a hundred times before and giving uninspired talks to people who had only vague memories of R.D. Laing. One conference, 'The Evolution of Psychotherapy', in Phoenix, Arizona in December of 1985, proved the exception to the increasingly routine and boring merry-go-round of the international lecture circuit. The conference, organized by Jeffrey Zeig, the director of Phoenix's Milton H. Erickson Foundation, marked the centenary of the establishment of Sigmund Freud's private practice in Vienna. Over 7,000 participants attended, all of whom were required to have a professional qualification of some kind or other. More than 3,000 people were turned away due to lack of space. Anybody who was somebody in the field of psychotherapy was there.

Ronnie was on form during this filmed conference and although

Virginia Satir proved to be the main attraction he was given one of the longest individual reviews in *The New York Times*:

> R.D. Laing, the British psychiatrist whose methods owe much to such existential philosophers as Sartre, interviewed a paranoid woman from a Phoenix shelter for the homeless. The interview seemed to be no more than mere conversation. It began with the woman stiffly telling Dr. Laing of a grand conspiracy against her while their conversation was broadcast by closed-circuit television to a nearby audience of more than 1,000 therapists.
>
> By the end of the interview, Dr. Laing and the woman had achieved such a rapport that she seemed much less troubled and spontaneously offered to join him on the podium in the nearby lecture hall, where she answered questions with lucidity from the assembled therapists.
>
> The elusive nature of the therapeutic exchange was highlighted by the fact that some people in the audience maintained that nothing much had happened in the interview, while Dr Minuchin, the family therapist, rose from the audience to praise the interview as an example of the highest clinical art. Still others objected to Dr. Laing's explanation that it is as important just to be with someone in deep rapport as it is to try to change them. That event seemed emblematic of the vast differences in perspective that plague the field.

For posterity *Time* magazine recorded Jay Haley asking the participants, 'Why are you all here?', to which one of them replied, 'We want to see you all before you die'.

When Ronnie reappeared in London at the beginning of 1986 he was in for a shock. While he was in the States, the General Medical Council, a sub-committee of the Privy Council which has disciplinary powers over UK registered doctors, had written to him. The letter informed Ronnie that the General Medical Council had received a complaint from an individual who had gone to see him as a patient in autumn of 1983. Ronnie was alleged to have been under the influence of alcohol and to have 'abused and assaulted' the complainant. The statutory declaration, dated December 1985, specified two occasions in September and October of 1983 during which Ronnie had spent a few minutes with this American in his consulting rooms at Eton Road. He had then suggested that they go for a drink in a public house outside of which Ronnie was alleged to have said, 'I think this is one place I have never been thrown out of.' They had a drink together and left without incident. Subsequently, on 19 October, the complainant turned up for another consultation, but instead of being given the undivided attention of Dr Laing he found himself in the middle of an ongoing crisis involving a young man who was obviously in a very disturbed condition. The complainant informed the Council that he was invited to 'come and join the party' by Dr Laing, who had quite obviously 'been drinking heavily' but was 'well under control' and 'very pleasant and affable'. The drinking continued, and after an hour or so the complainant decided to leave. Before he did so a dispute arose over the non-payment of his last visit. Finally Ronnie demanded in 'a drunken rage' that he depart. As he did so, the complaint continued, 'Dr Laing slammed the glass panelled door on me, catching my elbow'. The General Medical Council's letter of 17 December informed Ronnie that these allegations raised a question of 'serious professional misconduct', and invited him to make representations to the Preliminary Proceedings Committee, which would be meeting on 15 January. The letter also informed Ronnie that a question arose as to whether his fitness to practise 'was seriously impaired by reason of misuse or abuse of alcohol' and asked him to furnish medical evidence of his fitness to practise.

Ronnie came round to take advice from me and I told him that the matter should be put in the hands of a trusted and capable solicitor straight away. Ronnie attended the offices of Bernie Simons in Covent Garden and provided a sworn statement denying the allegations, which was sent on to the Council. In the meantime the Preliminary Proceedings Committee met as scheduled on 15 January and wrote to Ronnie on 3 February with their decision. They had decided to put the matter into the hands of the Preliminary Screener for health cases, who in turn had asked the Registrar of the Council to invite Ronnie to be examined by two or more medical examiners of his choosing. Ronnie was quite adamant that if he was to be examined in any way whatsoever then he wished to reserve the right to have the doctors who examined him examined by doctors of his own choosing. Not surprisingly the Council wrote back explaining that 'the Health Committee Rules make no provision for one medical examiner selected in accordance with Rule 6(3) to comment upon the selection of another'. The Preliminary Screener was, however, 'pleased to note Dr Laing's agreement to be examined by medical examiners chosen by him in accordance with the Health Committee Rules'.

Ronnie was beginning to wake up to the fact that he was in deep trouble. The General Medical Council were serious, very serious. Ronnie decided to take them on and his solicitor wrote to the Council in March, nominating Professor Ivor Browne of Dublin University, Professor Morris Carstairs and Professor Anthony Clare. Unfortunately it did not occur to Ronnie to let his nominees know what he had done. Nor did it sink in that this 'local difficulty' would not 'disappear'. The Council reared its head again in May, by which time they had decided to appoint two of their own doctors to examine Ronnie's fitness to practise. Unknown to Ronnie the complainant had contacted the General Medical Council prior to the date of this letter, informing them that he no longer wished to pursue the matter and was formally withdrawing his complaint. The Council again wrote to Ronnie's solicitor in June, reminding him that investigations were proceeding, but made no reference to the fact that the original ground for the complaint had been formally withdrawn. By this stage the complainant decided to inform Ronnie himself that he had withdrawn all allegations, whereupon Ronnie's solicitor wrote to the Council 'expressing great surprise that the General Medical Council should wish to proceed with this matter in view of the fact that Mr. [B], the Complainant, has apparently withdrawn his complaint'. Ronnie felt they would get him any which way and proposed to his lawyer that he should resign as a registered medical practitioner if that would bring the matter to an end. He was, however, persuaded to hang on and see it through. By late August Ronnie received another letter from the Council. The Preliminary Screener had decided to refer the matter back to Preliminary Proceedings Committee – a move of some importance within its own dimensions, and one that was thought to be the beginning of the end of the affair.

However, on 1 September 1986 the Council wrote to Ronnie again. This time the goal-posts had been subtly moved. The Council had decided to pursue the issue of Ronnie's fitness to practise despite the withdrawal of the original complaint. They had two new leads to pursue: Ronnie's conviction at Hampstead Magistrates' Court in November 1984 and the July 1985 radio interview with Anthony Clare. Ronnie's solicitor was not gearing himself up for a major confrontation and wrote asking for further details. The Council responded in November 1986 in order to clarify 'some misunderstanding'. The issue was Dr Laing's fitness to practise – he was not being asked to respond to any 'allegations against him'. They forwarded a copy of the transcript of the Anthony Clare interview but regarding the drugs issue the General Medical Council could not 'disclose . . . the information forwarded in confidence by the Metropolitan Police concerning Dr Laing's conviction on 27th November 1984. However I am able to inform you that the information supplied by the police included details of the circumstances of Dr Laing's arrest and of his conviction'.

Ronnie had put the matter out of his mind once he became aware that the complaint had been withdrawn and by late 1986 he was living quietly in Burch House in Littleton, New Hampshire. The community, a residential community established by David Goldblatt, was based on the principles of the Philadelphia Association. Ronnie wondered whether he need ever return to all the hassle in the UK.

As fate would have it, Ronnie received word that his mother had died on Monday 10 November. The funeral was arranged for the Friday and the action moved to Glasgow. The entire family dropped everything – this was going to be an old-fashioned beano of the highest order. Ronnie flew in from the States, I left in the middle of a court case, Paul came in from his work on the oil-rigs, Aunt Ethel made the journey from Largs. Anne, Fiona, Karen and her husband Tommy prepared themselves for R.D.'s performance to reach new disgraceful heights and Donald MacDonald took on the role of presiding minister. Ronnie's old drinking mates, Johnny Duffy and Lenny Davidson, prepared themselves, for a long session. The boys had waited a long time for this one and by now the Glasgow Laings were seasoned mourners. Expectations were high that Ronnie was going to disgrace himself, possibly beyond redemption.

As expected, Ronnie quickly stole the show by booking into the bridal suite of the Central Hotel adjacent to Glasgow Central Railway Station. I arrived late on Thursday night to find Ronnie entertaining as if hosting a banquet; endless trays of food and alcohol were being brought into his suite, people were laughing and joking and Ronnie himself was in fine fettle. However, a ferocious row was brewing up over Donald MacDonald's concern for Ronnie's health. Ronnie was on the verge of throwing the reverend out. In order to defuse matters Ronnie suggested that Donald take me down to the chapel to view the body, and I reluctantly agreed. Some time later Donald and I reappeared with a rather embarrassing story. Donald MacDonald had taken the lid off the coffin for me to share my last moment with Amelia but due to our inebriated condition neither of us could get the lid back on again. The evening became more and more raucous until the assembled crowd went their separate ways. The last thing anyone could remember was the sight of Ronnie's seventy-five-year-old Aunt Ethel dancing the Gay Gordons with me down the hotel corridor. An old Scottish adage states: 'A Glasgow funeral is more fun than an Edinburgh wedding.' Damn right it is.

Amelia was buried the next day. The Reverend Donald MacDonald delivered a short but touching speech in a small church off Sauchiehall Street during the course of which Ronnie started to sob his heart out. Perhaps for the first time he realized the pain his mother had felt. Perhaps he also remembered the last communication between him and his mother some years previously, shortly after his father's death. Amelia had written to her only child stating that she never wanted to see him again, and asked Ronnie to promise that he would never contact her. He wrote back on a single piece of paper on which he had drawn a large heart enclosing the words 'I Promise'. His crying became so loud and seemingly uncontrollable that the others became slightly agitated especially as it was aggravating with the collective hangover. A Glaswegian voice was heard distinctly above Ronnie's uninhibited sorrow: 'Eh, d'you think Ronnie's just got hit wi' the hotel bill?'

Ronnie returned to the States to find out that the General Medical Council issue was still a live one and would not go away. The Council wrote again on 28 January, this time informing Ronnie that the Preliminary Screener had referred his case to the Health Committee (not to be confused with the Preliminary Proceedings Committee), which would adjudicate on 26 February 1987. Ronnie was given the opportunity to attend but, unwisely, decided not to. The Health Committee duly met and concluded that on the evidence before them (i.e., a withdrawn complaint, a spent conditional discharge for 6.98 grams of hashish and the transcript of a public interview with Professor Anthony Clare), Ronnie's fitness to continue in medical practice was questionable. The Council wrote to Ronnie's solicitor in March to inform him of the decision. Ronnie believed, in all naïvety, that if he sent the Council a couple of video recordings of recent speeches they would see fit to drop the matter. But by now the fight was going against Ronnie and on 31 March the Council wrote to New Hampshire with a deal. Ronnie was asked to fill in a form – an Application for Removal of Name from Register. The registrar of the General Medical Council wrote: 'The Preliminary Screener has asked me to point out that, if your name were to be so removed from the Register, no further action would be taken at the present time in relation to Council's inquiries into your fitness to practise.' Ronnie was none the less reminded that he could apply at some future date to have his name restored to the register. 'However, before any such application from you would be granted, you would be asked to satisfy the Council of your fitness to resume medical practice.'

Ronnie sent a handwritten note to his solicitor on 28 April 1987 from his new abode in The Naropa Institute in Boulder, Colorado, enclosing the signed application form and adding, 'I have no intention to practice [sic] medicine again, having thought about it for some while'.

The matter finally came to an end when the Council wrote back on 27 May 1987 confirming that the name R.D. Laing was removed from the Medical Register on 20 May and reminding Ronnie that he could reapply 'any time in the future'. The final screw was turned in the penultimate paragraph: 'the Council would wish to be satisfied of your fitness to resume medical practice before acceding to any such application, and it is likely that you would be asked to undergo medical examination in order to provide evidence of your fitness to resume practice'.

After nearly thirty years the Establishment had finally got him.

During the various talks, workshops, lectures and experiences of 1985–6 and in the aftermath of the disappointment of *Wisdom, Madness and Folly*, the separation from Jutta, the sale of Eton Road and the death of his mother in late 1986, an idea for another blockbuster formed in Ronnie's mind. He was now, perhaps understandably, becoming increasingly concerned with 'the love of lies and the lies of love'. Evidence of a typical workshop which served as a sounding board for the intended material of this new book is afforded by an advertisement of two Canadian workshops, 'Schizophrenia and the Family' and 'Sex, Deception and Jealousy'.

By December of 1986 Ronnie had completed the first raw draft of 'The Lies of Love – A Study of Sexual Jealousy and Deception', which was still being worked on at the time of his death. Ronnie had always been taken with the writings of Michel Foucault; *Madness and Civilization*, *The Order of Things*, *The Birth of the Clinic* and *The Archaeology of Knowledge* were intellectual landmarks to him. *The History of Sexuality* (1978) was a breath of fresh air to Ronnie, who often said that Foucault's power and talent was to separate people into those whose could understand and appreciate his works and those who believed he was nothing other than a shallow charlatan, bereft of logic and lacking credibility. Ronnie wanted to join in the conversation initiated by *The History of Sexuality*, and his interest in the prevailing attitude towards sex was heightened by Foucault's dying of AIDS at age 57, on 25 June 1984, amid rumours of his indulgence in sado-masochism.

Various projects in the pipeline had previously pre-empted a serious study of this nature, but the time was now right, particularly with the growing world-wide attention being given to sexual activity and the doomsday attitude to AIDS. It was also Ronnie's belief that 'The Lies of Love' would make him a belated fortune. His divorce from Jutta had been costly in both emotional and financial terms. He was approaching sixty with no property, an insecure future and, after all the settlements were made following the sale of Eton Road, he was left with only £100,000. Due to his insistence on maintaining the lifestyle to which he had become accustomed, the money was rapidly disappearing and he was now faced with the real and immediate prospect of being completely insolvent. There was absolutely no possibility of his taking a job of any description; the royalties from his fifteen previous books were minimal (about £15,000 per year), and he was totally uprooted. To write a serious, well-written, well-researched, and controversial book about sex and deception was one of his last hopes.

The early draft of 'The Lies of Love' was broken down into seven chapters: 'The Lies of Love: the past in the present', 'Sex, Sin and Semen', 'Sexual Jealousy and the eternal triangle', 'Sexual Simulation', 'You Hate Me? You Love Me?', 'Lies of Love: the present' and 'The Sexual Spell'. The preface expressed the hope that 'this book will be a consolation for those who have been wounded in love, and food for thought for those who casually, callously, or cruelly, wound or kill with poisoned lies of love, and of interest and entertainment to those who have no idea what it is about.'

The first chapter was intended to be a survey of the lies of love from the ancient writings of Ovid, Plato, Apollonius of Rhodes, Aeschylus, Sophocles, Euripides, Kramer and Sprenger (authors of the *Malleus Maleficarum*), Boccaccio and Spinoza from the Western tradition and the *Kama Sutra* of Vatsyayana in the Eastern. The book would be written from the viewpoint of a cynical twentieth-century philosopher: 'Homer knew all about it. There were no flies on Plato. The old Indians were shrewd. Apollonius is as modern as Noël Coward. Ovid is more modern than anyone. Boccaccio still sets the pace. None of the greats are out of date.'

An entire chapter was dedicated to the detail of the *Malleus Maleficarum* (a fifteenth-century 'textbook' for the investigation of witches), which Ronnie believed 'deeply affected European jurisprudence for nearly three centuries. It lay on the bench of every judge, on the bench of every magistrate.' Specific passages provided Ronnie with tremendous fun during his lectures and were intended to be the source of focused attention in 'The Lies of Love'. For example:

> witches themselves have often been seen lying on their backs in the fields or woods, naked up to the very navel, and it has been apparent from the disposition of those limbs and members which pertain to the venereal act and orgasm, as also from the agitation of their legs and thighs, that, all invisibly to the bystanders, they have been copulating with Incubus devils. . . .

Another short passage provided a novel explanation for a man's inability to ejaculate: 'when a member is in no way stirred, and can never perform the act of coition, this is a sign of frigidity in nature: but when it is stirred and becomes erect but yet cannot perform it is a sign of witchcraft'.

Ronnie trawled over the dynamics of jealousy quoting from Spinoza's *Ethics*: 'If any one imagines that the thing loved is joined to another than himself with the same or a faster bond than that which binds it to him, he will be affected with hatred towards the object loved, and envy towards the other.' He used the technique used in *Knots* and *Do You Love Me*. The following example is based on recollections of conversations with his own mother:

> *You believe me?*
> *You love me?*

Then believe me.
You don't love me.

You don't love anyone
and
No one loves you

Except me

It's only because
I love you
I'm telling you this

Believe me

Don't believe me
because I say so

Look into your heart of hearts
And you'll see
That everything I'm telling you is true

Believe me.

Throughout this manuscript it becomes clear that Ronnie's main preoccupation is the 'down' side of love: deception, jealousy and revenge, the latter of which was epitomized in a story which had recently been told to Ronnie. A couturière in Paris was having sex with three men: her 'lord and master', a poet and a rich boyfriend. Each of the sexual relationships were 'secrets' except to the extent that the poet and the boyfriend were aware that she was having sex with her 'lord and master'. Her 'most delicious moment of "revenge"' occurred

on one particular occasion after being fucked by the poet before lunch, and being fucked by the boy-friend after a delicious lunch that the poet couldn't afford, and the lord and master hadn't the sensibility for, flying into the latter's arms, and being squeezed deliciously by him, by the door of the white Rolls-Royce, held open by the chauffeur, about four-thirty in the afternoon before taking off from the City for an evening to his chateau, and feeling the spunk of the poet and the business man ooze from her vulva down her thighs, as he squeezed her, so deliciously, in his repulsive embrace, by the door of the white Rolls-Royce, held open by his chauffeur.

Another example concerns a husband who knew of his wife's affair with another man. He asked a female friend who knew what was going on: 'Why am I finding it so difficult? Am I jealous? Am I making a fuss about nothing? What is she doing? What is *he* doing?' His lady friend replied: 'I'll tell you what *he's* doing. *He's* fucking *you* up the *arse*! That's what he's doing!' The punchline of the story: 'In one blinding flash, he knew she was right. Within a few seconds his marriage had ended.' Many such stories were told in the same uncompromising style, presumably designed either to shock or amuse depending on one's personal level of irreverence.

Whether the book would have been a great success is impossible to say. One of Ronnie's literary agents in London refused to handle the manuscript and publishers were approached to no avail. In all likelihood 'The Lies of Love' would have received the same brutal treatment afforded to *Do You Love Me?* and *Wisdom, Madness and Folly*. Certainly the *Knots* formula had worn thin, as evidenced by the reaction to *Do You Love Me?*. Ronnie had set himself an extremely high standard of writing with *The Divided Self*, and he was to a large extent forever burdened with having written his best book first. It would have been by reference to his first published work that 'The Lies of Love' was judged. In that context, the odds were that as with all Ronnie's works published since 1972, it would have been either predominantly ignored or ridiculed.

One of Ronnie's last published articles was, appropriately, about 'God and Psychiatry'. *The Times Literary Supplement* published a relatively short but extremely lucid piece by Ronnie in May 1986. It began:

I am invited to write on God, from the point of view of a practising and theoretical psychiatrist. But we can't really discuss the subject sensibly unless we have at least some vague consensus about what we mean by 'God' and by 'psychiatry'. Let's take the easy one first. I am a negative theologian. I can define God only by what he is not. He is not any definition I can think of. He is neither male nor female, nor both, nor neither, nor neither neither. Similarly he is not named any name we care to give him, including 'Him'. At the same time, I believe in God, because I can't possibly see how a Being beyond all my imagination, concepts or visions of such Being-as-Such, cannot, must not be. For want of a better word, I believe in God.

Ronnie's attention to God seemed to have increased since his 1984 and 1985 visits to Iona. At the service arranged in the Glasgow Cathedral a few days after Ronnie's death, the Reverend Donald MacDonald went so far to say that during the conversations he and Ronnie had on these occasions Ronnie 'returned to the Church'. The truth of this is difficult to assess. Throughout 1986, for example, Ronnie lived the sort of life that had developed over the years: attending conferences on wide ranging subjects (e.g., 'World Peace and the Individual' in Philadelphia during March and the Paisley Writers' Festival in April), writing and drinking. Overtly he was much the same Ronnie as before. But he was sending out clear signals to his close family and old friends that he wanted to 'come home'. He more than toyed with the idea of living permanently in Scotland and his search for a sanctuary was as much for himself as for others. He had been revered in Scotland ever since achieving his fame in London. Despite his wayward reputation and the occasional drunken débâcle, the fact remained that his portrait hung in the Scottish National Portrait Gallery, he had strong familial ties and many long-standing friends, most of whom lived in and around the Glasgow area. Even as late as October 1987 the *Glasgow Herald* published a full-page spread on 'the many faces of R.D. Laing' to celebrate his forthcoming sixtieth birthday. It described him as 'the Glasgow guru – Scotland's finest intellectual', whose first book 'The Divided Self, represents a landmark in twentieth-century psychology', and portrayed a man with 'tireless energy and ability' who has 'suffered the indignity of becoming a climate of opinion, and survived'.

It must have seemed a clarion call to come home. Death did not seem so far away; on two occasions during the mid-eighties Ronnie suffered minor heart attacks. In addition, his rectum was emitting blood. David Cooper died in Paris in July 1986, having drunk himself to an early death at the age of fifty-five. There is nothing more unsettling than the death of one's peers. Ronnie knew he was getting nearer the top of the queue.

By the spring of 1987 Ronnie still had not found a permanent base.

He roamed the States and even visited Bali in the hope of finding somewhere to settle. The pressure to stabilize his life was heightened by the confirmation of Marguerite's pregnancy and the subsequent birth of his tenth child, Charles, on 6 January 1988. He was sixty years old, the father of a new-born baby, with no reliable income, no home, a serious drinking problem and a debilitating feeling of depression bordering on despair. 'The Lies of Love' was in a rut and no other book was inside waiting to burst forth into the world.

By the end of 1988, one small step had been taken on the long road back to stability: Ronnie had given up drinking entirely and had found a small flat in the quiet town of Going, Austria. When Bernard Spalding visited him there it was apparent that Ronnie had turned over a new leaf: he was happy, sober and prone to long walks in the Austrian countryside. In Going, he could focus on the painstaking progression of 'The Lies of Love' and coordinate a new project that had come into his life. Bob Mullan, a director and producer at Anglia Television, had suggested a biography of Ronnie. This proposal appeared to solve several problems at a stroke: there was the possibility of serious money, so the idea and hassle of getting together Volume II of *Wisdom, Madness and Folly* could be scrapped. In addition, the research for the biography would provide an excellent excuse for meeting up with old friends and close family (in particular with his Aunt Ethel) and reacquainting himself with the 'Glasgow scene'.

A lot of Ronnie's time during 1988–9 was taken up with Bob Mullan's book, which was abandoned after Ronnie's death. His university friends were contacted, interviews were conducted with a large number of people in Ronnie's life ranging from his immediate family to former university acquaintances and colleagues at the Tavistock including John Bowlby who was not surprised to hear that Ronnie 'had run aground'.

The last time I saw Ronnie alive was in November 1988 when he came to my wedding in London. He behaved himself and delivered an appropriately amusing speech from the high table. We still maintained the habit of having the occasional conversation over the phone no matter where he found himself. In July 1989 we spoke for the last time. He tried to persuade me to cooperate with Bob Mullan, something I was reluctant to do despite our friendship. I had always made it clear to Ronnie that the day would come when I would write my own book. Besides, I was not impressed by the fact that Ronnie had signed a contract confirming his full cooperation in the 'authorized biography of R.D. Laing', for which he had received a paltry £2,000, in addition to a percentage of a percentage of the royalties. No, I would not cooperate: as far as I was concerned, Ronnie was being taken for a sucker.

In the last week of August 1989 Ronnie travelled from Going to St Tropez for a holiday. His host was a wealthy American, Bob Firestone, author of *The Fantasy Bond* and, perhaps more importantly, the owner of a luxurious ocean-going yacht. Adam and Natasha had agreed to meet up with him, both looking forward to seeing their dad and having a good time. On the afternoon of the 23rd, Ronnie agreed to have a game of tennis with Bob at a club on the mainland. They were well into the first set, and Ronnie was leading four games to one. Quite suddenly, he felt unwell and told Bob that he would need to rest for a bit. He lost his colour and his condition gave rise to immediate concern. Frantic calls were sent out to the yacht to contact Marguerite. Natasha arrived on the scene to find her dad had 'completely let go'. He was dead. Just a few moments previously Bob had asked Ronnie if he was all right. 'Do you want a doctor?' he enquired with some urgency. Ronnie replied, 'Doctor, what fucking doctor?'

Sources

R.D. Laing was an avid keeper of diaries, drafts of his books both published and unpublished,* notes, scribbles, loose thoughts, recollections of dreams, jottings, correspondence, tape-recordings, transcripts of tape-recordings and press cuttings. When he left Eton Road in early 1986 his material belongings were scattered among friends, storage depots, banks, accountants and lawyers. Collating all the background information used for the purpose of writing this book was therefore time-consuming but not impossible. I believe I have had access to nearly all such material partly due to my status as a lawyer in addition to being one of the administrators of the Laing estate.

Over the years Ronnie was prone to giving away drafts of speeches and books to close friends and relatives and I generally found such individuals were willing to provide me with copies.

As a son of R.D. Laing I had a wealth of memories to delve into and during the period I lived with his second family (June 1978 to August 1979) I kept my own diary.

I contacted many of the institutions that had, at some stage, been part of Ronnie's life or still retain relevant historical material: The Mitchell Library in Glasgow provided me with records relating to Cuthbertson's Primary School and the Scottish Record Office with information concerning Hutchesons' Grammar School. Glasgow University was extremely cooperative with regard to Ronnie's undergraduate days. Other institutions that assisted me with detail were The Royal College of Psychiatrists, The Tavistock Centre (which has a library containing papers Ronnie wrote during the early 1960s), The Institute of Psycho-Analysis and the Philadelphia Association.

Although there were over 200 individuals who agreed to speak or corre-

---

* In particular: 'Jung: A Biography' with Dr Gene Nameche (1976–9), 'The Politics of Birth' (1972–9), 'The Way of the Warrior' (1983–4) with Bob Aubrey, 'The Lies of Love and the Love of Lies' (1984–9). Dates in brackets indicate approximate dates during which Ronnie was involved in the work.

spond with me about my father there are a few who provided a considerable amount of their time in helping me unravel specific events: Ethel Laing (Ronnie's paternal aunt) was an invaluable source of family history; Sid Briskin and I spent many hours trawling over Kingsley Hall and he deserves special credit. Dr Joe Berke, to whom I became an accidental neighbour, was also extremely helpful. Dr Charles Rycroft was a unique source of information with regard to Ronnie's graduation from the Institute of Psycho-Analysis.

In addition to the written records of R.D. Laing there is a vast amount of film material featuring or concerning Ronnie, much of which was gathered by Robert Dando for a 'festival' of R.D. Laing held at the Institute of Contemporary Arts during August 1990.

Several people were willing to read drafts of this book during various stages of its preparation and provided me with invaluable criticism, corrections and advice: Ethel Laing, Sid Briskin, Dr Joe Berke, Dr James Templeton, Dr Aaron Esterson, Mary Garvey, Dr Ross Speck, Joan Speck, Dr Leon Redler, Dr Loren Mosher, Deborah Fosbrook, Dr Steve Ticktin, Jutta Laing and Bernard Spalding.

My father's intended biographer, Dr Bob Mullan, also interviewed many people, including Ronnie himself. I did not utilize this material as much as I might have, with the exception of a recorded interview with the late Dr John Bowlby conducted shortly before his death and for those insights I am particularly grateful. Others whose paths crossed Ronnie's have, during the course of the last four years, passed away: Ethel Laing, Dr Jock Sutherland, Lord MacLeod, Dr Marion Milner, Dr Lenny Davidson, the Reverend Donald MacDonald and Bernie Simons, all of whom provided valuable material for this book and deserve special mention.

Select Bibliography

BATESON, Gregory, *Steps to an Ecology of Mind*, New York: Chandler, 1972

BERKE, Joseph, and BARNES, Mary, *Two Accounts of a Journey Through Madness*, London: Free Association Books, 1972

BOYERS, Robert, ORRILL, Robert, eds., *Laing and Anti-Psychiatry*, London: Penguin, 1972

BOSZORMENYI-NAGY, Ivan, FRAMO, James L., eds., *Intensive Family Therapy: Theoretical and Practical Aspects by Fifteen Authors*, Maryland: Harper and Row, 1965

BROWN, Phil, *Radical Psychology*, New York: Harper and Row, 1973

CAMERON, J.L., McGHIE, A., LAING, R.D., 'Patient and Nurse: Effects of Environmental Changes in the Care of Chronic Schizophrenics', *The Lancet*, vol. 2, 1955, pp. 1384–6

CHARLESWORTH, Max, *The Existentialists and Jean-Paul Sartre*, Australia: University of Queensland Press, 1975

CLARE, Anthony, 'R.D. Laing Returns to the Fold', *The Spectator*, no. 7545, 3 February 1973, pp. 148–9

——, *Psychiatry in Dissent*, London: Tavistock, 1976.

——, 'Ronald David Laing 1927–1989: an appreciation', *Psychiatric Bulletin*, 14, 1990, pp. 87–8

——, *In the Psychiatrist's Chair*, London: Heinemann, 1992

COHEN, David, ed., *Psychologists on Psychology*, London: Routledge and Kegan Paul, 1977

——, 'R.D. Laing: The Divided Prophet', *New Society*, 5 May 1977, pp. 215–17

COLLIER, Andrew, *R.D. Laing: The Philosophy & Politics of Psychotherapy*, New York: Pantheon, 1977

COOPER, David, ESTERSON, Aaron, LAING, R.D., 'Results of Family-orientated Therapy with Hospitalised Schizophrenics', *British Medical Journal*, vol. 2, 18 December 1965, pp. 1462–5

COOPER, David, *Psychiatry and Anti-Psychiatry*, London: Tavistock, 1967

_____, ed., *To Free a Generation: The Dialectics of Liberation*, London: Penguin, 1968

_____, *The Death of the Family*, London: Pelican, 1971

COOPER, Robin, ed., *Thresholds Between Philosophy and Psychoanalysis*, London: Free Association Books, 1989

COTT, Jonathan, 'Knots, Tangles, Fankles, & Whiligogs: A Conversation with R.D. Laing', *Rolling Stone*, 30 August 1973, pp. 40–4

CARSTAIRS, G. Morris, 'The Sense of Incompleteness', *Times Literary Supplement*, 26 November 1974, p. 1474

DICKS, Henry V., *Fifty Years of the Tavistock Clinic*, London: Routledge and Kegan Paul, 1970

ESTERSON, Aaron, *Leaves of Spring*, London: Tavistock, 1970

EVANS, Richard I., *R.D. Laing: The Man and His Ideas*, New York: Dutton, 1976

FOUCAULT, Michel, *Madness and Civilization*, London: Tavistock, 1967

_____, *History of Sexuality*, New York: Pantheon

FRIEDENBERG, Edgar Z., *Laing*, (Modern Masters), London: Woburn Press, 1974

GORDON, James S., 'Who is Mad? Who is Sane? R.D. Laing: In Search of a New Psychiatry', *The Atlantic Monthly*, vol. 227, January 1971, pp. 50–66

HAMPSHIRE, Stuart, 'Philosophy and Madness', *The Listener*, vol. 78, no. 2006, 7 September 1967, pp. 289–92

HOWARTH-WILLIAMS, Martin, *R.D. Laing: His Work and its Relevance to Sociology*, London: Routledge and Kegan Paul, 1977

JACOBY, Russell, *Social Amnesia: A Critique of Conformist Psychology from Adler to Laing*, Boston: Harvester Press, 1975

KUMAR, Satish, ed., *The Schumacher Lectures*, London: Blond and Briggs, 1980

LAING, Adrian Charles, 'R.D. Laing: The First Five Years', *Journal of the Society of Existential Analysis*, volume 2, 1992, pp. 24–9

LAING, R.D., ESTERSON, Aaron, 'The Collusive Functioning of Pairing in Analytical Groups'. *British Journal of Medical Psychology*, vol. 31, Part 2, 1958, pp. 117–23

LAING, R.D., 'Philosophy and Medicine', *Surgo*, June 1949, pp. 134–6

_____, 'Health and Society', *Surgo*, Candlemas 1950, pp. 91–3

_____, 'An Instance of the Ganser Syndrome', *Journal of the Royal Army Medical Corps*, vol. 99, no. 4, 1953, pp. 169–72

_____, 'An Examination of Tillich's Theory of Anxiety and Neurosis', *British Journal of Medical Psychology*, vol. 30, 1957, pp. 88–91

_____, *The Divided Self*, London: Tavistock, 1960

_____, *Self and Others*, London: Tavistock, 1961

_____, 'Series and Nexus in the Family', *New Left Review*, no. 15, May–June 1962, pp. 7–14

_____, ESTERSON, A., *Sanity, Madness and the Family*, volume 1, London:

Tavistock, 1964

——, 'Schizophrenia and the Family', *New Society*, no. 81, 16 April 1964

——, 'Practice and Theory - The Present Situation', *Psychother. Psychosom*, 13, 1964, pp. 58-67

——, COOPER, D., *Reason and Violence*, London: Tavistock, 1964

——, 'Them', *Queen*, 26 August 1964, p. 21

——, 'Psychotherapy: Search for a New Theory', *New Society*, 1 October 1964, pp. 12-14

——, 'What is Schizophrenia?', *New Left Review*, no. 28, 1964, pp. 63-9

——, 'A Happy Hypomania to You All', *Queen*, 2 December 1964, p. 66

——, 'Is Schizophrenia a Disease?', *International Journal of Social Psychiatry*, vol. 10, no. 3, 1964

——, 'Violence and Love', *Journal of Existentialism*, vol. 5, no. 20, 1965, pp. 417-22

——, PHILLIPSON, Herbert, LEE, A. Russel, *Interpersonal Perception*, London: Tavistock, 1966

——, 'Ritualisation and Abnormal Behaviour', *Philosophical Transactions of the Royal Society of London*, Series B, *Biological Sciences*, vol. 251, no. 772, 1966, pp. 331-5

——, 'Schizophrenia. Heart of the Matter: Report of the Annual Conference of the National Association for Mental Health', 1966, pp. 74-8

——, *The Politics of Experience and The Bird of Paradise*, London: Penguin, 1967

——, *Knots*, London: Tavistock, 1970

——, *The Politics of the Family*, London: Tavistock, 1971

——, 'The Psychotherapist as Attendant', *Hyde Parker*, 1973, p. 16

——, *Do You Love Me?*, New York: Pantheon Books, 1976

——, *The Facts of Life*, London: Allen Lane, 1976

——, 'Memories and Madness', *The Listener*, 25 November 1976, pp. 673-5

——, *Conversations with Children*, London: Allen Lane, 1978

——, *Sonnets*, London: Michael Joseph, 1979

——, *The Voice of Experience*, New York: Pantheon, 1982

——, *Conversations with Children*, volume 2, Paris: Editions du Seuil, 1985

——, *Wisdom, Madness and Folly*, London: Macmillan, 1985

——, 'God and Psychiatry', *Times Literary Supplement*, May 23 1986

LEACH, Edmund, 'The Millennium', *The Listener*, vol. 85, no. 2203, 1971, pp. 669–71

LEARY, Timothy, *Flashbacks*, Los Angeles: J.P. Tarcher, Inc., 1983

LOMAS, Peter, ed., *The Predicament of the Family*, London: Hogarth Press, 1967

LUNT, Anthony, *Apollo Versus the Echomaker: Psychotherapy, Dreams and Shamanism, A Laingian Approach*, London: Element Books, 1990

MERCER, Derrik, ed., *Chronicle of the 20th Century*, London: Longman, 1988

MEZAN, Peter, 'After Freud and Jung, Now Comes R.D. Laing', *Esquire*, vol. 77, 1972, pp. 92–7, 160–78

NUTTALL, Jeff, *Bomb Culture*, London: Paladin, 1970

RUSSELL, Roberta, *R.D. Laing and Me: Lessons in Love*, New York: Hillgarth Press, 1992

SCRUTON, Roger, *Thinkers of the New Left*. London: Longman, 1986

SEDGWICK, Peter, *PsychoPolitics*, London: Pluto Press, 1982

SIEGLER, Miriam, OSMOND, Humphrey, MANN, Harriet, 'Laing's Models of Madness', *British Journal of Psychiatry* 115, 1969, pp. 947–58

SPECK, Ross, ATTNEAVE, Carolyn L., *Family Networks: A New Approach to Family Problems*, New York: Pantheon, 1973

STEINER, Claude, MEIGHAN, Spence, 'R.D. Laing: An Interview', *Issues in Radical Psychiatry*, vol. 3, no. 4, 1975, pp. 3–9

SZASZ, Thomas, *The Myth of Mental Illness*, London: Paladin, 1962

_____, 'Anti-Psychiatry: The Paradigm of the Plundered Mind', *The New Review*, vol. 3, no. 29, 1976, pp. 14-24

TICKTIN, Steve, ed., 'Asylum: R.D. Laing Memorial Issue', volume 4, no. 2, February 1990

TYSON, Alan, 'Homage to Catatonia', *The New York Review of Books*, 11 January 1971, pp. 3–6

Index